Foundation Joomla!

B.M. Harwani

friendsof

DESIGNER TO DESIGNER™

an Apress® company

T0091892

Foundation Joomla!

Copyright © 2009 by B. M. Harwani

All rights reserved. No part of this work may be reproduced or transmitted in any form or by any means, electronic or mechanical, including photocopying, recording, or by any information storage or retrieval system, without the prior written permission of the copyright owner and the publisher.

ISBN-13 (pbk): 978-1-4302-2375-7

ISBN-13 (electronic): 978-1-4302-2376-4

Printed and bound in the United States of America 9 8 7 6 5 4 3 2 1

Trademarked names may appear in this book. Rather than use a trademark symbol with every occurrence of a trademarked name, we use the names only in an editorial fashion and to the benefit of the trademark owner, with no intention of infringement of the trademark.

Distributed to the book trade worldwide by Springer-Verlag New York, Inc., 233 Spring Street, 6th Floor, New York, NY 10013. Phone 1-800-SPRINGER, fax 201-348-4505, e-mail orders-ny@springer-sbm.com, or visit www.springeronline.com.

For information on translations, please e-mail info@apress.com, or visit www.apress.com.

Apress and friends of ED books may be purchased in bulk for academic, corporate, or promotional use. eBook versions and licenses are also available for most titles. For more information, reference our Special Bulk Sales–eBook Licensing web page at http://www.apress.com/info/bulksales.

The information in this book is distributed on an "as is" basis, without warranty. Although every precaution has been taken in the preparation of this work, neither the author(s) nor Apress shall have any liability to any person or entity with respect to any loss or damage caused or alleged to be caused directly or indirectly by the information contained in this work.

The source code for this book is freely available to readers at www.friendsofed.com in the Downloads section.

Credits

Lead Editor: Ben Renow-Clarke

Technical Reviewer: Ian Piper

Editorial Board: Clay Andres, Steve Anglin, Mark Beckner, Ewan Buckingham, Tony Campbell, Gary Cornell, Jonathan Gennick, Michelle Lowman, Matthew Moodie, Jeffrey Pepper, Frank Pohlmann, Ben Renow-Clarke, Dominic Shakeshaft, Matt Wade, Tom Welsh

Project Managers: Beth Christmas and Candace English

Copy Editor: Damon Larsen

Production Editor: Brigid Duffy

Proofreader: Patrick Vincent

Indexers: Ann Rogers/Ron Strauss

Cover Image Designer: Corné van Dooren

Interior and Cover Designer: Anna Ishchenko

Manufacturing Director Tom Debolski

Dedicated to my mother, Mrs. Nita Harwani, and Peter Norton, the producer of one of the most popular PC tools, Norton Utilities.

My mother is next to God for me. Whatever I am today is just because of the moral values taught by her.

I have been highly impressed by Peter Norton ever since I took a computer engineering course. I was fascinated by his amazing tool, Norton Utilities. He is also author of many successful books and a great programmer, and he is an inspiration for me.

Contents at a Glance

Contents

About the Author

 **B. M. Harwani** is managing director of Computer Education Centre—Microchip Computer Education (MCE), based in Ajmer, India. He graduated with a BE in computer engineering from the University of Pune, and also has a C Level (master's diploma in computer technology) from DOEACC Society, Government of India. He has been involved with teaching since he was 15 years old, and he has developed the art of explaining even the most complicated topics in a manner that everybody can easily understand. He has written several successful books, including *Programming and Problem Solving through C* (BPB, 2004), *Learn Tally in Just Three Weeks* (Pragya, 2005), *Data Structures and Algorithms through C* (CBC, 2006), *Master Unix Shell Programming* (CBC, 2006), *Business Systems* (CBC, 2006), *Practical Java Projects* (Shroff, 2007), *Practical Web Services* (Shroff, 2007), *Java for Professionals* (Shroff, 2008), *C++ for Beginners* (Shroff, 2009), *Practical ASP.NET 3.5 Projects* (Shroff, 2009), and *JavaServer Faces: A Practical Approach for Beginners* (PHI, 2009). He also writes articles on a variety of computer subjects, which can be seen on a number of websites. To find out more, visit `http://bmharwani.com`.

About the Technical Reviewer

 **Ian Piper** is director and owner of Tellura Information Services, a UK-based information services consultancy. When not wrangling with the innards of Mac system software, he develops content-rich web applications and information system architectures, specializing in the design of taxonomies and metadata vocabularies. He has been designing and building websites based on content management systems such as Joomla far longer than he cares to remember.

About the Cover Image Designer

 **Corné van Dooren** designed the front cover image for this book. After taking a brief from friends of ED to create a new design for the Foundation series, he worked at combining technological and organic forms, with the results now appearing on this and other books' covers.

Corné spent his childhood drawing on everything at hand and then began exploring the infinite world of multimedia—and his journey of discovery hasn't stopped since. His mantra has always been, "The only limit to multimedia is the imagination"—a saying that keeps him moving forward constantly.

Corné works for many international clients, writes features for multimedia magazines, reviews and tests software, authors multimedia studies, and works on many other friends of ED books. You can see more of his work at and contact him through his website, at www.cornevandooren.com.

If you like Corné's work, be sure to check out his chapter in *New Masters of Photoshop: Volume 2* (friends of ED, 2004).

Acknowledgments

I owe a debt of gratitude to Steve Anglin, assistant editorial director, and Joohn Choe, assistant editor, for their initial acceptance of this book, and for giving me an opportunity to create this work. I am highly grateful to the whole team at Apress for their constant cooperation and contribution in the creation of this book.

I must express my gratitude to Ben Renow-Clarke who, as a senior editor, offered a significant amount of feedback that helped to improve the chapters. He played a vital role in improving the structure and quality of information.

I must thank Ian Piper, the technical reviewer, for his excellent, detailed reviewing of the work and the many helpful comments and suggestions he made.

Special thanks go to Caroline Rose, the developmental editor, and Damon Larson, the copy editor, for their first-class structural and language editing. I appreciate their efforts in enhancing the contents of the book and giving it a polished look.

I also thank Nancy Wright, the formatter, for doing excellent formatting and making the book dramatically better.

Big and ongoing thanks to Beth Christmas, senior project manager, for doing a great job and making a sincere effort with the whole team to get the book published on time.

I also want to give a great big thank you to the editorial and production staff, and the entire team at Apress, who worked tirelessly to produce this book. Really, I enjoyed working with each of you.

Introduction

Joomla is the world's most powerful open source content management system (CMS). It makes the job of website maintenance much easier by providing an easy-to-handle administrative interface. This book is a step-by-step, user-friendly guide to the ins and outs of Joomla. Beginning with the installation of Joomla, we then step through its configuration, and then on to setting up a site and managing its content. The whole lot is completely explained with screenshots at every step. I teach by example throughout, starting by modifying the default website installed by Joomla, and using that to demonstrate the functions of Joomla's various menu options. Once you have a firm grasp of what Joomla can do and how to move around in it, you'll discover how to build your own site in Joomla and really harness its power. If you have never used Joomla or any other CMS before, then this is the book for you, as it is purely for beginners. The book also explains how to make use of powerful Joomla add-ons and extensions to add features like e-commerce, chatting capabilities, and RSS feed readers to your website.

Who the book is for

This book is suitable for web developers, web designers, webmasters, trainers, bloggers, corporate content creators, and professionals who are looking to build a fully featured website easily and quickly without needing to spend years learning a complex programming language. Whether you're completely new to Joomla and CMSs, or you've dabbled in Joomla but are looking for a more thorough guide to its menus and controls, this book will give you all the information you need to push Joomla to the max.

What you will learn from this book

In this book, you will learn how to fully install and configure Joomla from scratch, beginning with where to download Joomla and how best to configure it on your system. You'll then install the default Joomla website and use that to practice creating, editing, and managing your website contents. With the contents of the site ready, you'll then explore creating and managing users and contacts so people can administer your site both locally and remotely, and so users can create their own articles and items to populate your site. We also look at how to set up banner clients, news feeds, and polls to further enhance your site. These dynamic and interactive elements will keep visitors returning to your site and increase the sense of community. We then look at all of the different menu types and modules provided as standard by Joomla. These enable you to add functionality to your website and build its functionality and richness. We also look at extending this further by installing third-party extensions and plug-ins. Finally, we look at how you can tinker with Joomla's global settings to increase the functionality of your website, including creating search engine–friendly URLs for the information on your site to increase your visibility to the world and help your marketing.

Layout conventions

To keep this book as clear and easy to follow as possible, the following text conventions are used throughout.

Important words or concepts are normally highlighted on the first appearance in **bold type**.

Code is presented in `fixed-width font`.

New or changed code is normally presented in **`bold fixed-width font`**.

Pseudocode and variable input are written in *`italic fixed-width font`*.

Menu commands are written in the form `Menu` ➤ `Submenu` ➤ `Submenu`.

Where I want to draw your attention to something, I've highlighted it like this:

> *Ahem, don't say I didn't warn you.*

Chapter 1

Introduction to Joomla!

Joomla is a CMS (content management system) that helps you build dynamic and functional websites with a minimum of effort. It is possible to make all kinds of websites with Joomla, from personal websites to blogs and discussion forums, and even fully functional professional websites such as e-commerce stores. All of this is possible because Joomla is supported with hundreds of freely available plug-ins and extensions that can be easily applied to a website to increase its capabilities. By default, Joomla provides all the standard website content, such as menus, articles, and modules, and all of these can be customized via the Administrator interface. Because of this system, the overhead of making a website from scratch is highly reduced.

In a CMS, the content of the website (such as articles, pictures, etc.) is stored in a database, and this makes creating and maintaining a website very simple. Traditional websites are often bulky and unwieldy because they consist of a large amount of content (several web pages) displaying different information to the visitor. The greater the number of web pages, the more difficult is to maintain that website. It is for this reason that the maintenance of a traditional website is usually done by a group of people. But in Joomla, since all the web content is maintained in a database, its maintenance cost is highly reduced, because, asyou'll see throughout this book, maintaining a database requires less effort than manually changing web content. Moreover, Joomla provides a user-friendly Administrator interface that guides the administrator through maintaining the website content stored in the database. Even a single person can easily maintain a website with the help of Joomla's easy-to-use, menu-driven administrative interface. With a little training, a web developer or administrator can easily administer a website, and change its content, navigation features, structure, and so on, with just a few clicks of the mouse. Let's dig a bit deeper into what a CMS is, and what makes Joomla so special.

What is a CMS?

As mentioned previously, *CMS* stands for *content management system*, and it is a software system that enables us to create, edit, and manage documents of different types. These documents can include data files, audio/video files, image files, and most other forms of web content. A CMS not only helps in managing all of this content (without requiring any technical knowledge of HTML), but it also defines different groups of users each with different roles and responsibilities. The idea is that more than one person in an organization can contribute to creating, editing, and managing content, while normal visitors are given limited access privileges—usually just permission to view the content. In short, we can make an easily maintainable website with the help of a CMS where creating, editing, and managing content is a simple task. In a CMS, the whole of the website is contained within a database. All of the links, articles, user information, images, and other parts of the website are maintained by the administrator using that database. All this talk of databases may sound a bit scary, but all of the website maintenance is carried out using the Administrator interface—a user-friendly menu-driven system that makes the task of updating or managing the content of the website very easy. The Administrator interface is accessed through your web browser and is simple to operate. All the changes that you make in the Administrator interface are reflected in the database where the content of the website is kept.

Making a website from scratch is usually a time-consuming task, and it requires expertise to develop all of the individual parts of a site. The coding and integration of all of these different parts are highly error prone, and need thorough testing procedures before new parts can be added to a website. In a traditional web application, you might have several different criteria for modules that you want to add to your site, such as the following:

- **Login system**: Provides a means of authenticating a user
- **Account Creation module**: Provides a user with a form to enter information, which is then stored in a database for future use
- **Forgotten Password module**: Helps users who have forgotten their password or user ID
- **Popular module**: Displays popular website content or services
- **Polling module**: Gets visitor feedback on a chosen subject
- **RSS Feed module**: Gets your website content syndicated for others to read
- **Feed Reader module**: Allows the reading of RSS feeds from different websites
- **Search box**: Enables users to search website content
- **Multilingual module**: Makes it possible to implement multilingual facilities in your website
- **Granting-and-Revoking-Permission module**: Facilitates assigning permissions to the user so as to allow them to view or block them from viewing certain information

In a CMS system, all of these modules are already built for you, and are easy to add to an existing site. You just need to configure them and decide on their position and appearance in your website. This makes creating a website very simple, and you can have a website ready in a couple of hours. Also, maintaining the content of the website doesn't take much effort. The configuration of the modules provided by a CMS and maintenance of the web content is all done using the easy-to-use Administrator interface.

Why are CMSs so popular?

There are many reasons why people choose to use a CMS rather than creating a site from scratch in code, so I'll run through a couple of the big ones. You will always need to update your website to keep viewers returning to it, and a CMS makes this very easy. For example, you may need to do things like

- Deliver new articles or information about your organization to visitors
- Inform readers about any forthcoming events
- Introduce new services or products

Besides this easy and quick updating, you might also need to add some extra features, such as

- Allowing users to sign up to your website with different privileges
- Adding a shopping cart module
- Adding multilingual support to your website
- Applying different dynamic styles to your website
- Adding a third-party module to provide extra features like Google Maps or a search box

To deal with all of these natural demands of webmasters, CMSs appeared as helping hands, as they store all the contents of the website in a database, and enable the webmaster to manipulate the database contents with an easy-to-operate browser-driven Administrator interface. So, in simple terms, using a CMS is a way to manage the content of a website with the click of a mouse button instead of hours spent typing in code. The popularity of CMSs lies in the fact that they separates the web content from the presentation. As a consequence, the content developer can concentrate on creating that content and the web designers can focus on giving that content a dynamic appearance by applying different templates, or developing their own custom templates, without interfering with each other. Hence, in a CMS, the content development and presentation process can proceed simultaneously.

What is Joomla!?

Joomla is one of the most powerful and popular open source CMSs available today. It is a free, open source framework and content publishing system designed for quickly creating highly interactive multilanguage websites, online communities, blogs, and e-commerce applications. It is a server-based application that maintains all the contents of the website in a database. A website built with Joomla can be easily administered via a web browser using Joomla's browser-driven Administrator interface.

Joomla provides several built-in modules and components for adding features to your websites, such as main menus, polls, popular items, search, RSS feeds, and so on. In addition to this, there are hundreds of third-party modules and components available on the Internet, such as shopping carts, news readers, language translators, and so on, that can be freely downloaded and added to your Joomla website.

One of the best features of Joomla is that it separates the content from the presentation—that is, the raw content stored in the database is given dynamic styling with the help of **templates** (collections of styles) before it is viewed by the visitor.

Joomla is very successful, and is a winner of the Open Source Content Management System Award. It has many more great features (some of which are explained in more detail following).

Structure of a Joomla website

Figure 1-1 shows that the raw contents of the website (i.e., the articles, pictures, user information, etc.) are stored in a database. When any visitor selects any link or menu item on a website, the desired data is retrieved from the database and is displayed to the visitor. But before the information is displayed to the user, there are several modules and components that are applied to it to filter the required information. For example, there may be several news feeds stored in the database, but only the news feed specified in the news feed module will be passed. There may be polls on several subjects, but only the subject specified in the poll module will be passed on to the visitor. Once it is decided what information is to be displayed, the selected template is applied to it. The template consists of styles that give an attractive look to the content. It also defines the design and structure of the website, as it contains the screen position of several modules, such as where the polls, search box, and popular links modules are supposed to appear on the website. Joomla provides three built-in templates to give a dynamic appearance to your website. However, you can always download more templates from the Internet and install them to be used in your website.

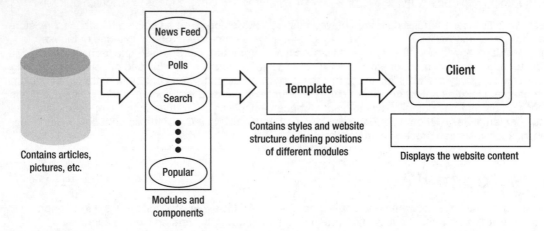

Figure 1-1. Structure of a Joomla website

It is also possible to make your own custom templates, but that is a more complex process, and is beyond the scope of this book.

Characteristics of Joomla!

Joomla is one of the most powerful open source CMSs around today, and it is heavily used in developing highly interactive multilanguage websites, blogs, discussion forums, online communities, e-commerce applications, and much more. Joomla has several characteristics that make it a highly demanded CMS. These include the following:

- Joomla offers a huge number of extensions. You can easily enhance features of your website by installing more extensions, some of which follow:

    - **Dynamic form builders**: These components helps us to take feedback from visitors and accordingly display a form back to them. For example, a visitor paying for a product in cash will be displayed a form that prompts him to fill in the bank name and account details, and a visitor paying via credit card will be displayed a form that has a list of credit cards to choose from and a field to enter the credit card number information.

    - **Image and multimedia galleries**: These components help you add images to your website, view image thumbnails, customize image size, apply special effects on images when the mouse is moved over them, and so on. Beside this, these components also allow you to add music and animations to you website.

    - **E-commerce and shopping cart engines**: These components help you create and manage shopping carts, complete with PayPal support, in minutes. Examples of these components are SimpleCaddy, VirtueMart, and EXP Shop.

    - **Forums and chat software**: Forums are used for discussing subjects, getting the views of visitors, replying to queries, and so on. FireBoard is a Joomla component that can add a forums facility to your website. Similarly, to enable visitors to chat or send private messages, there are several chat components available, including jPFChat and BlastChat.

    - **Calendars**: Calendar extensions can display monthly calendar information. You can switch to the calendar of any month and year, and the date on which you click will be retrieved for processing.

    - **Blogging software**: You can create your own blog with the help of this component. You can manage blog posts, write or edit the entries, view all entries with pagination, filter blogs on the basis of users or keywords, include RSS feeds to your blogs, and so on. There are several blogging extensions available for Joomla on the Internet, one of which is MyBlog, which is feature-filled, simple to use, user-friendly, and powerful.

    - **E-mail newsletters**: To contact visitors of your website and get their feedback, e-mail is the best communication medium. Joomla provides many e-mail marketing newsletter components for doing this job, including Mass Mail, Letterman, ANJEL, YaNC, and mosListMessenger.

- **Data collection and reporting tools**: These components search through data to collect the requested information and display reports, such as sales reports, market survey reports, and sales forecasting reports, in either tabular format or charts.
- **Banner advertising systems**: These components are used for managing and displaying advertising banners on your site. You can also specify the period for which the banner will be published on your website (e.g., for a specified number of hits or for an unlimited period).

- You can easily install any of these hundreds of extensions to increase functionality of our website.
- Joomla has an active community of more than 100,000 users and developers.
- Working with Joomla is very simple. Its user-friendly menu-driven system and tools allow even nontechnical users to add or edit content of a website.
- Joomla runs on Windows, Linux, FreeBSD, Mac OS X, Solaris, and AIX.
- With Joomla, you can build completely database-driven sites.
- With Joomla, you can upload images to be used anywhere in the site. Joomla has a Media Manager component that allows you to upload images. These uploaded images can then be used on any number of web pages (also called articles).
- Joomla contains image libraries that can store all type of picture formats, including PNG, GIF, and JPEG, along with other documents types, such as PDF, DOC, and XLS.
- Joomla contains an Automatic Path-Finder tool, which allows you to just place an image from the image library (Media Manager) and have Joomla set its path automatically.
- With Joomla's Remote author contribution tool, authors can add articles, news, links, and so on to your website remotely. Joomla supports different groups of users, each having different rights and permissions (e.g., authors, editors, publisher, managers, etc.). This allows authorized users to contribute to the website from anywhere.

- For every article, Joomla provides two options: "E-mail a friend" and "Print." This means that you don't have to write code for providing these facilities yourself.
- Joomla's provides two inline text editors for adding or editing articles and information: TinyMCE and XStandard Lite. These are WYSIWYG editors that help to apply different fonts, styles, and sizes to your text.
- Joomla supplies several ready-to-use modules that can be used directly in your website, including the following: Polls, Popular, RSS Feed, and Banner.
- With Joomla, you can change the sequence of appearance of modules on your website.
- Administrators can administer the website remotely with the help of a browser.
- You can apply different templates to give a dynamic look to your website. A template contains styles and screen positions for placing modules and components. Joomla provides several templates by default that you can immediately apply, and you can download many more.

Advantages of Joomla!

There are several advantages of using Joomla for building your website. A few of them follow:

- It is absolutely free.
- It offers a huge amount of extensions to enhance the features of your website. For example, in just a few minutes you could add extensions providing discussion forums, chat features, or shopping carts to your site.
- It supports multiple languages.
- It can be controlled remotely using a web browser. A Joomla website can be easily maintained from anywhere using its browser-based Administrator interface.
- It supports XAMP technology. (The *X* in *XAMP* designates the three operating systems that it supports—Windows, Linux, and Mac OS X—and the *AMP* refers to the three pieces of server software that it is built upon: Apache, MySQL, and PHP.)
- Joomla can manage website content using any of the popular web browsers. It is fully tested on Firefox 2.0+, Internet Explorer 6 and 7, Safari 3.0+, Opera 9.0+, and Camino 1.0+.

Summary

In this chapter, you saw how Joomla has influenced the web development industry, and why it is such a powerful tool. Some points that you should remember are as follows:

- Joomla is a CMS that enables you to create a fully featured website in a few hours. It is supported with hundreds of extensions and plug-ins, and any kind of website can be easily made with it.
- Joomla provides a GUI-based Administrator interface that makes the process of website maintenance easy.
- A CMS reduces the cost of website maintenance because all the web content is organized in a database, making it easier to maintain than it would be in individual web pages.
- In Joomla, you don't have to make a website from scratch because it provides a default website with menus, articles, and modules in it that can be easily customized to suit your needs.
- Joomla supports most operating systems, including Windows, Linux, and MAC OS X.
- Joomla is free, supports multiple languages, stores all types of picture formats, and is compatible with most web browsers.

In Chapter 2, we will run through the Joomla installation process, covering both local as well as remote servers. For local installation, we will be installing and using the XAMPP software. The characteristics of XAMPP and how it is installed and configured are covered in detail.

Chapter 2

Installing Joomla!

You now know that Joomla is a CMS that stores all the information of a website in a database, and it provides a bundle of built-in modules that can be readily added to make a rich web application in a couple of hours. So, let's go ahead and install Joomla and start playing around with the possibilities that it provides. In this chapter, you will learn how to install Joomla on a local server as well as on a remote server. A **remote server** is a machine containing special software that is used for hosting your website. These servers are called remote servers because they are found in another location (often a long way away) from where you are, and you usually access them using FTP client software. While the website is under construction, there is no need to run everything on a remote server, and it is much quicker and easier to run the site from your everyday (local) machine. This can be made possible by installing some software on your machine that will make it into a local server ready to test your website on. So, let's look at setting up a local server, and setting up Joomla to run on that machine.

Prerequisites to installing Joomla! on the local server

Joomla is a server-based application made in PHP (a popular web scripting language) that has to be installed on a web server, as discussed earlier. It also requires a database server, another piece of software running remotely or locally to help maintain the database, in order to store the contents of the website. So, before installing Joomla, you need to have the following applications installed on your local PC:

- **The web server**: Apache web server (version 1.3 or higher)

- **The PHP scripting language**: PHP (version 4.3.x or higher)

- **The database server**: MySQL (version 3.23.x or higher)

> *You are free to choose any other web server that is compatible with PHP if you'd prefer not to use Apache.*

What a lot of complex-sounding things to install! Luckily, instead of downloading and installing these three applications individually (which is a difficult task), you can download and install just one application: XAMPP. XAMPP is a project that provides a complete web development environment in one easy package—perfect for your needs. Let's find out a little more about XAMPP.

Joomla is platform independent and can run on several OSs, including Linux, Mac OS X, Windows (98, 2000, 2003, Me, XP, and Vista), and Unix.

The prerequisite of installing Joomla on a Linux platform may depend on the distribution that you are using. You may have Apache, PHP, and MySQL packages preinstalled, and you may not need to install XAMPP at all. Even if any of the packages are not installed, the process of their installation is quite simple.

Similarly, on Mac OS X, you have a default web server (Apache) in your system that just needs to be activated. You only need to download the PHP Apache module and executable versions of MySQL for Mac OS X, and install them.

Web request life cycle

Before diving into the Joomla installation prerequisites, it's important to have some background on the web request life cycle. Web applications normally work in a request-response mode. The user (usually called a client) sends a request for some information to the web server via a web browser. The web server processes the request by executing certain scripts/programs that may involve fetching desired information or updating the RDBMS. The web server then sends the response in the form of an HTML document back to the client as shown in Figure 2-1.

In terms of Apache PHP and MySQL, the following list describes the steps in the web request life cycle:

1. The client sends the request to the Apache web server in terms of HTTP GET or POST messages.
2. The Apache web server parses the request, locates the desired PHP script, and executes it.
3. Depending on the user's request, the PHP script either fetches the desired information from the MySQL database or updates its contents.
4. The MySQL database returns the desired information and the status of the database to the PHP script.

5. The PHP script combines the database information with an HTML template and sends it to the Apache web server program.

6. Apache sends an HTTP response in the form of the HTML document to the user's browser.

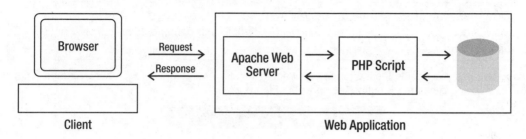

Figure 2-1. Web request life cycle

XAMPP

As discussed, to develop any websites with Joomla, you need a web server, a database, and the PHP language installed on your computer. XAMPP is an Apache distribution developed by Kai "Oswald" Seidler and Kay Vogelgesang that contains Apache, MySQL, and PHP. In fact, that's what the *AMP* in XAMPP stands for—Apache, MySQL, and PHP. The final *P* is for Perl, another scripting language. The first letter in the acronym, *X*, means *cross-platform*, and implies that XAMPP is available for the Windows, Mac, and Linux operating systems. XAMPP is very easy to install, and it will automatically configure the Apache web server along with MySQL, PHP, and Perl.

Installation of XAMPP doesn't makes any changes to the Windows registry, which makes removing it from the system an easy task—you can just delete its folder from the disk drive (though removing using Control Panel is considered better). Also, XAMPP is a compilation of free software, and it's free to copy under the terms of the GNU General Public License (GPL). To make it convenient for developers, XAMPP is configured with all features turned on.

XAMPP installation

XAMPP is very easy to install. Just navigate to www.apachefriends.org, click the XAMPP link on the website, and then click the correct version for your operating system. Scroll down to the Download section and click the Installer file download under the Basic Package heading. I downloaded the Windows version, XAMPP 1.7.1; at the time of this writing, this is the latest available Windows version. The downloaded file is named xampp-win32-1.7.1-installer.exe. Just double-click this EXE file to install it.

On Vista, you get a message about UAC warning to not install XAMPP in the *Program Files* directory. So, it is a better option to install it at the root of the local disk drive. I have used disk drive *C:*.

The first screen lets you decide the language you want to install XAMPP in. Choose your language (in this case English), and click the OK button, as shown in Figure 2-2.

Figure 2-2. Selecting the language for installation

You'll get a welcome screen, as shown in Figure 2-3.

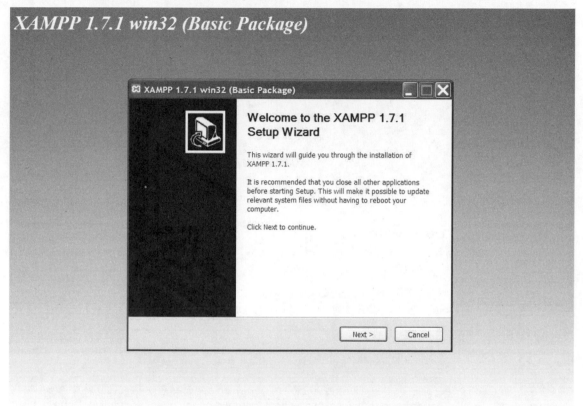

Figure 2-3. Welcome screen of XAMPP installation wizard

Click the Next button. You will be prompted to specify the location to install XAMPP. Specify the c:\xampp folder, as shown in Figure 2-4 (note that you can install it in any folder you choose).

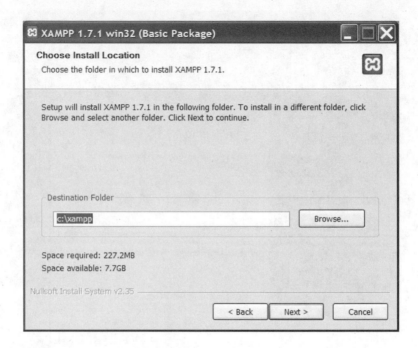

Figure 2-4. Specifying the folder to install XAMPP

Click `Next`, and you'll see a dialog box allowing you to specify which services you want to install. A service is an executable file that performs specific functions without the need of any user intervention. Usually, the services are **auto-starts**, meaning they automatically start when the operating system is booted, and run in the background as long as the system is running.

Apache and MySQL are essential requirements for Joomla, so you must select the two check boxes `Install Apache as service` and `Install MySQL as service`. You can also select the `Install Filezilla as service` check box, as shown in Figure 2-5, but this is optional.

> **FileZilla** is an FTP server used for remote administration. It is used if you need to transfer files to your web server from a remote computer. If you already have an FTP server installed on your machine, then you can skip it. You just have to carefully handle the server address and FTP username and password to avoid any unauthorized access.

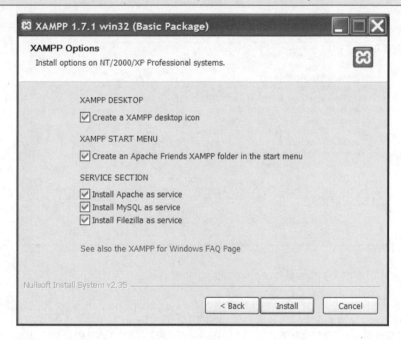

Figure 2-5. Selecting the services to be installed

Click `Install`, and XAMPP will start extracting the files, as shown in Figure 2-6.

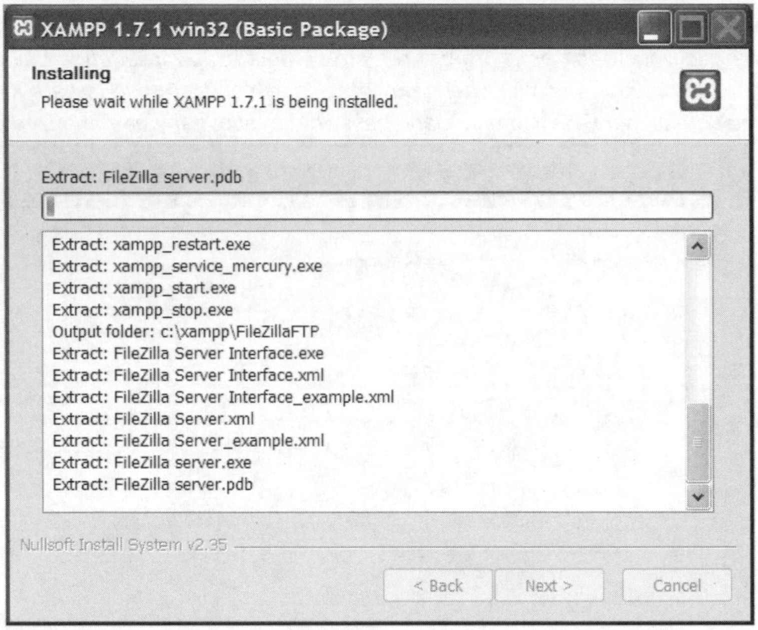

Figure 2-6. XAMPP files being copied to the specified folder

XAMPP requires port 80 to work. If you already have a server occupying port 80 (e.g., ColdFusion Server, IIS Server, Skype, etc.), you will not be able to launch XAMPP after installing it due to a port-binding conflict. For example, if you have Skype installed on your machine, then you may get an error saying that port 80 is already in use, as shown in Figure 2-7.

Figure 2-7. Port conflict error

To fix this common error, you need to open Skype and select the `Tools` ➤ `Options` ➤ `Advanced` ➤ `Connection` option. You may get a screen like the one shown in Figure 2-8.

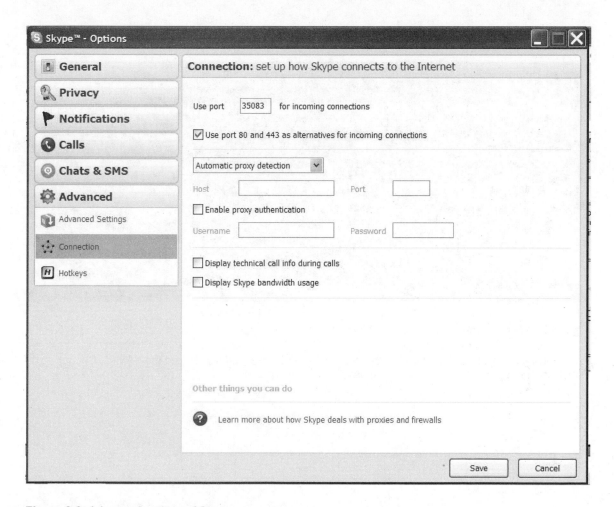

Figure 2-8. Advanced options of Skype

You will find the check box Use port 80 and 443 as alternatives for incoming connections selected. Just uncheck this check box to make this port free for XAMPP to work. Then save the changes in Skype and click OK (refer to Figure 2-7), and you will find that the port conflict error disappears, and a splash window appears showing that it is configuring XAMPP (see Figure 2-9).

> *To avoid the port-binding conflict with any server running on our machine, it is a better option to stop the services of other servers (if any) from the Control Panel.*

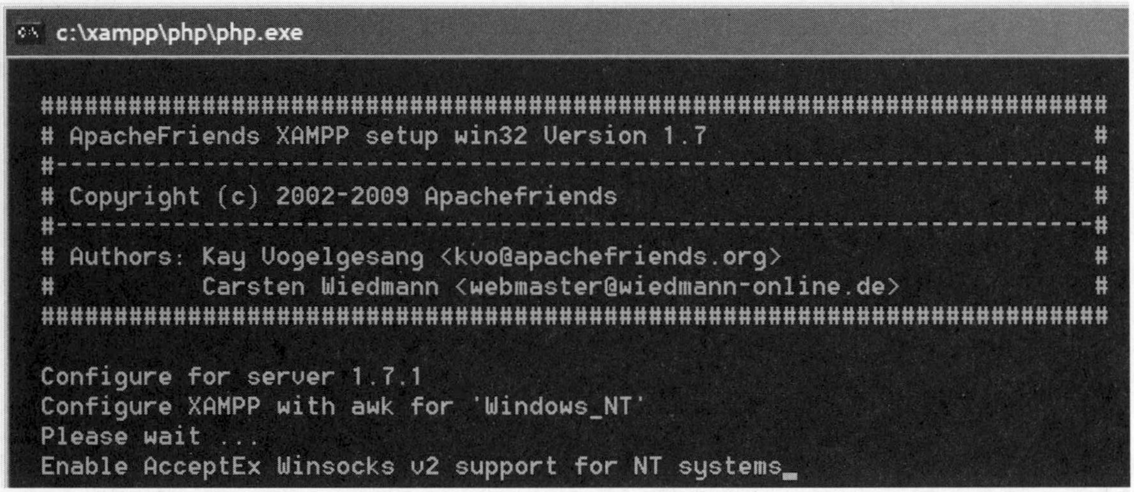

```
c:\xampp\php\php.exe

################################################################################
# ApacheFriends XAMPP setup win32 Version 1.7                                  #
#------------------------------------------------------------------------------#
# Copyright (c) 2002-2009 Apachefriends                                        #
#------------------------------------------------------------------------------#
# Authors: Kay Vogelgesang <kvo@apachefriends.org>                             #
#          Carsten Wiedmann <webmaster@wiedmann-online.de>                     #
################################################################################

Configure for server 1.7.1
Configure XAMPP with awk for 'Windows_NT'
Please wait ...
Enable AcceptEx Winsocks v2 support for NT systems_
```

Figure 2-9. XAMPP configuration splash window

Then you'll get a dialog box mentioning that the service installation is finished and the XAMPP Control Panel can be used for managing services, as shown in Figure 2-10.

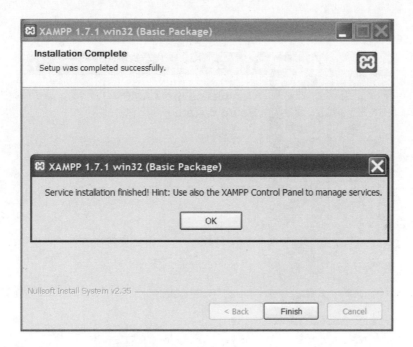

Figure 2-10. Service installation success message

On clicking `Finish`, you'll get a screen showing that the XAMPP installation is complete, as shown in Figure 2-11.

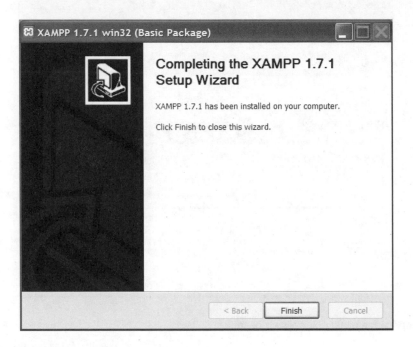

Figure 2-11. Finishing the XAMPP setup wizard

Click `Finish` to complete the installation. You get a dialog box asking whether to start the XAMPP Control Panel, as shown in Figure 2-12. The XAMPP Control Panel is the main steering panel from where you can control the workings of Apache as well as MySQL. You can also work with phpMyAdmin through this panel. phpMyAdmin is software for creating and maintaining MySQL databases. You can access your MySQL account using phpMyAdmin.

XAMPP comes packed with phpMyAdmin and an FTP server.

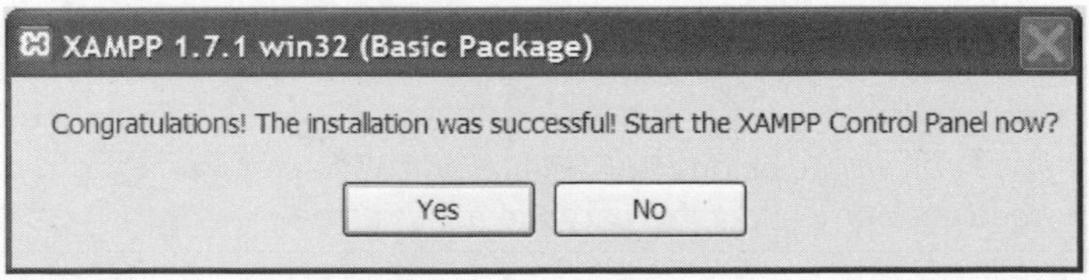

Figure 2-12. Congratulations message for successful installation of XAMPP

The installation of XAMPP is simple if there are no port conflicts—just double-click its installer file. You may see a number of informational messages and dialogs during the installation. Just accept the default options. Finally, you will see a dialog confirming a successful installation. Click `Yes`, and the XAMPP Control Panel will be displayed, as shown in Figure 2-13.

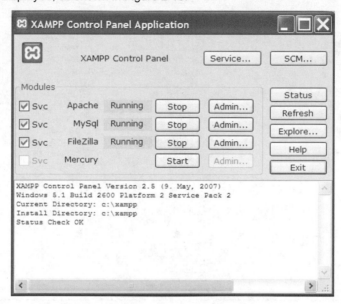

Figure 2-13. XAMPP Control Panel showing the status of services

On the XAMPP Control Panel, you should see that Apache, MySQL, and FileZilla are running (assuming this is what you selected while installing XAMPP). With successful installation of XAMPP, you are assured that your PC now contains Apache, PHP, and MySQL, which are necessary for Joomla installation.

> *Mercury bundled with XAMPP is a mail transport mechanism that provides your website users with message boxes so that they can communicate with each other and/or receive autogenerated messages. It is very straightforward to use. To get started, just click the* `Start` *button in the* `Mercury` *section of the Control Panel. Then click the* `Admin` *button to add users. After managing user accounts, a couple of steps configure this package and make it ready for use. Your website visitors will then be able to send/receive e-mails. But since you will be using the PHP mailer function for managing e-mail on your website, you need not worry about this package at this stage.*

From the XAMPP Control Panel, if you click `Explore`, you'll get a list of all the subfolders under the xampp installation folder, as well as the files required to start and stop XAMPP, as shown in Figure 2-14.

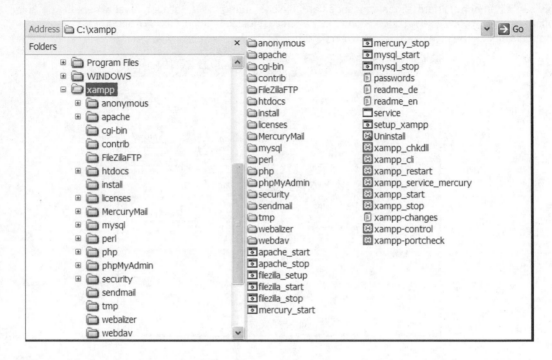

Figure 2-14. List of files and folders in xampp directory

In the XAMPP Control Panel, if you click the `Admin` button in the `MySql` section, you get a screen displaying the environment, server, client, host, and other information of MySQL. You can administer MySQL and set its environment from that page. However, since you don't have to do any administration in MySQL, just click the `Admin` button next to the Apache service in the XAMPP Control Panel. Your default browser will open up, showing a screen asking you to select the language in which you want to administer XAMPP, as shown in Figure 2-15.

Address http://localhost/xampp/splash.php ⌄ ➔ Go Links

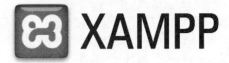

English / Deutsch / Francais / Nederlands / Polski / Italiano / Norwegian / Español / ☐☐ / Português (Brasil) / ☐☐☐

Figure 2-15. Selecting the language to administer XAMPP

Click the appropriate link to display the administration options in the language of your choice. The first page that opens up is a welcome page. On the left side is a navigation bar, as shown in Figure 2-16.

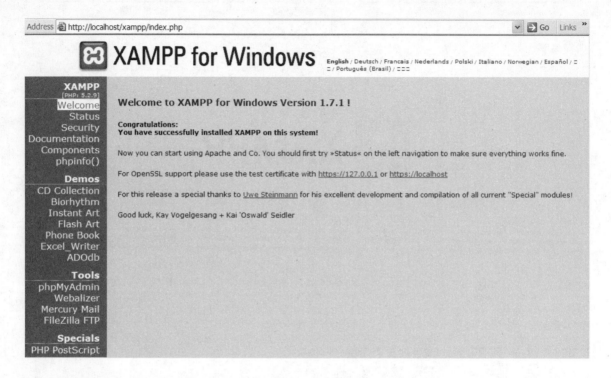

Figure 2-16. Welcome screen displayed upon opening XAMPP

Click the `Status` link on the navigation bar to display the status of the service(s) running on your computer, as shown in Figure 2-17.

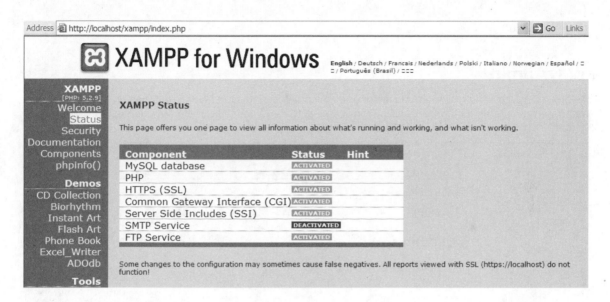

Figure 2-17. Displaying the status of all the services

You can see that MySQL, PHP, HTTPS, Common Gateway Interface (CGI), Server Side Includes (SSI), and FTP Service are all activated. Only SMTP Service (required for sending/receiving e-mails) is not working. Currently, you shouldn't be worried about any other services except PHP and MySQL (required for installing Joomla), so your job is done.

If you click the phpMyAdmin button from the navigation bar on the left side, it will open phpMyAdmin, a software package used for creating and maintaining MySQL databases. Let's take a look at that now.

phpMyAdmin

As previously stated, phpMyAdmin is used for creating and maintaining MySQL databases. The initial database management interface screen (shown in Figure 2-18) can look a little bewildering, but you don't need to worry about a lot of that information for now.

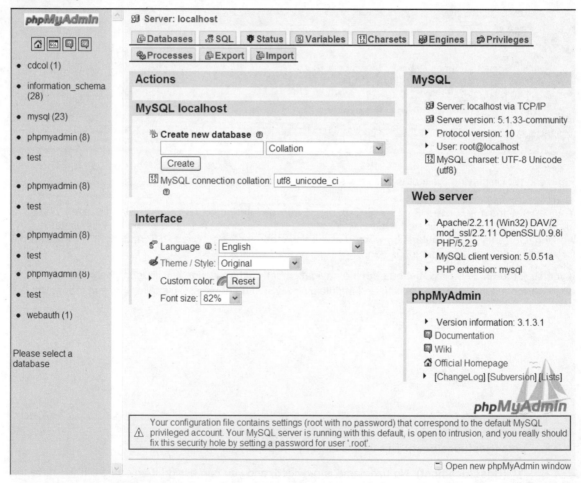

Figure 2-18. The opening screen of phpMyAdmin

The left-hand frame in phpMyAdmin is used for navigation. The databases that you create are displayed in this area, along with the tables (if any) under the respective database names. You can click any database or table to work with it. By default, six databases are provided—namely `cdcol`, `information_schema`, `mysql`, `phpmyadmin`, `test`, and `webauth`. The number in parentheses next to the database name is the number of tables in that database. For example, `mysql (23)` designates that the database name is `mysql` and there are 23 tables in it. If you select the `mysql` database from the navigation bar, you get the list of tables in it, as shown in Figure 2-19.

mysql (23)									
	☐ tables_priv					✕	4	MyISAM	utf8_bin
columns_priv	☐ time_zone					✕	546	MyISAM	utf8_general_ci
db									
event	☐ time_zone_leap_second					✕	23	MyISAM	utf8_general_ci
func	☐ time_zone_name					✕	546	MyISAM	utf8_general_ci
general_log									
help_category	☐ time_zone_transition					✕	37,739	MyISAM	utf8_general_ci
help_keyword	☐ time_zone_transition_type					✕	2,510	MyISAM	utf8_general_ci
help_relation									
help_topic	☑ user					✕	4	MyISAM	utf8_bin
host	23 table(s)			Sum			43,368	**MyISAM**	latin1_swedish_ci
ndb_binlog_index	↑ Check All / Uncheck All / Check tables having overhead						With selected: ▾		
plugin									
proc									
procs_priv									

Figure 2-19. The default tables in the mysql database automatically provided in XAMPP

To see the list of default users of the `mysql` database, you need to browse the contents of the `user` table within it. Just select the check box next to the `user` table, as shown in Figure 2-16, and click the `Browse` icon in that row (it's the first button next to the table name). You'll find that there are four rows in the `user` table, as shown in Figure 2-20. This shows that by default there are four users of the `mysql` database. Users are the people who are authorized to access the `mysql` database. You can edit the contents of these rows to change the username and password, and you can also add new users and delete existing users. The four default users are as follows:

- **root (Host:localhost)**: This user can only access the `mysql` database locally.

- **root (Host:127.0.0.1)**: This user can access the `mysql` database locally and from the Internet. That is, a person can log in remotely and access the `mysql` database. In that case, the host column in the user table of the `mysql` database should be set to the IP address of the remote MySQL server.

- **pma (Host:localhost)**: This user is used by the phpMyAdmin application.

- **" " (Host:localhost)**: No username is provided, and you can assign it any name. It will have the same priviledges as pma and can be used to perform necessary database functions via phpMyAdmin.

For security reasons, you should change the password of root (keeping default passwords is too risky). Since you will be accessing the mysql database locally, you will edit the root user that has the value localhost in its Host column.

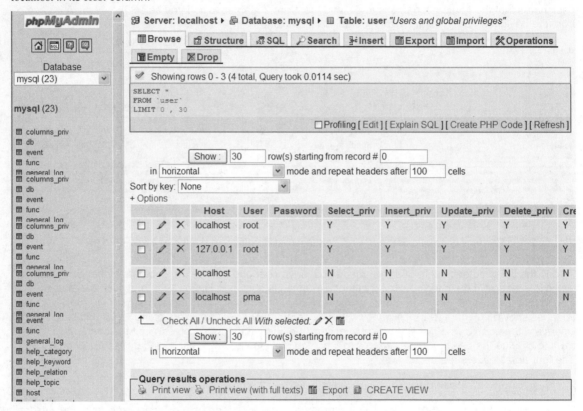

Figure 2-20. Browsing the records in the user table of the MySQL database

Select the first row (which has the value root in its User column and localhost in its Host column) by checking the box for this row, and select the Edit tool in that row (the Edit tool looks like a pen). The table will open in edit mode, and you can alter its contents, as shown in Figure 2-21.

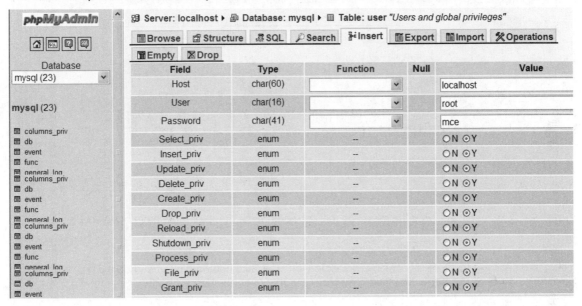

Figure 2-21. Changing the root user's password

Enter a password for the root user. I have used "mce" here, but you can use whatever you like. Click the Go button at the bottom to save the password.

> *If you don't want the password to be stored in the user table as plain text, you can use the PASSWORD function from the Function drop-down box. This will encrypt the password.*

You need to change the default password of the mysql database for security reasons. After saving the password, you'll get a screen like the one shown in Figure 2-22.

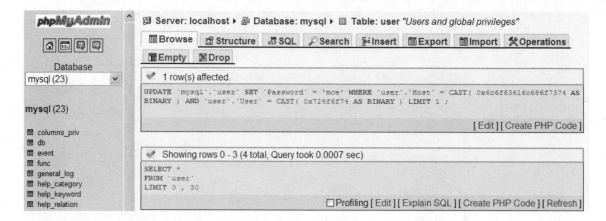

Figure 2-22. Screen displaying the message that the contents of the user table have been successfully modified

You get a message that one row has been updated, and the SQL command that carried it out is displayed below. The message confirms that the password of the root user has been changed.

Creating a database

Since Joomla will store all the raw contents of your website (articles, images, user information, etc.) in a database, you should now create a database. I'll show you how to create a database in MySQL. I'm going to call mine joomladb, but you can use any name you like. So, open the initial screen of phpMyAdmin by clicking the Home button at the top left underneath the phpMyAdmin banner. Then type the name of the database to be created in the Create new database text box, and click the Create button, as shown in Figure 2-23. Don't worry about the rest of the settings; you'll leave everything else as is for now.

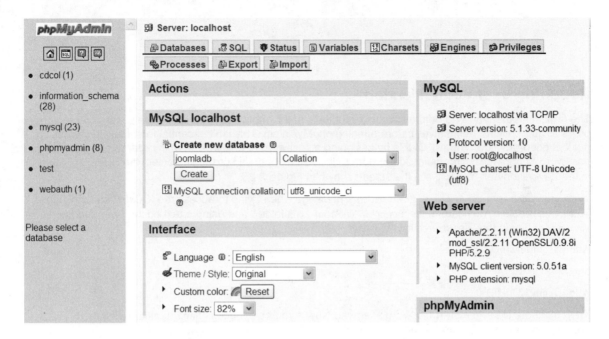

Figure 2-23. Creating a database by name: joomladb

You'll get a message informing you that the database has been successfully created, and a message that the database created (which I'll refer to as joomladb from here on) has no tables in it, as shown in Figure 2-24. However, you don't need to create any tables manually, because it will all be done automatically by Joomla when you start adding features to your website.

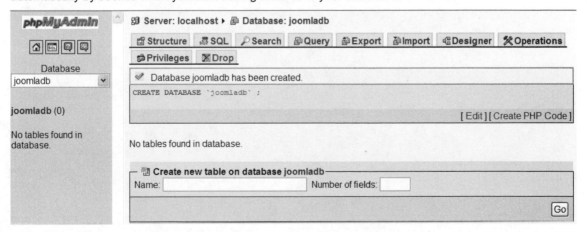

Figure 2-24. Window displaying message of successful creation of the database

Requiring user authentication

The final thing that you'll do before installing Joomla is make phpMyAdmin a little more secure by requiring users to authenticate themselves before opening phpMyAdmin. This isn't essential for installing Joomla, but it is good practice. You will do this by assigning a password to phpMyAdmin. In order to assign a password to phpMyAdmin, you need to return to the XAMPP admin screen and select the `Security` tab in the navigation bar. You will see the screen shown in Figure 2-25.

Vista users may get an `Access forbidden!` message when trying to access the XAMPP security page. To fix this problem, navigate to the xampp\apache\conf\extra folder, and using a text editor, open the httpd-xampp.conf file. In this file, search for the line

Allow from localhost

and change it to

Allow from 127.0.0.1

Then save the file and restart the XAMPP server. Now if you try to access http://localhost/security/lang.php?en, the XAMPP security page will open.

> *If the page still doesn't open, try going into the Apache Services Control Panel and restarting Apache.*

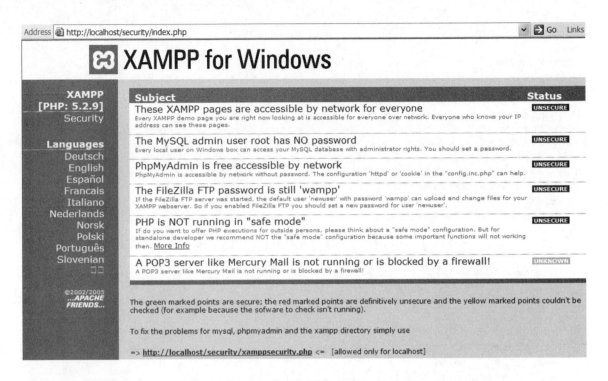

Figure 2-25. Screen showing the security status of MySQL and phpMyAdmin

Click the http://localhost/security/xamppsecurity.php link to open the security console, as shown in Figure 2-26. Specify the password for MySQL SuperUser: root in both the New password and Repeat the new password text boxes.

> The **superuser** is the user who has all the privileges for maintaining the databases. The superuser can create more users, delete existing users, assign and revoke permissions to other users, create backups, and even restore databases in case of system crashes.

Enter any password you like, but make sure that it is something you can remember. Then select either the `http` or `cookie` radio button for `PhpMyAdmin authentification`, and click the `Password changing` button to save the password.

HTTP and **cookie** are authentication modes used in a multiuser environment where you want users to be able to access their own database only. These modes also determine how phpMyAdmin connects to MySQL as the root superuser. By default, cookie mode is used, in which the password is stored in a cookie. Alternatively, you can use HTTP mode, for which you will be prompted to enter the root password every time you access phpMyAdmin. Typically, cookie mode is preferred, since with this mode, the password is stored in encrypted form.

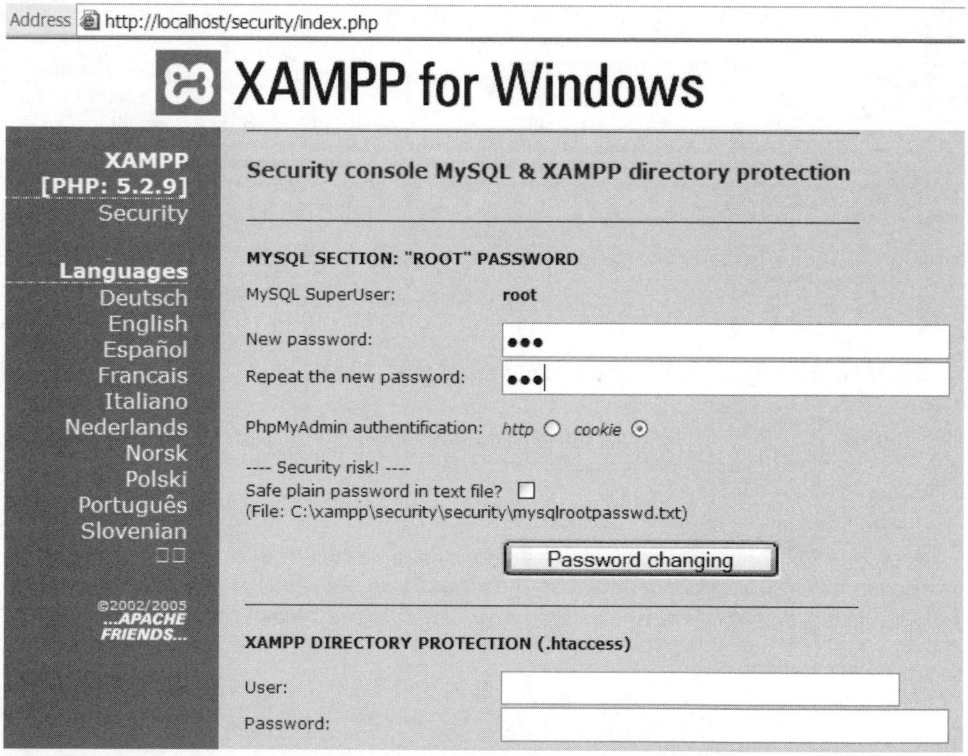

Figure 2-26. Specifying the option for phpMyAdmin authentication and root password

You should now get a confirmation message telling you that the MySQL root password change was successful, as well as a message informing you to restart MySQL so that the change will take effect, as shown in Figure 2-27.

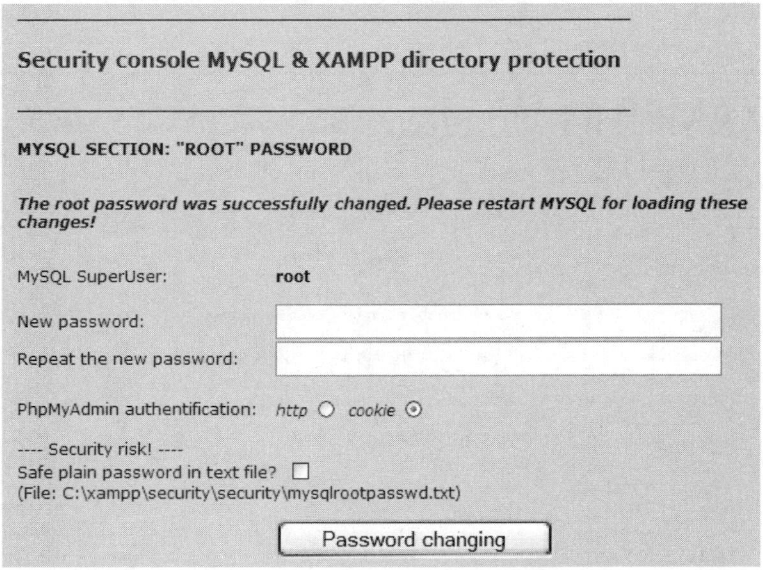

Security console MySQL & XAMPP directory protection

MYSQL SECTION: "ROOT" PASSWORD

The root password was successfully changed. Please restart MYSQL for loading these changes!

MySQL SuperUser: **root**

New password: [   ]

Repeat the new password: [   ]

PhpMyAdmin authentification: *http* ○ *cookie* ◉

---- Security risk! ----
Safe plain password in text file? ☐
(File: C:\xampp\security\security\mysqlrootpasswd.txt)

[Password changing]

Figure 2-27. *Message displaying the successful change of the MySQL root password*

Restart MySQL by clicking the `Stop` button in the `MySql` section of the XAMPP Control Panel (refer to Figure 2-13). The MySQL server is stopped, and the button will change to `Start`. Click it to restart MySQL. To invoke the XAMPP project, click the `Admin` button in the `Apache` section of the XAMPP Control Panel. The XAMPP project will be invoked, and its welcome screen will be displayed, as shown in Figure 2-28.

If you find some error here, it means something is wrong with the password you entered. To fix that error, go to the phpmyadmin directory of the xampp directory and open the config.inc.php file. In it, search for the following line:

find $cfg['Servers'][$i]['password'] = '';

and add your password in the single quotes after the = (equal) sign. For example, if you want to set the password to world2009, then the line will be changed to the following:

$cfg['Servers'][$i]['password'] = 'world2009';

Save the file and you will be able to invoke the XAMPP project. The welcome screen that may appear is as shown in Figure 2-28.

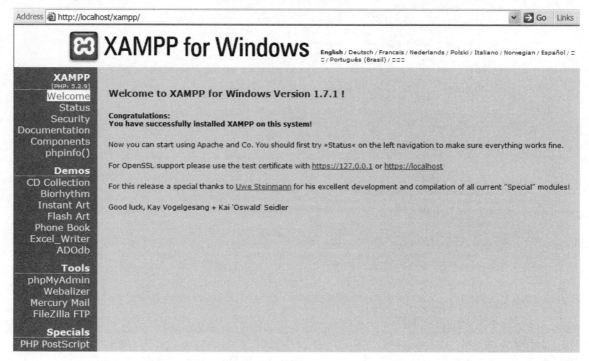

Figure 2-28. Welcome screen of the XAMPP project

Now, if you invoke phpMyAdmin by clicking the `phpMyAdmin` button from the navigation bar, it will not open directly as before, but will prompt the user to enter the password for the root user, as shown in Figure 2-29.

Figure 2-29. Login screen for opening phpMyAdmin

Until you enter the correct password in the preceding page (you have to enter the same password that you specified in the security console—refer to Figure 2-26), phpMyAdmin will not open, and you will not be able to maintain the MySQL database.

Now that the prerequisite conditions of Joomla installation have been successfully met (i.e., you've installed XAMPP, which has automatically installed PHP, MySQL, and Apache), you can go ahead and install Joomla on the local server (Apache) installed on your PC.

Installing Joomla! locally

To install Joomla on a local server, you have to unzip the Joomla ZIP file into a subfolder of the htdocs directory of XAMPP. That is, you have to first make a subfolder inside the htdocs directory of your XAMPP project, where you will store all of the Joomla files and folders. Recall that you have installed your XAMPP project in the default c:\xampp folder, so open this folder and go to its htdocs directory. Now make a subfolder in the c:\xampp\htdocs directory. I called mine "joomlasite," but the name doesn't matter. The only thing left to do now is to copy the Joomla files and folder into this `joomlasite` subfolder.

Download the latest Joomla package from the Internet by going to www.joomla.org and clicking the `Download Joomla` button. It is packaged in a ZIP file, so you'll need to have appropriate software, such as WinZip, in order to unpack it. I have downloaded the Joomla package, and it is in the form of a Joomla_1.5.10-Stable-Full_Package.zip file, but this may vary depending on the latest release available on the Internet. Unzip the file to any folder and copy all the unzipped files and folders of the Joomla package into the joomlasite subfolder (created in the c:\xampp\htdocs directory).

Joomla version 1.5 is certainly an upgraded version of Joomla 1.0. It includes the following added features:

- It allows you to preview your website after making changes.

- It has an improved user interface that allows you to manage media files (images, songs, videos, etc.) easily.

- It includes a new plug-in manager.

- It allows multi-CSS file editing.

- It has full support for Atom 1.0 and RSS 2.0 feeds.

- It has better internationalization support, including full UTF-8 support, RTL support, and translation using INI files.

- It contains several components that help in developing Ajax applications easily.

Joomla is installed using a browser. So, open your browser and point it to the following address: http://localhost/joomlasite/installation (assuming you have copied the Joomla files and folder into the joomlasite subfolder of the htdocs folder). The first screen that you'll get is the `Choose Language` screen, from which you can select the language to be used for the installation steps. Select `English`, and then click `Next`, as shown in Figure 2-30.

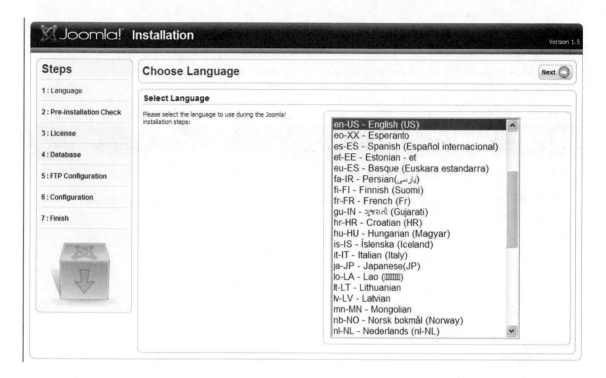

Figure 2-30. Selecting a language to install Joomla

Next, you'll get the `Pre-installation Check` screen (shown in Figure 2-31), which checks whether your system has all the prerequisite software and items required for successful installation of Joomla. The list of items that are required but are not currently supported by your system will be marked `No` so that you can configure your system before proceeding.

> Usually, all the required options will be marked `Yes` if XAMPP is installed and configured properly; if any option is marked `No`, it is always better to reinstall XAMPP.

This screen also displays the recommended settings for PHP for making it fully compatible with Joomla. You don't have to worry too much about these, as they will not hamper Joomla operations if your settings do not match. Click Next.

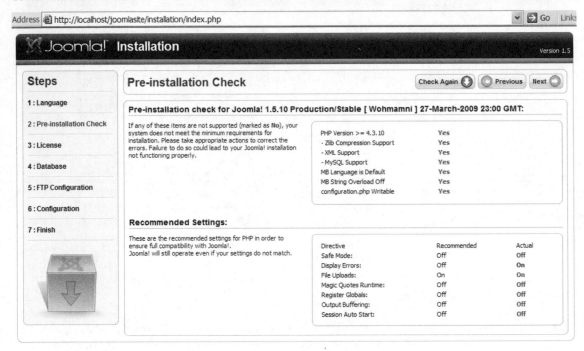

Figure 2-31. Screen that checks the preinstalled software and displays recommended settings

Next, you'll be taken to the `License` screen (see Figure 2-32), which explains that Joomla is released under the GNU General Public License (GPL). Read the terms and conditions of using this open source project that is mutually developed by thousands of developers around the world, and then click `Next`.

Figure 2-32. Screen displaying the Joomla GPL

The next screen is `Database Configuration`, as shown in Figure 2-33. Here, you specify the information for the database you created via phpMyAdmin in MySQL earlier. Recall that you created a MySQL database called joomladb via phpMyAdmin, and also set the root user's password to "mce" (or whatver password you chose) by altering the contents of the user table of your mysql database. Specify the `Host Name` as `localhost` here because you are installing Joomla on the local server. Also, enter the MySQL username and password that you defined earlier—in my case it's `root` and `mce`. In the `Database Name` text box, enter `joomladb`. This database will now be used for storing the contents of your Joomla website. Click `Next`.

> *When you install Joomla on the remote server, the host name, username, and password are provided by the hosting company.*
>
> *Having your website **hosted** involves the procedure of uploading your website to a public server to be viewed and accessed by the rest of world. It gives you the ability to show your presence on Internet. Website hosting has become the most common medium to advertise the services, facilities, and products provided by an organization. It has also become a great medium to get feedback from customers around the globe. The server space for hosting websites is provided by various web hosting companies.*
>
> *Web hosting companies offer an environment where people can have their piece of cyberspace on the Internet 24/7 without the great cost. These companies provide the space where you can keep your website, news, bulletins, documents, data, and post office (mail server) to accept mail. You just need to pay for the disk space used on the server and any extra charges for database support. The core components in a web hosting environment are the web server, FTP server, mail server, and database server.*

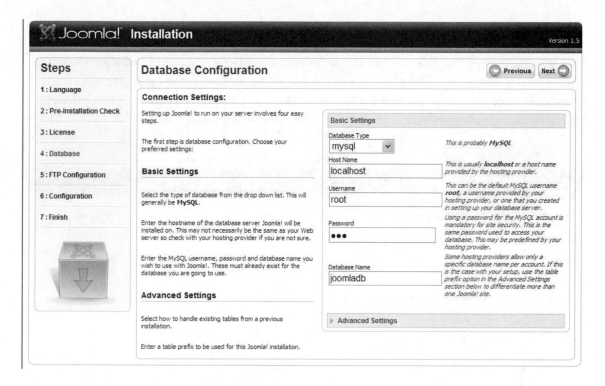

Figure 2-33. Screen for specifying database configuration settings

Next, you get the `FTP Configuration` screen, as shown in Figure 2-34. Since you are installing Joomla on the local server, you don't have to enter anything on this screen—just skip this step and click `Next`. Also, if you want to provide FTP information in the future, you can do so by accessing the global configuration settings anytime (explained in detail in Chapter 10).

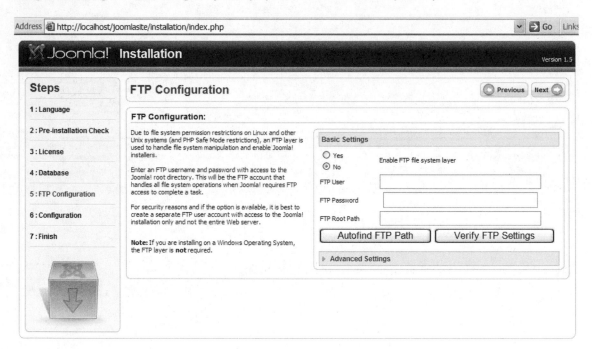

Figure 2-34. Screen for specifying FTP configuration settings

The final step is the `Main Configuration` screen (shown in Figure 2-35), which asks the name of your Joomla site. I'm using the name harwanibm.net, but you can use whatever name you'd like for your site. Also, you have to specify the e-mail ID of the super-administrator, so enter your own e-mail address here. The e-mail ID informs the website owner about maintenance tasks that are performed on the server (it is usually used while doing remote Joomla installation). The username of the super-administrator is set to "admin" by default, and you can't change it. You do have to specify the password for admin, though. Enter a password that you'll remember in this field, and confirm it in the field below.

This `Main Configuration` page also helps beginners by providing sample data. This sample data includes a set of menus, navigation links, sections, and categories, and is extremely useful for beginners learning the workings of Joomla and its different modules. So, select the `Install Default Sample Data` radio button, and then click the `Install Sample Data` button. This will create a sample website for you. You will be using and modifying this website throughout the book to get a feel for how Joomla works. At the end of the book, you will create a new website of your own from scratch using all of the skills that you've learned.

You may also select the option `Load Migration Script` to load and execute the SQL script containing the backup of the website (if the Joomla website was made earlier and you want to restore it).

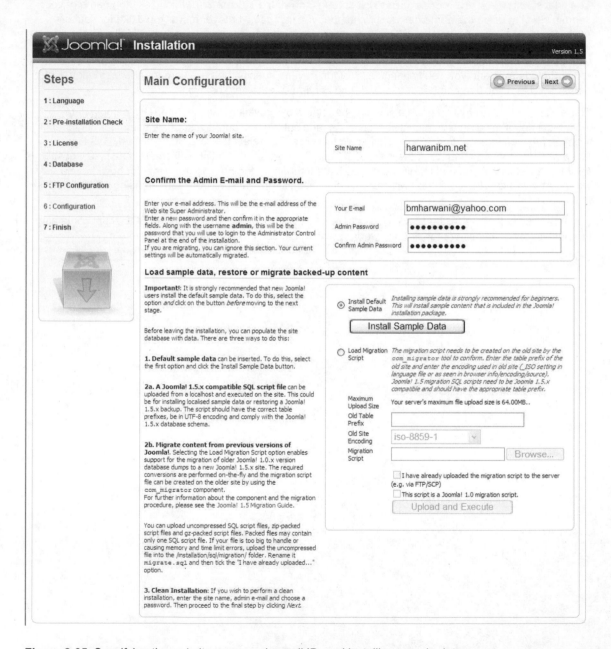

Figure 2-35. Specifying the website name and e-mail ID, and installing sample data

Once you click the `Install Sample Data` button, you'll get a message that reads `Sample data installed successfully,` as shown in Figure 2-36.

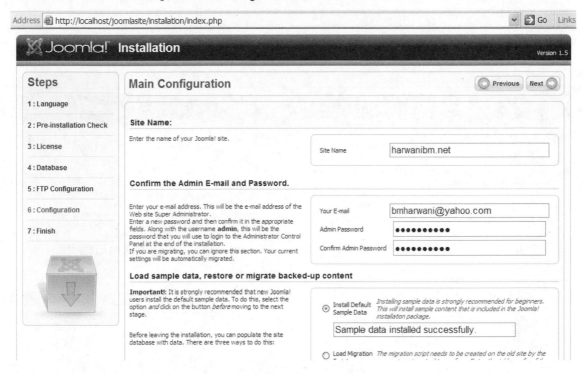

Figure 2-36. Message that the sample data has been installed successfully

Finally, you'll get a `Finish` screen displaying the message, `Congratulations! Joomla! is now installed`. You'll also get a message telling you to remove the installation directory from the joomlasite subfolder (in the c:\xampp\htdocs directory), as shown in Figure 2-37. This is a compulsory condition for successful installation of Joomla because of security reasons.

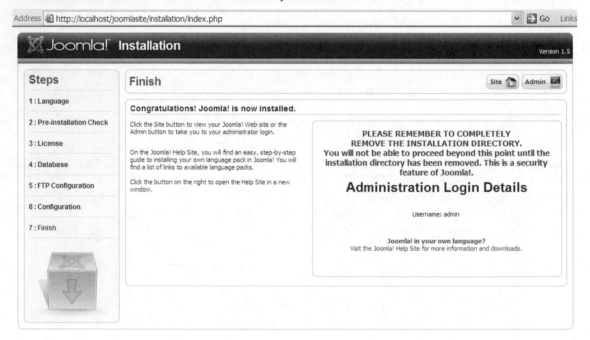

Figure 2-37. Screen displaying the message of successful Joomla installation and a note for deleting the installation directory

You cannot delete the installation folder from within Joomla. You need to do it either with Windows Explorer or with the command line. To do so via Windows Explorer, open the joomlasite subfolder of the c:\xampp\htdocs directory and search for the installation directory (shown in Figure 2-38).

Figure 2-38. The installation folder to be deleted

Select the installation folder and delete it. Return to the installer screen (Figure 2-37) and click the Site button at the top-right corner.

The page that appears is actually your new website (it should look something like Figure 2-39). The reason that all of that content is already there is because you clicked the Install Sample Data button earlier. You'll be changing this website throughout the rest of the book to make it something of your own. This website can now be accessed anytime by pointing the browser at http://localhost/joomlasite, replacing joomlasite with whatever you called your website earlier.

> *I'll be using joomlasite throughout the book, so remember to change the name to whatever you called your own website whenever you see it appear.*

Figure 2-39. The first welcome screen of the Joomla website made by you

To administer this Joomla website and manage its content, you have to use the Administrator interface, which you can open by pointing the browser at the following address: http://localhost/joomlasite/administrator. Before opening the Administrator interface, you will be prompted to specify the super-administrator's username (admin) and password (the password you entered during the Joomla installation earlier), as shown in Figure 2-40.

The default super-administrator's username is "admin."

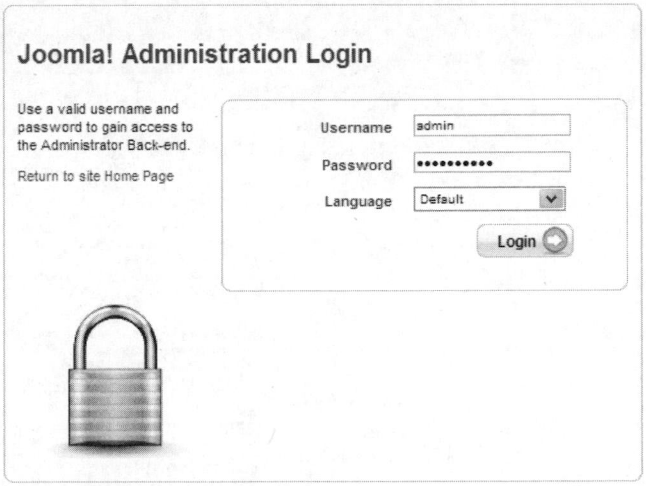

Figure 2-40. Opening the Joomla Administrator interface by entering the username and password

In the Administrator interface, you find a control panel and menus to manage the website contents, as shown in Figure 2-41.

Figure 2-41. Screen showing different managers and menus of the Joomla Administrator interface

From Chapter 3 onward, you will learn how to use these managers and menus to maintain your Joomla website.

That's it for installing Joomla on your local machine. The next thing you need to do if you want the rest of the world to be able to see your Joomla site is to install Joomla on a remote server.

Installing Joomla! on a remote server

In order to install Joomla on a remote server, you need to do two things:

- Register a domain name

- Book a web space on a server

If you do not already own a domain name, there are a great many services available on the Web that will enable you to register one. I have registered a domain by name (bmharwani.net) and booked around 2GB of space on a server via a web hosting provider company.

Before you proceed, you should know the following things about your hosted account:

- PHP is installed and enabled.

- You have a MySQL database for the website and you know the MySQL database name, usename, and password.

You just need to upload the Joomla ZIP file to the public_html folder on the remote server (or whatever folder is provided by your hosting company), and then unpack it. You can even use File Manager to extract the files. Then you open the browser and type in your domain name (in my case www.bmharwani.net), after which you will get the first Joomla installation screen. The rest of the procedure should then be exactly the same as a local installation.

Another way to install Joomla is to use the Fantastico tool provided by the web hosting service provider, available in the control panel.

Fantastico is an easy-to-use tool that facilitates the installation of many open source applications on web hosting accounts. With just a few clicks of the mouse, it uploads files and configures databases. With the help of this tool, you can easily install a large number of CMSs, blogs, forums, shopping carts, galleries, and so on.

Fantastico, being an autoinstaller script, provides a step-by-step wizard to install Joomla on the remote server. To execute Fantastico tool, you have to first access the control panel.

The control panel, called **cPanel**, is a premier software package that makes life easier for web hosts and website owners. It offers easy-to-use, powerful tools that perform essential tasks easily. It provides a GUI interface to help website owners manage their sites. It also includes video tutorials and onscreen help that allows hosting customers to manage their own accounts without requiring any help from the support staff. Also, it includes virus protection, rootkit detection, and a host of other tools to keep servers secure. To access cPanel, open the browser and point it at the following address: www.bmharwani.net/cpanel.

You will be asked to specify the username and password. Enter the username and password supplied to you by the web hosting service provider while booking the web space. After entering the correct username and password, cPanel will open. Select the option `Fantastico Home` from the `Navigation` menu, and you should get a screen similar to Figure 2-42.

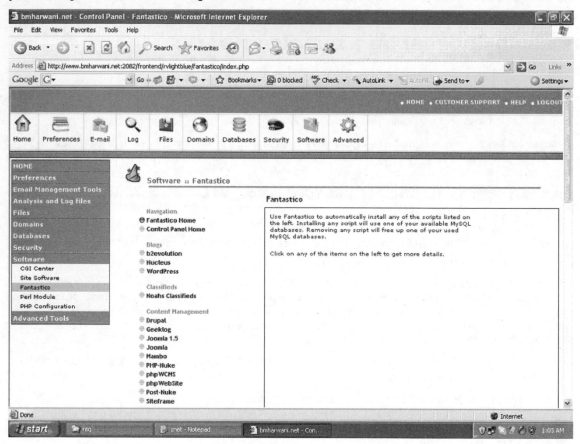

Figure 2-42. Screen showing the control panel

From the `Content Management` category, select the `Joomla1.5` link. You'll get a screen displaying a small introduction to Joomla along with its home page link, as shown in Figure 2-43.

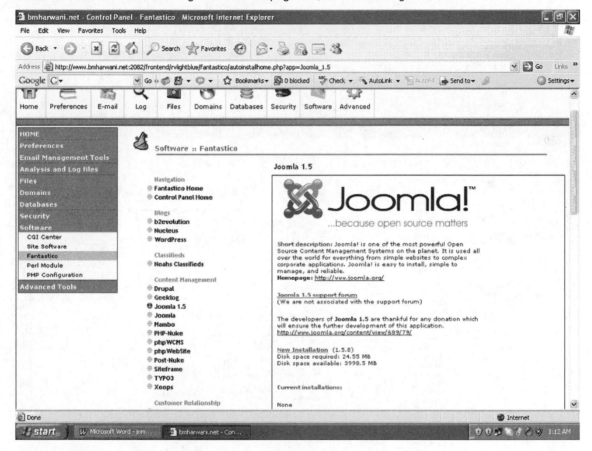

Figure 2-43. The Joomla 1.5 introduction page

Select the `New Installation` link, as you are installing Joomla for the first time in your web space. You will be asked to specify certain information, including the following (see Figure 2-44):

- **The domain name to install Joomla on**: Enter the name of your web domain here (mine is bmharwani.net).

- **The administrator username and password**: You will be prompted to enter the username and password whenever you open the Administrator interface for your Joomla website.

- **The e-mail ID of the administrator**: Enter your e-mail address.

- **The full name of the administrator**: Enter your name here.

- **The website name**: Enter your website name here (mine is bmharwani.net).

- **The sample content to install**: Select the `Install Sample Data?` check box to install your sample content (menus, articles, modules, etc.).

After entering all the preceding information, click the `Install Joomla 1.5` button.

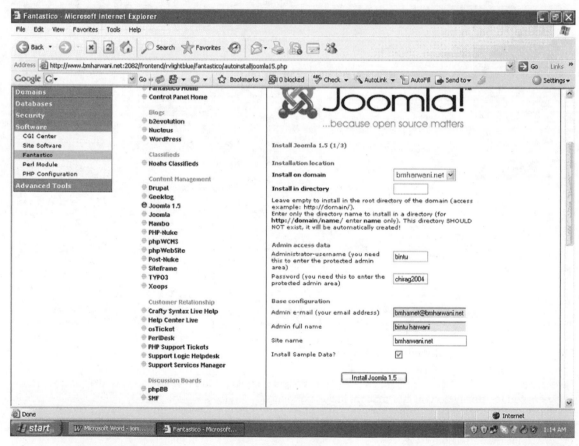

Figure 2-44. Screen for specifying Joomla website information and administrator details

As shown in Figure 2-45, you'll get a message that the MySQL database and MySQL user are being created as bmharnet_jo151 (this name is provided by the web hosting service provider, and it may vary). That is, the MySQL database is created as bmharnet_jo151, and the MySQL user is created as bmharnet_jo151 as well. This also means that your Joomla website will be stored in the bmharnet_jo151 database on the remote MySQL server of the web hosting service provider.

> *You need to remember this database name, as it may be required for future maintenance tasks.*

The URL to access the Joomla website is also provided: http://bmharwani.net. Click Finish installation.

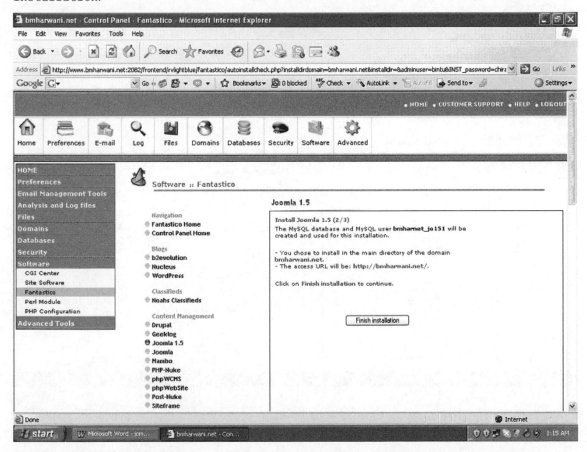

Figure 2-45. Screen displaying the MySQL database name, username, and URL to access the Joomla website

The last screen that you got, as shown in Figure 2-46, displays a message that Joomla is installed. Also, you are provided the URLs to access the website and the Administrator interface—they are http://bmharwani.net/ and http://bmharwani.net/administrator/, respectively. That is, to see your Joomla website, you point the browser at address http://bmharwani.net/, and to manage its content, you open its Administrator interface by pointing the browser at http://bmharwani.net/administrator/.

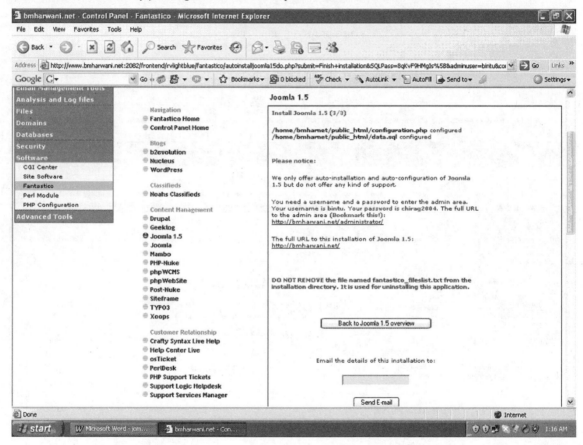

Figure 2-46. Screen showing that the Joomla website has been created and displaying the URLs for the website and Administrator interface

While opening the Administrator interface, you will be prompted to enter the administrator username and password (that you entered in Figure 2-44). If you enter the correct username and password, as shown in Figure 2-47, then the Administrator interface will be invoked.

Figure 2-47. Opening the Administrator interface of your Joomla website

When the Administrator interface opens, you'll be shown a control panel that has a list of managers and menus used for maintaining the website content, as shown in Figure 2-48.

Figure 2-48. Control panel screen with its managers and menus displayed

To see the Joomla website, point the browser at http://bmharwani.net/, and you should see a fully functional website, as shown in Figure 2-49. The content and modules that you see are provided as sample data, which you can remove through the Administrator interface anytime.

If the Joomla site doesn't open, and you get some "Hello" message instead, it means that there is a file named index.html in your home directory that is preventing your index.php file (the home page of your Joomla website) to execute. Usually every web hosting company provides a default opening file—index.html—on creating your web space account. This index.html file just displays a "Hello" or "Welcome" message. This file has to be deleted in order to invoke the opening web page—index.php—of your Joomla site. The location of the home directory is specified by the web hosting service provider, and is usually public_html. Connect to your domain with some FTP client software, go to the public_html folder, and delete any file with the primary name index.

After you take care of this, your job should be done! Just refresh the browser, and a fully functional Joomla website will be displayed on the screen.

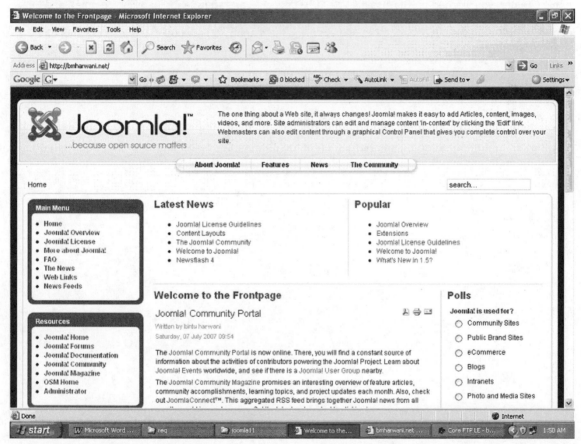

Figure 2-49. Fully functional Joomla website with default content

Summary

In this chapter, you learned how to install an XAMPP project (a prerequisite for installing Joomla), and took a step-by-step walkthrough of installing Joomla on a local as well as a remote server. The next step is learning to maintain your Joomla website content using the managers provided in the control panel of the Administrator interface.

Chapter 3

Your First Steps in Joomla!

In the previous chapter, we looked in detail at the installation of the XAMPP framework and the Joomla package. While installing Joomla, you were prompted to specify the name of the Joomla website you wanted to create (in this case, harwanibm.net). As a result, Joomla created a full fledged website that already contains menus, links, search boxes, articles, polls, news feeds, and so on, and all of these features are functional. This automatically generated content can be updated, deleted, and added to at any time.

> *As mentioned in Chapter 2, the entire content of the website so far is stored in the MySQL database named joomladb (although you could have called it anything) that you created when you installed Joomla. This is what is meant by a content management system (CMS): the whole website is managed in one place, and what could be a better place than a database?*

Before we get started, there are two important terms that will crop up again and again throughout this book, and it will be useful to define them now. They are *front end* and *back end*.

Front end refers to the website itself; the part that's accessed by users or visitors and that displays the content of the website itself. The front end is called up by opening a browser window and pointing at the address (in this case http://localhost/joomlasite—remember that joomlasite was the folder where we unpackaged Joomla, and at this stage we are dealing with the local server). The front end of your Joomla website will appear as shown in Figure 3-1.

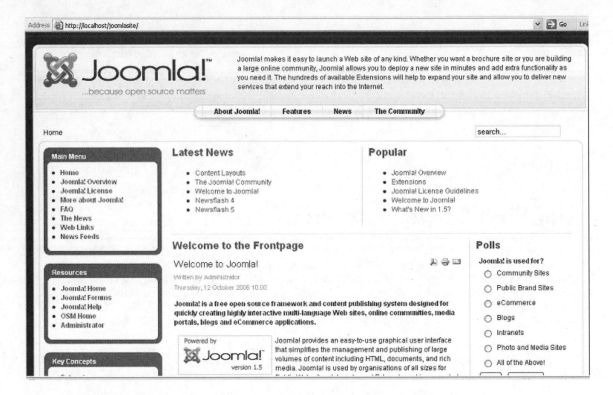

Figure 3-1. The default Joomla website

The **back end** is the Administrator interface, which you use to manipulate the contents of your website. It provides a control panel and other tools essential for maintaining your website. To reach the Administrator interface, open a browser window and point it at the address http://localhost/joomlasite/administrator.

With those terms defined, you're now ready to move on and get your first proper taste of Joomla. In this chapter, we are going to cover the following:

- A brief introduction to the Administrator interface

- The front page: What it is, and why it's important

- The impact of templates on a Joomla website

The elements of the Administrator interface

A CMS (content management system), as we discussed in Chapter 1, is a computer software system for organizing and managing documents, including web content. Joomla, being a CMS, provides a control panel and tools for you to manage your website and its contents, and this control panel can be accessed by using the Joomla Administrator interface. The Joomla Administrator interface enables you to add or edit content, upload images, and manage website data. To open the Joomla Administrator interface, open your browser and point it at http://localhost/joomlasite/administrator.

So, from now onward, you will have two windows open on your computer system: one with the browser pointing at http://localhost/joomlasite (showing your Joomla website), and the other pointing at http://localhost/joomlsite/administrator (displaying the administrator tools and managers). You'll manage the web contents through the Administrator interface, and switch to the Joomla website browser window and refresh it to see the effect of the changes made to your Joomla website. You can also view your updated Joomla website directly from the Administrator interface. The Preview link at the top right quickly opens up the home page of your Joomla website in a new window (in Internet Explorer) or a new tab (in Firefox).

Before the Administrator interface opens, you will be prompted to log in, as shown in Figure 3-2. Enter the administrator name and password that you specified while installing Joomla.

Figure 3-2. Login screen of the Administrator interface

The first screen that you'll see upon opening the Administrator interface is shown in Figure 3-3. This screen contains a set of buttons for the various Joomla managers, which are collectively called the **control panel**, and menus to manage your website contents.

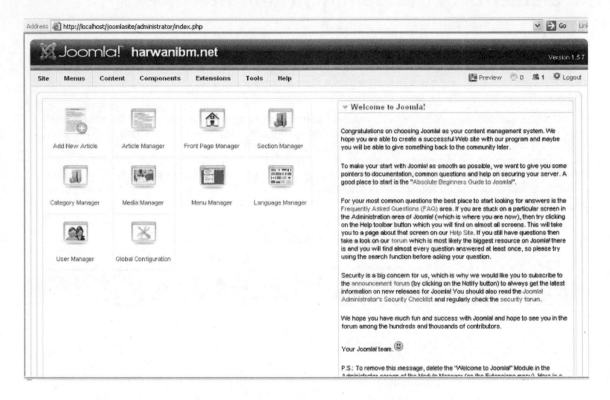

Figure 3-3. Administrator screen displaying the control panel (managers) and menus

This panel is where some of the most important features of Joomla can be found, and you'll be spending a lot of your time here. It is a sort of control tower for your website, where you can maintain its content and appearance. Each of the managers in the interface has a specific function, so let's take a look at them and see what they can do.

The Control Panel

In the control panel, you'll find a menu bar that contains drop-down menu items allowing access to all of the main Joomla functions. It also has a set of buttons that represent the most common actions, providing shortcuts to some of the menu items. Finally, it provides a utility toolbar at the top right that, among other things, allows you to view the front end of your Joomla website (the way it will appear to the user).

The control panel contains the following managers:

- Add New Article

- Article Manager

- Front Page Manager

- Section Manager

- Category Manager

- Media Manager

- Menu Manager

- Language Manager

- User Manager

- Global Configuration

Instead of running through all of these managers sequentially, I'll focus on those managers that will enable you to quickly get up and running and develop some content for your Joomla website. Before creating the content, let's take a look at the relationship between five key parts of Joomla that you'll need to understand to get the most out of the Administrator interface: menu items, menus, sections, categories, and articles.

A **menu item** appears as a link on a website that when selected displays some kind of information. Several menu items are collectively placed under one menu heading. In other words, a **menu** is a collection of several menu items. For example, Figure 3-5 shows two menus: Main Menu and Key Concepts; each has its respective menu items underneath it. For example, the Main Menu consists of the menu items Home, Joomla! Overview, Joomla! License, More about Joomla!, and so on.

A **section** is a collection of related **categories**. Suppose that on your website you want to display information about electronic and digital products, where electronic products consist of categories such as Camera and Cell Phone, and digital products consists of categories like Computer and Pen Drive. In that case, you need to create two sections for your website, namely Electronics and Digital. The Electronics section will have two categories to start with—Camera and Cell Phone—and the Digital section will have two categories—Computer and Pen Drive—as shown in Figure 3-4.

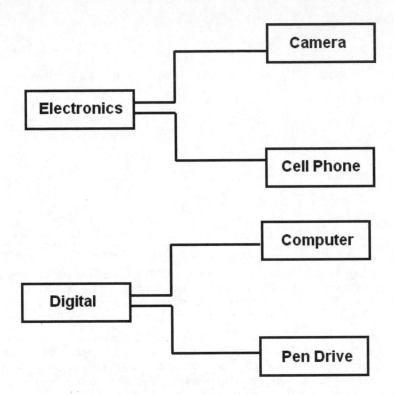

Figure 3-4. Electronics and Digital sections with two categories each

To display information for different types of computers (for your Computer category), you create one or more **articles** and link them with the Computer category of the Digital section. An article is a web page that can contain text, images, and animations to provide information about a product or service. You can create several articles for a category. So, a section consists of one or more categories and a category may store one or more articles

Using the Section, Category, Article, and Menu Item Managers

Let's make a website that looks something like the one shown in Figure 3-5. As shown in the figure, you'll add a new menu item, `New Electronics Products arrival`. When selected, this menu item will display the Camera category of the Electronics section.

> Joomla provides several default sections, categories, and articles in you website to give you an idea of how they are related. You can unpublish any of them to remove them from the website and create your own contents instead.

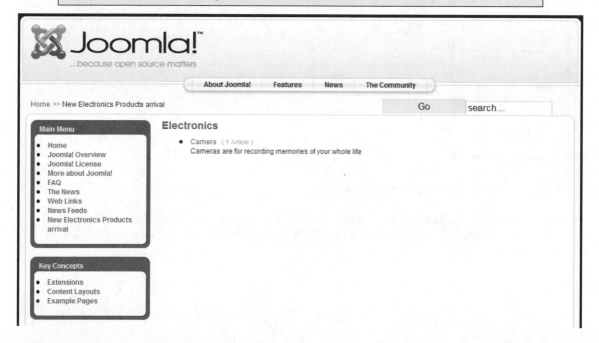

Figure 3-5. Menu item displaying the Camera category of the Electronics section

Before we get started, I'll give a brief overview of what your example website will look like and how it will function. Though you can create several sections and categories in your website, for this exercise, we'll keep it simple and just create one of each: a Camera category inside an Electronics section. When your visitor selects the Camera category, he will see the list of articles in that category, as shown in Figure 3-6.

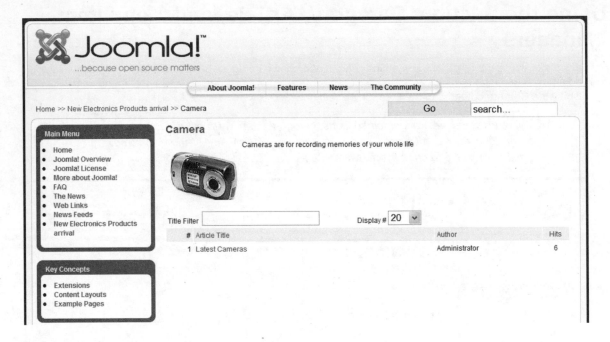

Figure 3-6. List of articles in the Camera category

Again, to keep the example simple, you'll also just display a single article when the Camera category is selected: "Latest Cameras." When the article title is selected, it will display the content of that article, as shown in Figure 3-7.

Figure 3-7. Content of the "Latest Cameras" article

To create some simple content for your example website, you'll make use of three managers found in the control panel: the Section Manager, the Category Manager, and the Article Manager. To create this simple content, you'll perform the following steps:

1. Create the Electronics section using the Section Manager.
2. Create the Camera category in the Electronics section using the Category Manager.
3. Create an article ("Latest Cameras") in the Camera category using the Article Manager.
4. Create a menu item (`New Electronics Products arrival`) using the Menu Manager and linking it to the Electronics section.

Creating a section (Section Manager)

Now, I'll show you how to build the Electronics section for your website using the Section Manager. Click the `Section Manager` button in the control panel, and the Section Manager will open, as shown in Figure 3-8. Notice that each manager window has a title in a consistent location to help you in locating your position in the Joomla environment. Also, most managers have a similar toolbar button layout and behavior. The Section Manager, as the name suggests, is used for managing sections, which entails the following:

- Creating new sections.

- Editing or deleting existing sections. A section cannot be deleted unless it is empty (i.e., before deleting any section, you have to first erase all its categories along with their contents so that you don't delete a section by mistake).

- Copying a category along with its articles from one section to another. When copying a category, you'll be prompted to specify the section to which the selected category's contents are to be copied.

- Publishing or unpublishing selected sections. If you unpublish a section, its articles will no longer be visible on your website.

- Setting the order (sequence) that the sections will be displayed on the front page.

- Setting the access level of the section (i.e., deciding whether the articles of the section can be viewed publicly or are meant to be viewed by only a specific group of users).

- Displaying the number of categories in each section.

Figure 3-8. Section Manager

Table 3-1 gives a description of all the columns in the Section Manager.

Table 3-1. Brief explanation of the Section Manager columns

Column	Description
Title	Displays the title of the section.
Published	Shows whether the section is currently in the published or unpublished state. A check mark indicates that the section is published (i.e., its categories and their corresponding articles will be visible on the website), and a red *X* indicates that the section is unpublished.
Order	Shows the order in which the section items are displayed on the front page, and enables you to change the order (by using the up and down arrows or typing in the sequence number). After changing the sequence number of a section, you can save it by clicking the Save button (floppy disk image) in the column heading.
Access Level	Displays the access level of the section—that is, which level of users can access the section. The access levels are as follows: Public: Anyone can access it. Registered: Only registered users can access it. Special: Only users with author status or higher can access it.
Categories	Displays the number of categories in the section.
Active	Displays the number of published content items in the section.
Trash	Displays the number of content items of the section that are deleted and are currently in the trash.
ID	Displays the identification number of the section as defined in the database.

Now click the New button in the toolbar at the top right of the Section Manager to create a new section. When you click the New button, you'll get a screen to specify information for the new section, as shown in Figure 3-9. On this screen, you can specify a variety of information for the section, including the title, access level, image, and description.

Figure 3-9. Creating a new section

For the `Title`, enter the name for your new section: Electronics. The `Alias` is a sort of secondary name for the section that is used internally by Joomla. You can leave it blank here (and anywhere else) and Joomla will fill it in automatically, or you can give it your own meaningful name. If you specify it, it must be lowercase, and it cannot contain any spaces (hyphens are the only allowed symbol—they should be substituted for spaces). Basically, the alias is used in SEF (search engine–friendly) URLs (which help search engines display your website content and also help you control the text that you want to appear in the URL). For this exercise, enter `electronics` for the alias.

Set the `Published` option to `Yes` to make the section visible on the website (unpublished sections don't appear on the website), and set the `Access Level` to `Public` to make the section accessible to anyone.

From the `Image` drop-down list, select an image to represent the section. The drop-down list shows the list of images present in the Media Manager. The Media Manager stores the images provided by default by Joomla, as well as those that are uploaded by the user. The `Image Position` allows you to specify whether you want the image to appear on the left or right side of the section title. For this exercise, choose `Left`.

In the `Description` text box, you can enter a few lines to describe the section. You can also insert an image into the description using the `Image` button at the bottom. Click the `Image` button, and you'll be presented with the images available in the Media Manager. Joomla provides some images by default, but you can also upload your own images into the Media Manager.

It is very easy to upload new images into the Media Manager. Just click the `Browse` button in the `Upload` section, as shown in Figure 3-10, to locate the folder that contains the image file to upload (preferably in PNG or JPG format). Assuming that you have a camera.jpg file on your local drive, select it, and then click the `Start Upload` button to upload the image into the Media Manager.

> *Generally, it is best to upload all the images that you are going to use on your website to the Media Manager before creating the website contents, as all the images for your website are accessed from the Media Manager.*

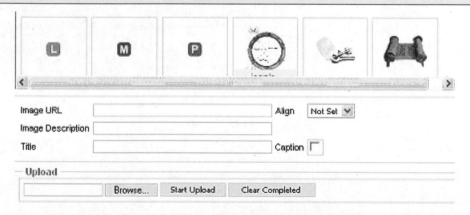

Figure 3-10. Uploading new images

When you select an image thumbnail, the URL of the image will be displayed in the `Image URL` field. In the `Image Description` field, you can enter a short description of the image. In the `Title` field, you enter the title of the image, which will be displayed when a visitor hovers the mouse over the image. Check the `Caption` check box if you want the title of the image to appear as its caption below the image.

After selecting the image to be uploaded to the Media Manager, when you click the Start Upload button, the image will be uploaded to the Joomla's images/stories folder, and a Completed message will appear to show that the uploading is done. Click the Clear Completed button to clear the Completed message.

Select the camera.jpg file and click the Insert button, and the image will appear in the Description region of the section.

After you've finished, click the Save button to save the Electronics section. You'll get the message Section Saved, and the newly added section will appear in the Section Manager list (see Figure 3-11).

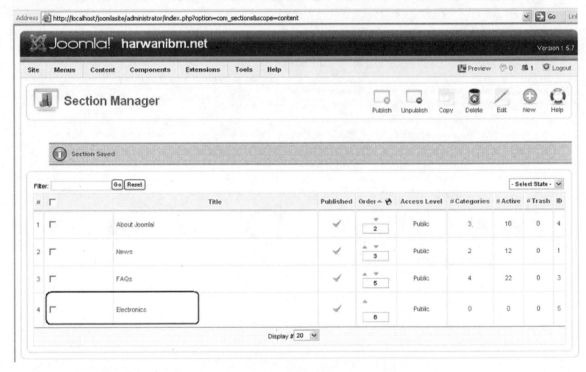

Figure 3-11. A new section added in the Section Manager

Now that you've learned how to add a new section, let's look at how to add a new category.

Creating a category (Category Manager)

Recall that categories are used to categorize the contents of a website and are set up as a part of a section. To create categories, you use the Category Manager. There are two ways of opening the Category Manager. You can either leave the Section Manager and open the control panel by selecting `Site` ➤ `Control Panel`, and then click the `Category Manager` icon; or you can select the `Content` ➤ `Category Manager` option from the current location. The Category Manager displays a table of existing categories of articles (provided by Joomla) and provides tools to manage them, as shown in Figure 3-12. It does the following jobs:

- Creating new categories under a given section

- Editing or deleting an existing category. Before deleting a category, it is essential that the category is empty, meaning that all of its articles are removed.

- Moving and copying a category (along with its contents) from one section to another.

- Publishing or unpublishing a selected category. Unpublishing a category makes all the articles within that category invisible on the website

- Setting the order (sequence) in which categories and their contents are displayed

- Setting the group of users that are allowed to view the contents of the specific category

- Displaying the section name to which the category belongs

Figure 3-12. Category Manager

To create a new category, click `New` button in the toolbar. You'll get a screen with a few fields for specifying the details of the category being created, as shown in Figure 3-13.

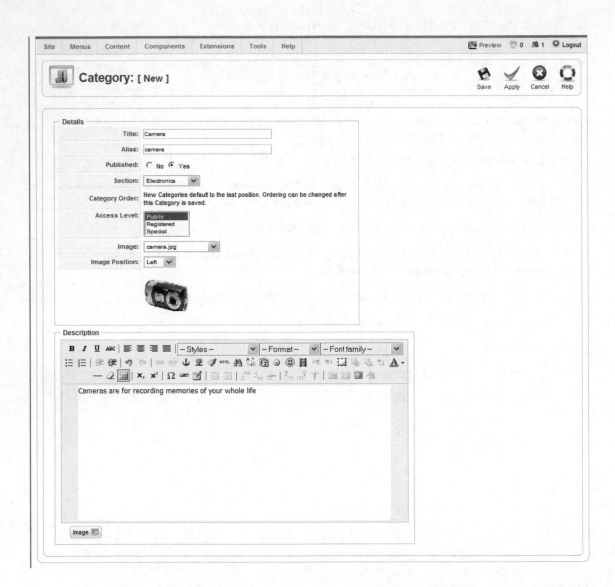

Figure 3-13. Creating a new category

In the `Title` field, you enter the name of your new category (in this case, `Camera`). As mentioned in the previous section, the alias is a sort of secondary name, and can be left blank. However, for the purposes of this exercise, enter `camera` here (remember that the alias must be lowercase and cannot contain spaces [use hyphens instead]). Set the `Published` option to `Yes` to make the category visible on the website. From the `Section` drop-down list, select the section to which you want the category to belong—in this case, `Electronics`. Set `Access Level` to `Public` to make the category visible to all users of the website. From the `Image` drop-down list, select camera.jpg to represent the category. Choose `Left` for `Image Position` so that the image will appear to the left of the category title. In the `Description` text box, you can enter a few lines to describe your category, and insert an image using the `Image` button at the bottom.

After inserting the necessary information for the new category, click the `Save` button in the toolbar to save it. Your newly created category, Camera, will be displayed in the Category Manager, which shows all the categories of all the sections. If you want to see only the categories of a particular section, select that section from the `Select Section` drop-down list. Go ahead and select `Electronics` from this list so that only that section will be displayed, as shown in Figure 3-14.

Figure 3-14. A new category added in the Category Manager

The columns in the category Manager are quite similar to those for the Section Manager, and the information is almost identical. Refer back to Table 3-1 if you need clarification of any column. Only one column is different: `Section`, which displays the title of the section to which the category belongs.

Now that you've created a section and a category, it's time to create an article.

Creating an article (Article Manager) and publishing it in a category

Articles contain the actual information or content that you want your website visitors to see. Besides text, articles can contain images and other multimedia content. The information in your articles may appear on the front page (home page) of the website so that visitors can view the article directly on opening the website, or it may appear when a visitor selects a particular menu item or link on the website.

Since you'll be displaying some content that provides information about new cameras, you'll write an article and attach it to the Camera category. To do so, you need to open the Article Manager, so either select `Content` ➤ `Article Manager` or click the `Article Manager` button in the control panel. The Article Manager will open and display a list of articles under different categories and sections (provided by Joomla in the default website), as shown in Figure 3-15.

The Article Manager, as the name suggests, is used to manage articles. It contains tools with which users of certain groups (e.g., administrators) can add new articles, edit existing articles, unpublish the article(s) (making them disappear from the website), move or copy the articles from one category or section to another, and so on.

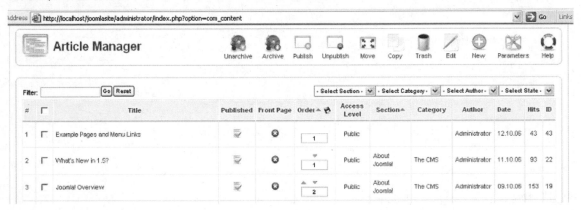

Figure 3-15. Article Manager

The Article Manager table contains some important information about each article, such as the author of the article, the access level (which sets whether the article is for public view or only for users belonging to certain groups), whether the article should be displayed on the front page (the first page of the website), the date the article was created, and the number of times it has been accessed by visitors.

To add a new article, you can either click the New button from the toolbar or the Add New Article button in the control panel. An editor box will appear allowing you to type the content for the article, as shown in Figure 3-16. In the Title box, specify Latest Cameras as the name of the article. For the alias, specify latest-cameras. Set the Published option to Yes to make the article visible on the website. Set the Front Page option to No, as you don't want the article to appear directly on the opening screen of your website, but only when a menu item is selected on the website. From the Section drop-down, choose Electronics, and from the category drop-down, choose Camera.

> *While adding an article, you must specify a section and category in which the article will be displayed.*

The editor provides formatting tools for formatting your text, and a variety of buttons that allow you to perform various tasks. If you're used to using a word processing application, then you'll find the buttons here fairly straightforward. However, I'll quickly run through a few of the ones that may be unfamiliar to you—namely, the buttons for inserting images, page breaks, and Read more links.

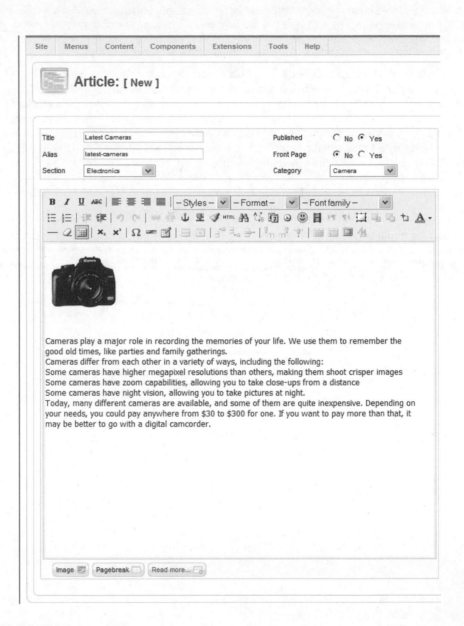

Figure 3-16. Creating a new article

There are two buttons for inserting images into an article. One is the Image button in the TinyMCE editor toolbar. (see Figure 3-17), and the other is the Image button at the bottom left of the editor (refer to Figure 3-16).

Figure 3-17. Image button in the TinyMCE editor

The button in the editor toolbar is a bit difficult to use, as it requires the URL of the image to insert, and it doesn't allow you to add new images in Media Manager. When you click the Image button in the toolbar, the Insert/edit image dialog will be displayed, as shown in Figure 3-18.

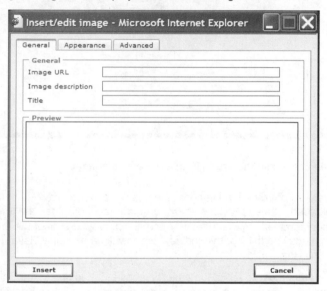

Figure 3-18. Insert/edit image dialog

In the Image URL field, you can specify the URL of an image available on the Internet, and you can also specify the URL of an image already uploaded to the Media Manager. Assuming that an image called cam1.jpg already exists in the Media Manager, you can insert it by specifying its URL here as c:\xampp\htdocs\joomlasite\images/stories/cam1.jpg, and then clicking the Insert button.

On the other hand, if you select the Image button at the bottom of the editor, you'll get a screen like the one shown in Figure 3-19. This dialog box allows you to upload new images to the Media Manager as well as insert selected images into the article.

Figure 3-19. Inserting an image into the article from the Media Manager

This dialog box provides a list of predefined images (the images that are provided by Joomla as well as those that you have uploaded). It also provides an `Upload` interface to upload the images from other directories into the Media Manager's `images` directory (the directory where all of the images for the website are kept, except for templates and third-party modules, which will be explained later). The uploaded images can be inserted into the article.

The `Pagebreak` button (at the bottom left of the editor) places a dotted line in the article as you are editing it. When viewing your website, the visitor is shown only the part of the article up until the page break line, and a `Next Page` link is shown at the end of the page. The portion of the article after the page break is displayed when the `Next Page` link is clicked, and this runs until the next page break or the end of the article.

The `Read more` button is used when you have a large article and you want to display a brief summary or introduction of the article first, and then include a link for the reader to read more. If interested, the reader can click the `Read more` link to see the whole article.

After entering the information for your article, click the `Save` button to save it. The message `Successfully Saved Article` will appear, and the article name will be listed in the Article Manager, as shown in Figure 3-20.

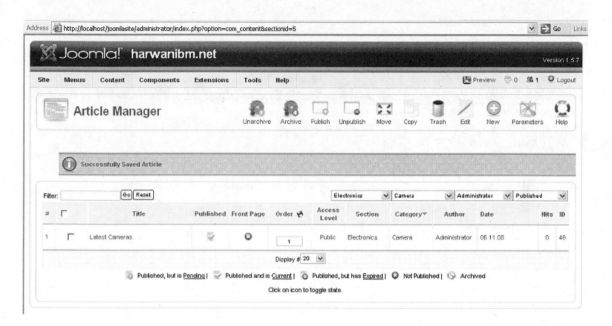

Figure 3-20. The "Latest Cameras" article added

Creating a menu item to access the section

A menu item is a link that appears on the website that users can select to see the desired information. To create a menu item, open the Menu Manager by clicking its button in the control panel. A range of menus will be provided by Joomla by default, as shown in Figure 3-21. Each menu is a collection of certain menu items. Every menu item is defined as a specific **menu item type**, and it is the menu item type that decides what kind of information the menu item is supposed to display (explained in detail in Chapter 7).

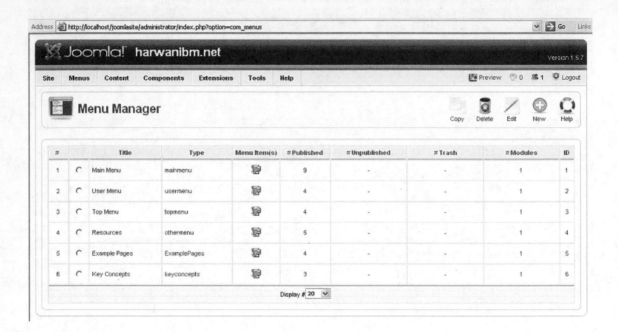

Figure 3-21. Menu Manager

You can create a menu item in any of the menus in the Menu Manager. Let's create a menu item in the Main Menu. Just click the Menu Items button in the Menu Item(s) column of the Main Menu row. You'll get all the menu items under the Main Menu that are provided by Joomla, as shown in Figure 3-22.

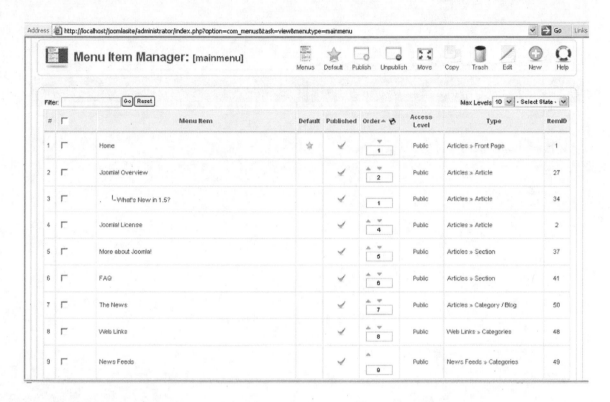

Figure 3-22. Menu items under the Main Menu

To add a new menu item, click the New button. You'll see a screen for specifying the menu type, as shown in Figure 3-23. The menu type plays a major role in deciding how to display the information (i.e., when the menu item is selected, whether to display the article directly, to display all the article titles of a particular category, or to display all the category names of a particular section). If the user selects the menu type that displays all the article titles of a particular category, then the contents of the article will be displayed when the user selects the title of the article. If the user selects the menu type that displays all the category names of a particular section, then to see the list of articles under any category, the user must select the category title.

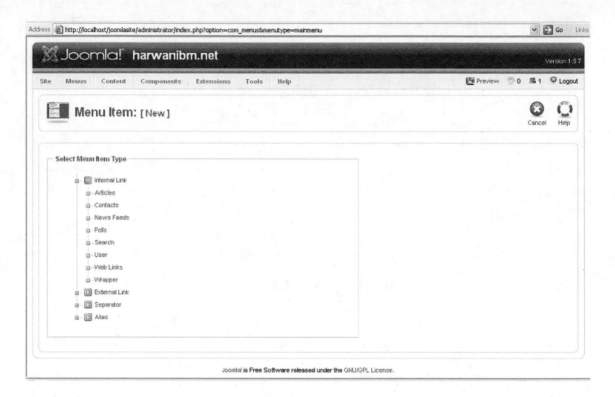

Figure 3-23. List of menu types

The list in Figure 3-23 shows that menu items can point to a variety of contents, including articles, contacts, news feeds, and so on. Let's see the available options in the `Articles` node. Select the `Articles` node, and you'll be presented with the options shown in Figure 3-24.

Figure 3-24. Expanding the Articles node

Select the Section Layout menu type, which will display all the categories of the selected section. When a category is selected, it will display the list of articles in that category, and when the title of an article is selected, it will display the information stored in that article. After selecting Section Layout, you'll be presented with a screen for specifying the rest of the information of the menu item, as shown in Figure 3-25.

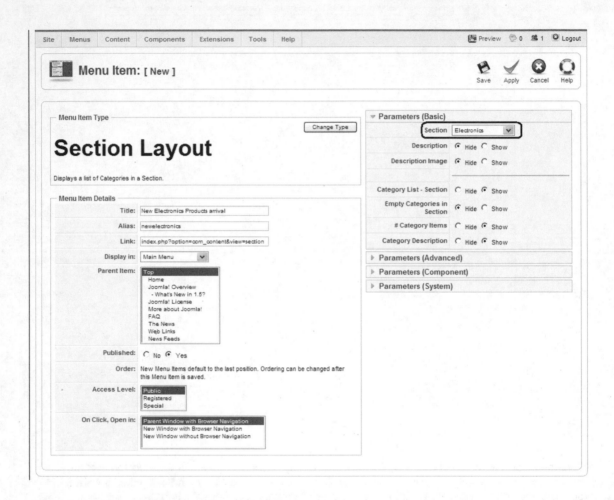

Figure 3-25. Specifying the menu item information

In the `Title` field, enter the menu item that you want to appear in the `Main Menu`—in this case, `New Electronics Products arrival`. The alias is optional. The text in the `Link` field appears automatically, and is dependent on the menu type selected. This text lets the menu item know which object it is linked to, and it cannot be edited. From the `Display in` drop-down list, you select the menu in which this menu item is supposed to appear. In this case, select `Main Menu`. In the `Parent Item` list box, you select the menu item that will act as a parent of the menu item that you are creating (used when creating sub–menu items). In this case, select `Top`, as you want to create an independent menu item. Set the `Published` option to `Yes` to make it visible on the website. `Order` is for setting the sequence of the menu item in the `Main Menu`. Leave it at the default so that the menu item will appear at the last position in the `Main Menu`. Set the `Access Level` to `Public` to make the menu item publicly accessible. In the `On Click, Open in` list box, you specify where the information will be displayed when the menu item is selected. Select the option `Parent Window with Browser Navigation` to make the information appear in the same window as the menu item (the front page), thus replacing the existing information being displayed. From the `Parameters (Basic)` section, select the section for which the information will be displayed (in this case, `Electronics`).

After you've entered the information as described (and shown in Figure 3-25), click the `Save` button to save the menu item. The menu item will be saved and added to the menu item list, as shown in Figure 3-26. Notice that the `Type` column displays `Articles > Section`, meaning that the menu item will display the categories of the specified section.

Figure 3-26. Menu item created

Viewing the Contents

Now that you've performed all the steps to create the website contents, its time to see the result. Open the browser window pointing to your website and refresh it, or just click the `Preview` button at the top right of the Menu Item Manager. On the front end, you'll find that the menu item `New Electronic Products arrival` appears in the `Main Menu`. Select this menu item, and it will display the categories under the Electronics section and the number of articles that these categories have, as shown in Figure 3-27.

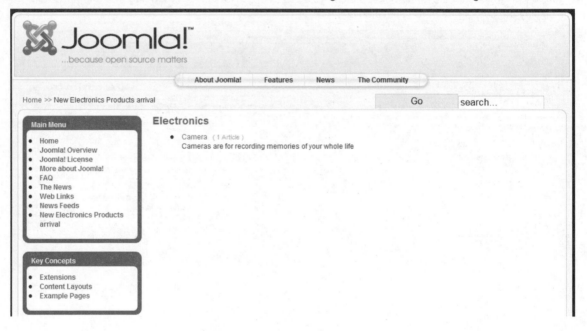

Figure 3-27. Menu item displaying the category of the section

Select the Camera category of the Electonics section, and the titles of all the articles under this category will be displayed, as shown in Figure 3-28.

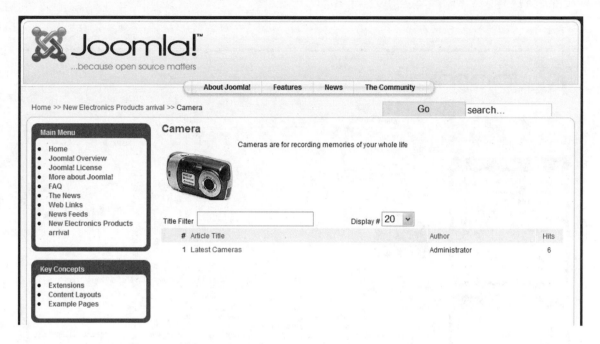

Figure 3-28. Article under the Camera category

Select the link for the "Latest Cameras" article, and its content will be displayed on the screen, as shown in Figure 3-29.

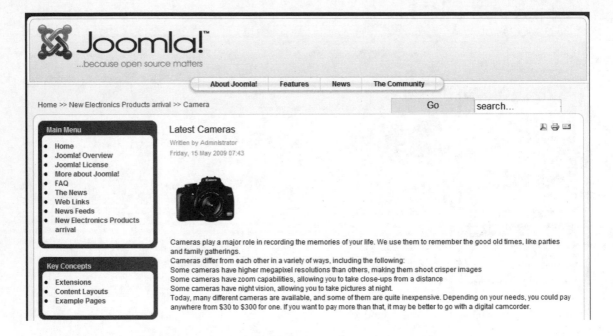

Figure 3-29. Displaying the content of the article

> You can also set the article to be displayed on the front page of the website by selecting `Yes` in the `Front Page` field of the new article creation screen (refer back to Figure 3-16).

Since you selected `Section Layout` for the menu item type (refer back to Figure 3-24), you first got the Category (Camera) of the selected section (Electronics) on selecting the `New Electronic Products arrival` menu item from the `Main Menu`. When you selected the `Camera` category, the title of the article ("Latest Cameras") in that category was displayed, and when you selected the article title, the information stored in that article was displayed. But if you want a list of all the articles (of all the categories) of the selected section directly on selecting the menu item, you need to set the menu item type to `Section Blog Layout`, as shown in Figure 3-30.

Figure 3-30. Selecting Section Blog Layout for the menu item type

If you select `Section Blog Layout` and then run the web application, you'll get the initial screen shown in Figure 3-31. The screen displays the `New Electronic Products arrival` menu item in the `Main Menu`.

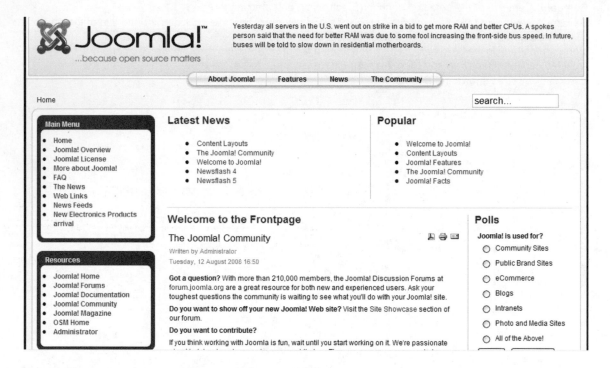

Figure 3-31. Your new menu item listed in the Main Menu

Now if you select the `New Electronic Products arrival` menu item from the `Main Menu`, it will not display the categories of the Electronics section; instead it will display the content of the "Latest Cameras" article directly. This happens because the menu item is set to point to the Electronics section and the menu item type is `Section Blog Layout`, meaning that the articles under the Electronics section will be directly displayed.

After this quick start on how to create content in your Joomla website, let's take a quick look through the rest of the buttons available in the control panel. You can use this chapter for reference if you ever need to remind yourself what the various managers do.

The Other Control Panel Managers

There are a number of other managers in the control panel that haven't been covered yet, including the Front Page Manager, the Media Manager, the Language Manager, the User Manager, Global Configuration, and the Template Manager. I'll describe them in the following sections.

Front Page Manager

The front page is the home page or first welcome screen of the website, and the Front Page Manager is used to manage the articles that should be published on this home page. The articles of a website can be of two types: those that you want to be visible the moment a visitor enters the website (these articles are set to `Published` mode in the Front Page Manager), and those that you want the visitor to view when a particular menu item is selected. The latter, as described previously, are linked with menu items (refer to Figure 3-5), and are set to `Unpublished` mode in the Front Page Manager. The Front Page Manager shows all the articles in a table, as shown in Figure 3-32. This table also displays the author of the article, the section and category to which the article belongs, the order in which the articles will appear on the front page, and the access level.

Figure 3-32. Front Page Manager

Media Manager

The `Media Manager` is used to maintain the images of the website. All the images are stored and maintained in joomla_root/images, with the exception that extensions, plug-ins, and templates keep their images in their own image directories.

*A **plug-in** is used for adding small functions to an existing component or module. For example, a search plug-in can be used to search a desired product from a shopping cart component, and a bookmark plug-in can be used to place bookmarks on the desired content. A **component** is an independent application (having its own functionality, database, and presentation). Adding a component to your website is like adding an application. Examples of components are shopping carts and guest books. **Modules** are meant for adding new features to an existing component (application) of your website (e.g., you might add a login module or a digital counter module to your shopping cart component).*

The images directory already contains some default subdirectories with images in them. Using the Media Manager, you can upload images from other directories into the joomla_root/images folder, and you can also delete any undesired images. The Media Manager with its default directories and images appears as shown in Figure 3-33.

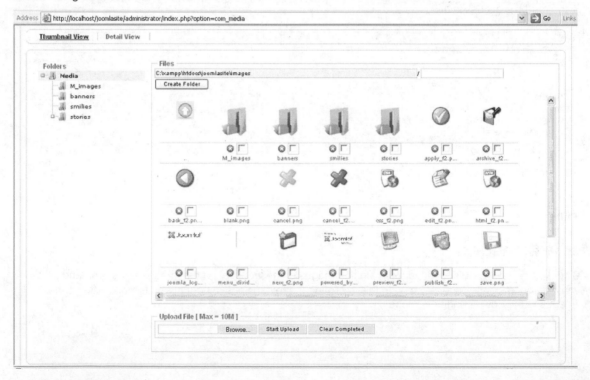

Figure 3-33. Media Manager

Language Manager

The Language Manager is used to manage the installed languages. You can define the default language for your website with this manager. This is the language used in the Administrator interface. The example Language Manager in Figure 3-34 shows that only one language is currently displayed (English), but you can always install more languages by using the `Extensions ➤ Install/Uninstall` option.

Figure 3-34. Language Manager

User Manager

The User Manager is for managing users. A **user** might be a simple visitor who's registered at your website, an employee of your organization, or even you. When you create users, you assign them to **groups**, which decides the permissions assigned to them (e.g., whether they can edit or add new articles to the website, or just view them). With the User Manager, you can create users, delete existing users, edit user information (password, e-mail ID, group membership, etc.), block existing users from accessing your website, and so on. The `User Manager` displays a list of all of the current users, as shown in Figure 3-35. The table in the User Manager displays the following information:

- Username (the ID by which the user logs in).

- Status of the user (whether the user is logged in or logged out).

- State of the user (whether the user is enabled or blocked).

- Group of the user. A user can be assigned any of the groups described following. Each group has certain privileges assigned to it that define the limits or rights of the user in that group. The list of groups in ascending order of their privileges is as follows:

    - **Registered**: Users of this group cannot edit or submit articles, and can only access the contents that are assigned the Registered access level.

    - **Author**: Users of this group can submit new articles, but these articles must be approved by a member of the Publisher group or higher. Users of this group cannot edit existing articles.

- **Editor**: Users of this group can submit new articles or edit existing articles. The articles must be approved by a member of the Publisher group or higher.

- **Publisher**: Users of this group can submit, edit, and publish articles.

- **Manager, Administrator, and Super Administrator**: Users of this group can do all of the above actions, and in addition they can log into the back end for better control over the website.

- E-mail ID of the user.

- The date when the user last visited the site.

Figure 3-35. User Manager

Global Configuration

Global Configuration is used for specifying certain configuration settings that can have a deep impact on the overall appearance and operation of your website. You can perform a variety of functions for your website with this tool, such as:

- Specifying the website metadata that is used by search engines to locate your website. Metadata contains keywords that describe your website.

- Specifying the lifetime of the session. The session is created when a user logs into your site, and is deleted when that user logs out. When you specify the lifetime of the session, the session is deleted automatically after the specified time. The lifetime is important for visitors who forget to log out of the website. By default, the value of the `Session Lifetime` field is 15 minutes, and the user is automatically logged out if there is no activity during this time period. (While working on the exercises in this book, I'd suggest increasing this time limit to avoid having to log in repeatedly.)

- Specifying the mail settings to indicate the mailer to use for e-mailing (e.g., PHP, Sendmail, SMTP, etc.). If you use SMTP as a mail server, you can also specify the SMTP username and password. Specifying the mail settings is required if you want to send and receive e-mail from your website.

- Allowing or disallowing new user registration on your website.

- Enabling or disabling web services (e.g., Google Search, Google Maps, etc.). **Web services** are facilities provided in the form of web methods that can be invoked by your application to add more functionality to your website. For example, invoking Google Search will allow your visitors to search the Net from your site, and they will get exactly the same output that they would get while searching from Google.

- Allowing or disallowing the FTP facility. If FTP is allowed, then you can specify the FTP username and password here.

- Specifying the location of media files and temporary files.

- Specifying the database name (to store the contents of your website), its type, and its hostname

Working with the front page

The front page is the first welcome page (home page) that opens up when you open any website. It can be any other page also, but usually it is the first page of the website, as shown in Figure 3-36.

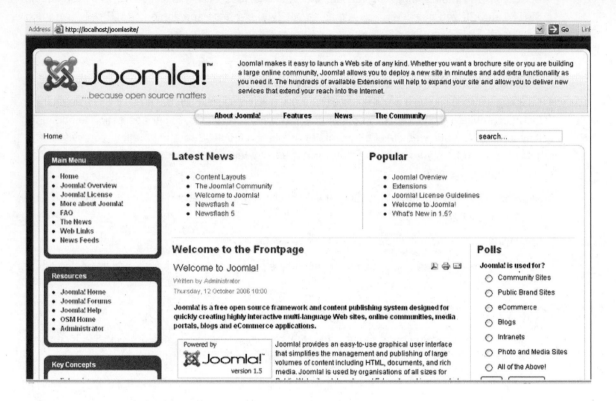

Figure 3-36. Front page

Open the Administrator interface, and from the `Main Menu`, select `Content ➤ Front Page Manager`. You'll see the screen shown in Figure 3-37. The articles shown in the figure are provided by default by Joomla. (You can always delete or unpublish the undesired articles).

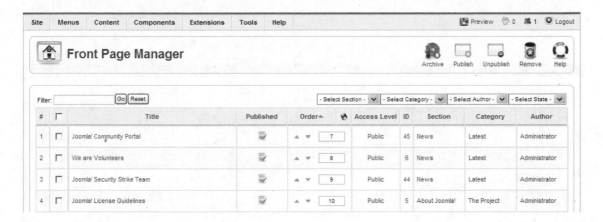

Figure 3-37. Front Page Manager

Suppose you want the three articles "Joomla! Community Portal," "We are Volunteers," and "Joomla! License Guidelines" to be removed from the front page. Just select the check boxes of these three articles and click the `Unpublish` button in the toolbar. You'll find that the check mark in the `Published` column of the selected articles changes to a red *X*, as shown in Figure 3-38, meaning that these articles will no longer be shown on the font page.

Figure 3-38. Unpublishing undesired contents

To see the effect in your website, open the website browser window and click the `Refresh` button. You'll see the result shown in Figure 3-39, in which all of the articles except those that you set to `Unpublish` are visible.

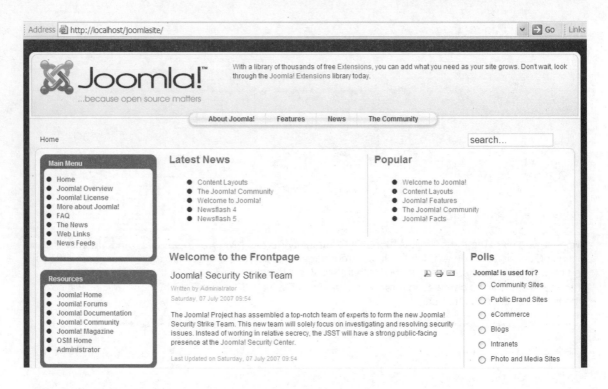

Figure 3-39. Website after removing certain contents from the front page

OK, you have a basic website, but it doesn't look very exciting yet. The easiest way to change the appearance of a Joomla site is by applying a template. There are hundreds of templates available covering every kind of design, so I'm sure you'll find something that suits you. For now, though, we'll start by looking at the templates that came preinstalled with Joomla.

Applying a different template

Templates are the predefined structure that gives a dynamic look to a website. A template consists of cascading style sheets and a layout that defines the positions of components and modules in it. When a template is applied to a website, the location of the modules and components are relocated according to the layout in it, and the styles are applied to the content of the website.

Three templates are automatically installed with Joomla: beez, JA_Purity, and rhuk_milkyway. rhuk_milkyway is the template that is already applied by default, and it is because of this template that your Joomla website initially appears as shown in Figure 3-40.

Figure 3-40. Impact of the rhuk_milkyway template

Let's apply some other template. Open the window displaying the Administrator interface (point your browser at http://localhost/joomlasite/administrator), and from the Main Menu, select Extensions ➤ Template Manager. As mentioned, you'll find that rhuk_milkyway is the template selected by default. To change this, select JA_Purity, and click the Default button in the toolbar, as shown in Figure 3-41.

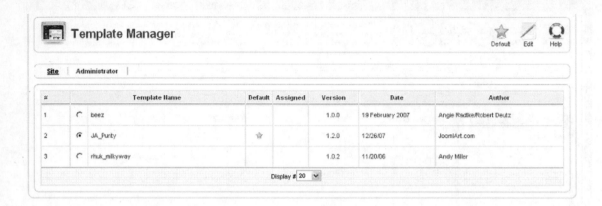

Figure 3-41. Selecting the JA_Purity template in the Template Manager

Switch to the browser window that is displaying your website (the one pointing at http://localhost/joomlasite) and click Refresh. The effect of the template on the Joomla website will appear, as shown in Figure 3-42. Notice that the location of the modules and contents has changed, and the cascading style sheets present in the current template have changed the appearance of the website altogether.

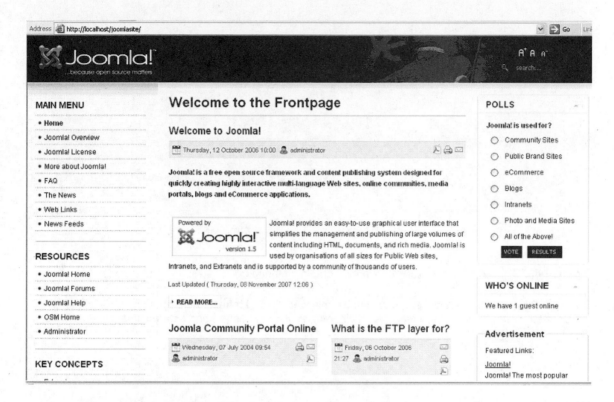

Figure 3-42. Impact of the JA_Purity template

Now let's see the effect of applying the beez template. Switch to the browser window displaying the Administrator interface, and in the Template Manager, select the check box of the `beez` template and click the `Default` button in the toolbar. The screen should appear as shown in Figure 3-43.

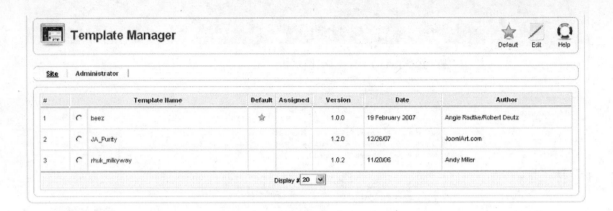

Figure 3-43. Selecting the beez template in the Template Manager

Switch to the browser window displaying your Joomla website and refresh the page to see the impact of the beez template. You'll get a screen with a different layout and banner, and different images and styles, as shown in Figure 3-44.

Figure 3-44. Impact of the beez template

You can also download third-party templates, and you can even create your own templates—but I'll cover all that in later chapters. From the introduction point of view, this is enough for the templates.

Summary

This chapter has given you an introduction to the managers of the control panel found in the Administrator interface. Additionally, you've learned how to publish and unpublish articles from the front page of the website, and you've learned how to change the default template used by your website.

In the next chapter, you will learn about the Media Manager. You will also learn to create banner categories, enter information for banner clients, and create a banner for a client. Finally, you will learn to use the Banner module to display a banner on your website.

Chapter 4

Managing Images and Banners

In the previous chapter, you saw how to create sections, categories, and above all, real content in the form of articles. You also learned how to make articles appear on the front page of the website and how to link them to menu items. In this chapter, you'll learn how to add colors to your website and make it a source of income for you. You're going to learn

- What the Media Manager is

- How to make categories for your banners

- How to enter information for your banner clients

- How to create a banner for your client

- How to use the Banners module to make the banner appear on the website

What is the Media Manager?

The Media Manager is a component that enables you to manage all the images used in your website in articles, menus, categories, sections, and so on. Using this manager, new images can be uploaded, existing images can be edited, and new directories can be created.

All the images in your website are stored in the joomla_root/images folder, except for the images for any extensions, which are stored in their respective image directories. The term **extensions** refers collectively to the components, modules, plug-ins, and templates that are installed in a Joomla website to enhance its features. A **template** is a collection of styles for giving a dynamic appearence to your website. The remaining types of extensions—components, modules, and plug-ins—are closely related:

- A **component** is an independent application with its own functionality, database, and presentation. Installing a component in your website is like adding an application to the site. A forum, shopping cart, newsletter, and guest book are all examples of a component. A component may consist of one or more modules.

- A **module** is used for adding new functions (features) to a component (application) of your website—for example, a login module, a sign-in module of a guest book component, or a subscription module of a newsletter component. A module isn't a stand-alone application, but a running unit of an application.

- A **plug-in** is a function that can be applied to a particular component or complete website—for example, a search plug-in that visitors can use to search your forum, or a bookmark plug-in to place bookmarks on the desired contents of your Joomla website. Plug-ins were called mambots in Joomla 1.0, but have been called plug-ins since Joomla 1.5.

Let's look at an example that combines all three. A shopping cart is a component that has several modules, including those for maintaining inventory, storing payment information, and printing bills. Plug-ins can be added to this component, such as a plug-in to change the price of a particular product, or a search plug-in to search for a desired product from the shopping cart.

To open the Media Manager, point the browser to the Administrator interface—that is, the address http://localhost/joomlasite/administrator. In the Administrator interface, select Site ➤ Media Manager from the menu bar, and the Media Manager will open, as shown in Figure 4-1. You can see that it already contains images in the folders M_images, banners, smiles, and stories. Joomla provides these images in the default website, and you can use them directly in your website.

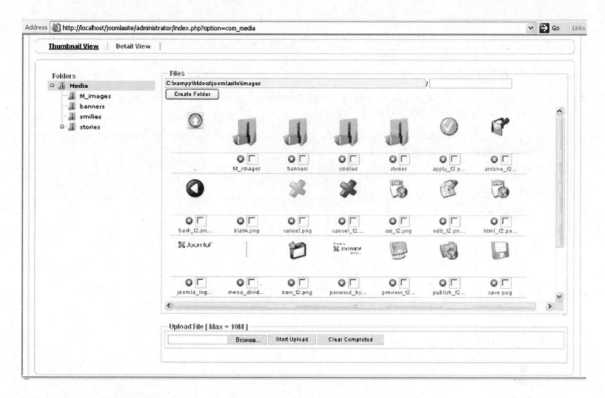

Figure 4-1. Media Manager

You can also upload new images. To do that, the first step is to create a folder in the Media Manager.

> *Moving or copying images between folders is not possible in the Media Manager.*

Creating a folder

It's best to create a separate folder for any new images uploaded in the Media Manager. To create a folder within the joomla_root/images folder, do the following:

1. In the Media Manager, type the name of the new folder in the `Files` text box to the right of the slash (/). Call your folder trialimg.
2. Click the `Create Folder` button, as shown in Figure 4-2.

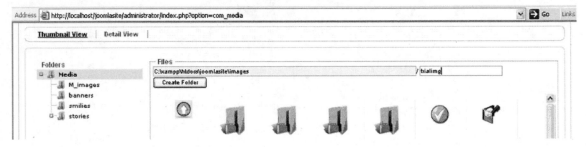

Figure 4-2. Creating the trialimg folder

A new folder named trialimg will appear in the `Folders` list, as shown in Figure 4-3.

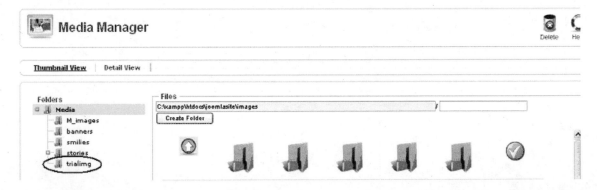

Figure 4-3. The trialimg folder added to the Folders list

3. To upload images to the trialimg folder, you need to make it the active folder by clicking it in the Folder list. Since it currently contains no images, it will appear blank, as shown in Figure 4-4.

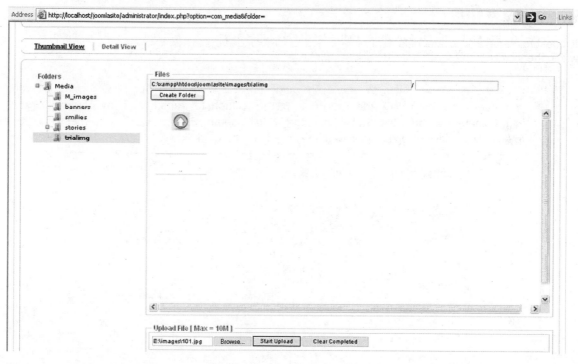

Figure 4-4. The trialimg folder contains no images.

Uploading a file

To upload an image from your computer to the Media Manager's active folder (in this case trialimg, a subdirectory of the joomla_root/images directory), you use the Upload File section at the bottom of the window.

1. Click the Browse button to locate an image (in JPG, GIF, BMP, or PNG format) on your computer, and then click the Start Upload button to transfer a copy of the file from your computer to the active trialimg directory. You'll see an Upload Complete message if the transfer is successful, and a preview of the image, as shown in Figure 4-5.

Figure 4-5. Image loaded into the trialimg folder

2. Upload one more image file—in this example, I'm using an image named 201.jpg from the images directory on the E: drive—and click the Start Upload button, as shown in Figure 4-6.

Figure 4-6. Uploading an image file

You now have two images, 101.jpg and 201.jpg, uploaded in the trialimg subdirectory of the joomla_root/images folder, as shown in Figure 4-7.

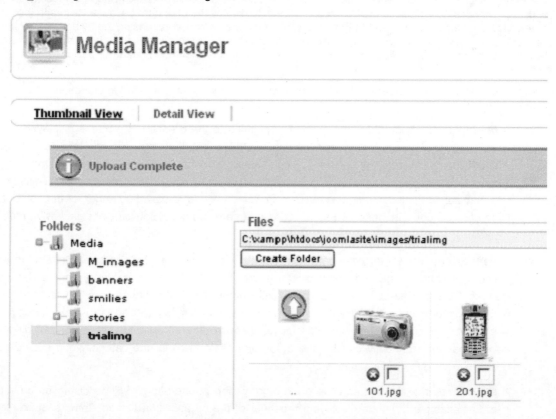

Figure 4-7. Two images loaded in the trialimg folder

These images can now be easily inserted into any article, menu, category, or section. When you create the contents of your website via the Administrator interface, you'll see a button for inserting images. When clicked, the button will only display the images found within the Media Manager, so if you want to add an image to your site, you have to first add it to the Media Manager like you did here.

Displaying a banner ad

Websites have become a good source of advertisements, and many organizations look out for high-traffic sites that can display their banner (an image that carries the logo of the organization and advertises its products or services). Organizations pay website owners to display their banners because visitors to the site who click the banner will be sent to that organization's website, hence increasing the awareness of their products or services and eventually increasing their business. The organizations whose banners you will be displaying on your site are called **clients**. There can be more than one banner for a client, and you can choose to display the banners of several clients.

Before you proceed with the steps for displaying banners on your website, you need to understand the following terms:

- A *banner* is an image file (with a hyperlink pointing to the client's URL) that is displayed on a website. If, for example, an organization named Chirag that deals with cameras and camcorders wanted you to display the banners of both these products randomly, you would make two banners—for example, named Chirag camera banner and Chirag camcorder banner. Similarly, if an organization named Johny Electronics also wanted you to display the banner for their product, Camera, you could name that banner Johny camera banner. (You can assign any name to a banner.)

- A *banner category* is for categorizing similar banners. For example, all banners related to the Camera product (of any organization) can be assigned to a banner category named Camera Banner. Similarly, all banners related to luxury hotels can be assigned to a banner category named Luxury Hotels. The idea behind keeping the banners categorized is to make it easy for you to find specific banners while assigning them to different clients. Also, you can display several banners randomly one by one by placing all of them in one category and setting the Banners module to display banners of that category.

- A *banner client* refers to the name of an organization whose banner will be displayed on your site. For example, if you're displaying a banner of the organization Chirag Camera Store, you create a banner client by the same name. Similarly, if you display a banner for the client Johny Electronics, you create a banner client named Johny Electronics. Note that a banner client can have multiple banners.

Displaying a client's banners

To display your client's banners on your website, you'll take following steps:

1. Upload the client's banner image file to the banners folder of the Media Manager.
2. Create a category for the banner using the Banner Category Manager.
3. Create a banner client using the Banner Client Manager.
4. Create a banner using the Banner Manager.
5. Use the Banners module to display the banner on the website.

Uploading the client's banner image file

To display the client's banner on your website, you must upload its banner image to the banners folder of the Media Manager. To do so, click the folder in the `Folders` list in the Media Manager to make it the active folder. You'll see all the banner images it already contains (provided as sample data by Joomla), as shown in Figure 4-8.

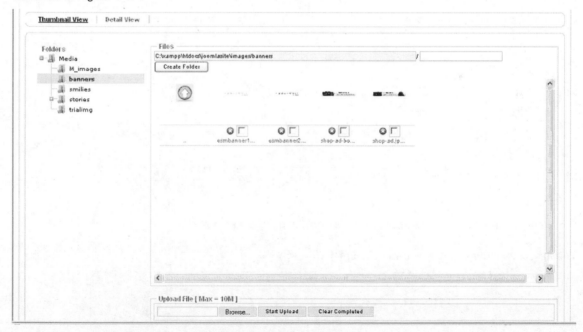

Figure 4-8. Banners in the joomla_root/images/banners folder

Let's assume that you want to display the banner for your Chirag Camera Store client, and that its banner image file is on your local computer and is named ch.jpg. You'll upload it into the banners folder of your joomla_root/images directory using the `Upload File` section.

> *The default banner size is 468 pixels in width and 60 pixels in height. So, to maintain compatiblity, it's best to make the banner using the same dimensions for your clients, too.*

You can upload the banner image file in the same way that you uploaded the camera image earlier. Once you upload it, you'll be able to see it in the banners folder of the Media Manager, as shown in Figure 4-9.

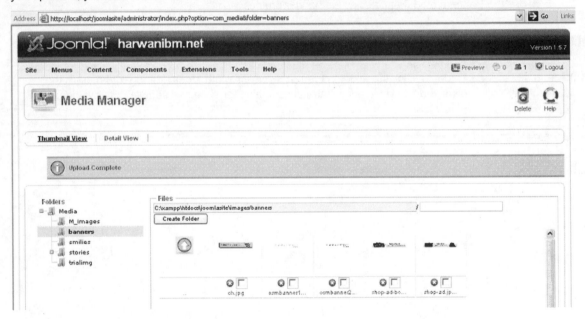

Figure 4-9. A new banner added to the joomla_root/images/banners folder

The full-size banner image is shown in Figure 4-10.

Figure 4-10. Actual view of the new banner added

After uploading the banner image, your next step is to define a category for it. You categorize banners so that similar banners can be found in one place.

Creating a category for the banner using the Banner Category Manager

The idea behind creating a banner category is to categorize similar banners. For example, you can keep all banners advertising the latest cellular phones in a category named Cellular Banner and all banners advertising the latest cameras in a category named Camera Banner. You can also create banner categories with names that describe their sizes, such as Standard Banner, Half Banner, Narrow/Wide Skyscraper, Box, Rectangle, and so on.

To create categories for banners, you need to open the Banner Category Manager, using either of two methods. The first method is to open the Banner Manager (by selecting `Components` ➤ `Banner` ➤ `Banners` from the menu bar), and then, from the Banner Manager, click the `Categories` link. The second method is to open the Banner Category Manager directly by selecting `Components` ➤ `Banner` ➤ `Categories` from the menu bar.

Let's open the Banner Category Manager via the Banner Manager. So, from the menu bar, select `Components` ➤ `Banner` ➤ `Banners`. But before you go further, let's take a quick look at the `Components` menu and its options.

The `Components` menu helps you invoke different components in your website. **Components** are the content elements that help in adding various features to your website; they include banners, contacts, news feeds, polls, and web links. These components increase the functionality of Joomla. Their main purposes are to

- Advertise for the clients

- Get feedback from visitors

- Develop interaction with visitors

- Share data from other providers in the form of RSS feeds

- Provide links to other, similar web content

Now let's return to your banner category creation process. When you select `Components` ➤ `Banner` ➤ `Banners`, the Banner Manager opens, as shown in Figure 4-11. You can see that the Banner Manager lists the banners of a client named Open Source Matters. Joomla provides this client by default in your website, but you can unpublish it if you don't want it to appear. Note the different banner categories that have already been set up: Joomla, Text Ads, and Joomla! Promo.

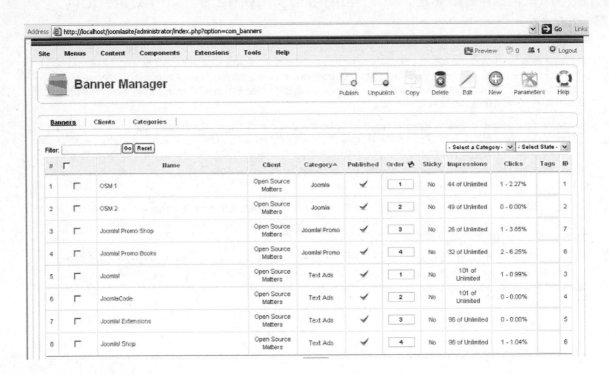

Figure 4-11. Banner Manager

The Banner Manager deals with banners that are used for displaying content provided by clients or sponsors for the purpose of advertisement. In Joomla, you can easily configure banners. You can set the placement of the banner, set it to display for either an unilimited or a defined number of user clicks, and define the categories in which banners of similar types can be stored.

If you click the Categories link, you'll see Category Manager: [Banner], also called the Banner Category Manager, as shown in Figure 4-12. It displays a list of banner categories. The three categories you see in the figure (Joomla, Text Ads, and Joomla! Promo) are provided by Joomla in the default website, but you can unpublish them at any time.

Figure 4-12. Banner Category Manager

Let's create a category named Camera Banner for storing banners advertising the latest cameras of different clients. Click the New icon in the toolbar. You'll see a screen for entering information about the new category, as shown in Figure 4-13.

Figure 4-13. Adding a new banner category

Category Manager listing. Enter `Camera Banner` as the title for this banner category. The `Alias` field is for a sort of secondary name or internal name of the item. Usually it is left blank, but if specified, it has to be lowercase and cannot include spaces. If you leave it blank, Joomla creates an alias for you out of the title by lowercasing it and replacing the spaces with hyphens. That is, if you leave this field blank, Joomla will create the alias camera-banner for you. The alias is used in the URL when SEF is activated. **SEF (Search Engine Friendly)** is the concept by which your website links are presented and optimized so that search engines can access more of your site. It is enabled from the `SEO` tab in the `Global Configuration` section (explained in Chapter 10). Aliases are used when SEF is activated, which makes Joomla produce friendly URLs rather than normal database-generated URLs.

Set the `Published` option to `Yes` to make the banners of this category visible on your website. The `Section` field displays `N/A` (for "not applicable") because sections are not used for banners. Nothing needs to be entered here. The `Category Order` field indicates the sequence number of this category in the Banner Category Manager listing. Usually the newly created category appears in the last position in the list by default, but you can change the order from the Banner Category Manager once the category is saved.

The `Access Level` field is used to specify which level of users can access this banner category. As usual, the access levels are as follows:

- **Public**: Everybody can access this category.

- **Registered**: Only registered users can access this category.

- **Special**: Only users with author or higher status can access this category.

Set the access level of this banner category to `Public` since you want it to be viewed by every visitor of your website.

The `Image` field is used for selecting the image to be displayed when the banner category description is viewed. All the images available in the Media Manager (from the joomla_root/images/stories folder—refer to Figure 4-1) will be displayed, from which you can select an image to represent this banner category. The selected image's preview appears immediately. The `Image Position` field decides the location of the image when displayed; the image has to appear to the left or right of the category title. The default is `Left`, and you can leave it as such.

In the `Description` box, you can write an introductory description of the category. Several tools are provided for formatting the description. The one I'll discuss here is the `Image` icon, which is used to insert images in the description. The list of images that you see upon clicking this icon are those that are available in the `Media Manager`. You can even upload new images to the Media Manager with this icon.

After entering the information for the new category, as shown in Figure 4-13, click the `Save` icon to save it. You'll see the message `Category saved`, and the new category, Camera Banner, will appear in the Banner Category Manager list, as shown in Figure 4-14.

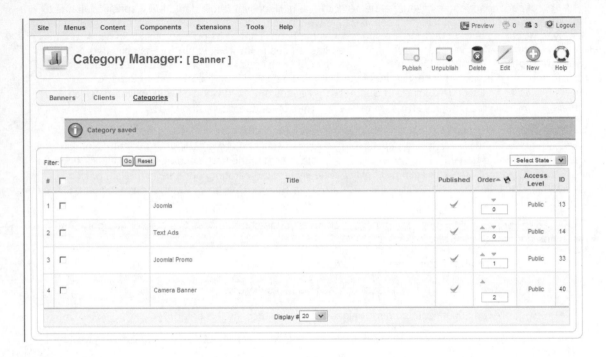

Figure 4-14. New banner category, Camera Banner, created

Now you need to define the client for whom you'll be displaying the banner on your website.

Creating a banner client using the Banner Client Manager

The banner client stores the information for the organization whose banner you're going to display on your website. To create clients for your banners, you use the Banner Client Manager. To open the Banner Client Manager, either click the `Clients` link in the Banner Category Manager or select `Components` ➤ `Banner` ➤ `Clients` from the menu bar. You'll see the Banner Client Manager, as shown in Figure 4-15. It displays a list of all the banner clients and their information, and lets you add new clients or edit or delete existing clients. You can see that a client named Open Source Matters (provided by Joomla) already exists in the default website; you can delete it if you don't want it by selecting its check box and clicking `Delete` in the toolbar. But before deleting a client, you need to delete all the banners of that client first. That is, you cannot delete a client that has a banner associated with it.

Figure 4-15. Banner Client Manager

The icons in the Banner Client Manager toolbar are fairly self-explanatory. For example, the `Delete` icon is used to delete a banner client. Users just need to select the check box of the client to delete, and click this icon. The user is prompted to confirm before deleting the client. The client details will be permanently deleted from the server. Similarly, the `Edit` icon is meant for editing client information (client name, contact name, e-mail ID, etc.). The `New` icon is used to create a new banner client. It displays a screen for entering information about the new client. The `Help` icon is used for displaying help screens from Joomla's help server.

For understanding the usage of each column of Banner Client Manager, see Table 4-1.

Table 4-1. Brief explanation of the columns of the Banner Client Manager

Column	Description
Client Name	Displays the name of the client for whom you want to display the banners.
Contact	Displays the name of the person who is authorized from the client's organization to deal with any issues that may arise.
Banners	Displays the total number of banners (whether in the published or unpublished state) currently available in the the Banner Manager for this client.
ID	Displays the unique client identification number that Joomla has assigned to this client. The ID is automatically assigned by Joomla and is not editable.

To create a new client, you click the `New` icon in the toolbar of the Banner Client Manager. You'll be shown a screen for entering the client's information, as shown in Figure 4-16.

Figure 4-16. Adding a new banner client

In the `Client Name` field, you enter the company or organization name whose banner you are going to publish. Enter a dummy banner client name—say, `Chirag Camera Store`. In the `Contact Name` field, you specify the name of the authorized contact person in the organization. Enter the name of the person who will be contacted for payments and other purposes in this field (in my case, I entered `chirag harwani`). In the `Contact E-mail` field, enter the e-mail address of the contact person. Assuming the e-mail address of Chirag Harwani is chirag@gmail.com, enter the same in this field. This e-mail ID may be used to inform clients of contract expiration, remind them for contract renewal, and so on. The `Extra Information` box is for entering other (optional) information about the organization.

After entering the information for the client, click the `Save` icon to save it. You'll see the message `Item saved`, and the client organization's name, Chirag Camera Store, will appear in the Banner Client Manager list, as shown in Figure 4-17.

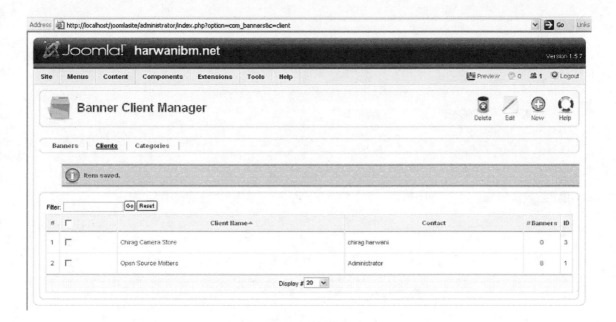

Figure 4-17. New banner client Chirag Camera Store added

Now that you've created the client (`Chirag Camera Store`) and the banner category (Camera Banner), you can open the Banner Manager to actually create a banner for your client.

Creating a banner using the Banner Manager

The banner is the actual content that you're going to display on your website and for which the client is going to pay you. The banner is in the form of an image file (uploaded in the Media Manager) with a hyperlink attached to it that navigates the visitor to the client's home page if the banner is clicked. A banner is associated with a banner category and a banner client, so both must exist before you create a banner. Let's open the Banner Manager to create the client's banner.

From the menu bar, select `Components` ➤ `Banner` ➤ `Banners` to see the Banner Manager, as shown in Figure 4-18. It displays a list of the default banners provided by Joomla.

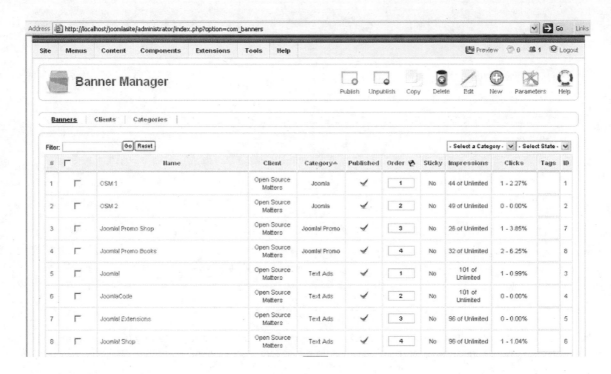

Figure 4-18. Banner Manager

In the toolbar of the Banner Manager are several icons. The `Publish` icon is used to make banners visible on the website. To publish a banner, you simply need to select the check box of the banner(s) and click this icon. Similarly, the `Unpublish` icon is for making banners invisible on the website.

The `Copy` icon is for making copies of an existing banner. You just need to select the check box of the banner you want to make a copy of and select the `Copy` icon from the toolbar. This will make a copy of the banner with the original banner name preceded by "Copy of." Let's make a copy of an existing banner: `OSM 1`. Select it and click the `Copy` icon, and a banner by the name of Copy of OSM 1 will appear in the Banner Manager, as shown in Figure 4-19. You can select this copy to edit it and change its name and other information later.

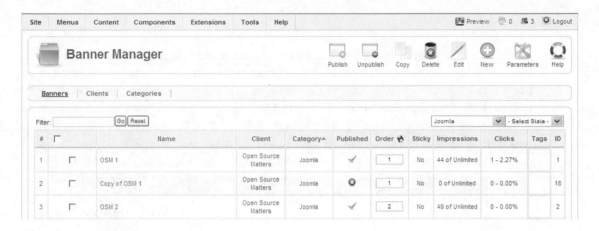

Figure 4-19. Making a copy of a banner

The `Delete` icon is used to permanently delete a banner. Before the banner is deleted, you'll be prompted for confirmation. The `Edit` icon is used to edit the information about the banner that was entered when the banner was created. Information such as the banner name, image, category, and client's name can be edited. After editing the banner information, you must save the changes by clicking the `Save` icon. The `New` icon is used to create a new banner. A screen is presented, on which you include information about the banner, such as its image file name, client name, category, and number of impressions.

The `Parameters` icon opens the banner's Global Configuration window, which allows you to set default parameters for banners, as shown in Figure 4-20. The parameters that you set in this dialog box play a major role in deciding when to display a particular banner and how long it will be visible on your website. The options are as follows:

- `Track Banner Impression Times`: You use this option to decide whether you want to count how many times a banner has been displayed. You should set this option to `Yes` if the client purchases a fixed number of impressions (wants the banner to be displayed a specific number of times), and set it to `No` if you want to display the banner an unlimited number of times.

- `Track Banner Click Times`: This option can be used to count how many times a client's banner is clicked. Assuming that the client's banner will be displayed an unlimited number of times, you set the values of both the options `Track Banner Impression Times` and `Track Banner Click Times` to `No`.

135

- `Tag Prefix`: Usually all the banners of a particular client and category are displayed randomly. But sometimes you only want to display the banner that relates to the type of content (article) being viewed by the user. For example, if the visitor is reading an article on cameras, then it is wise to display camera-related banners only. In this field, you enter the prefix for the tags you are going to insert in the banner's `Tags` field (refer to Figure 4-21). Enter `advt_` as the tag prefix to designate it as related to advertisement. (You will soon see how this field is going to help in choosing to display the banner on the basis of the content being viewed on your website.)

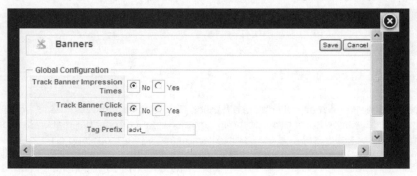

Figure 4-20. Parameters of a banner

Finally, the `Help` icon is for opening the Joomla help website.

Let's create a banner. Click the `New` icon in the toolbar, and you'll see a screen for entering information about the banner you want to create, as shown in Figure 4-21.

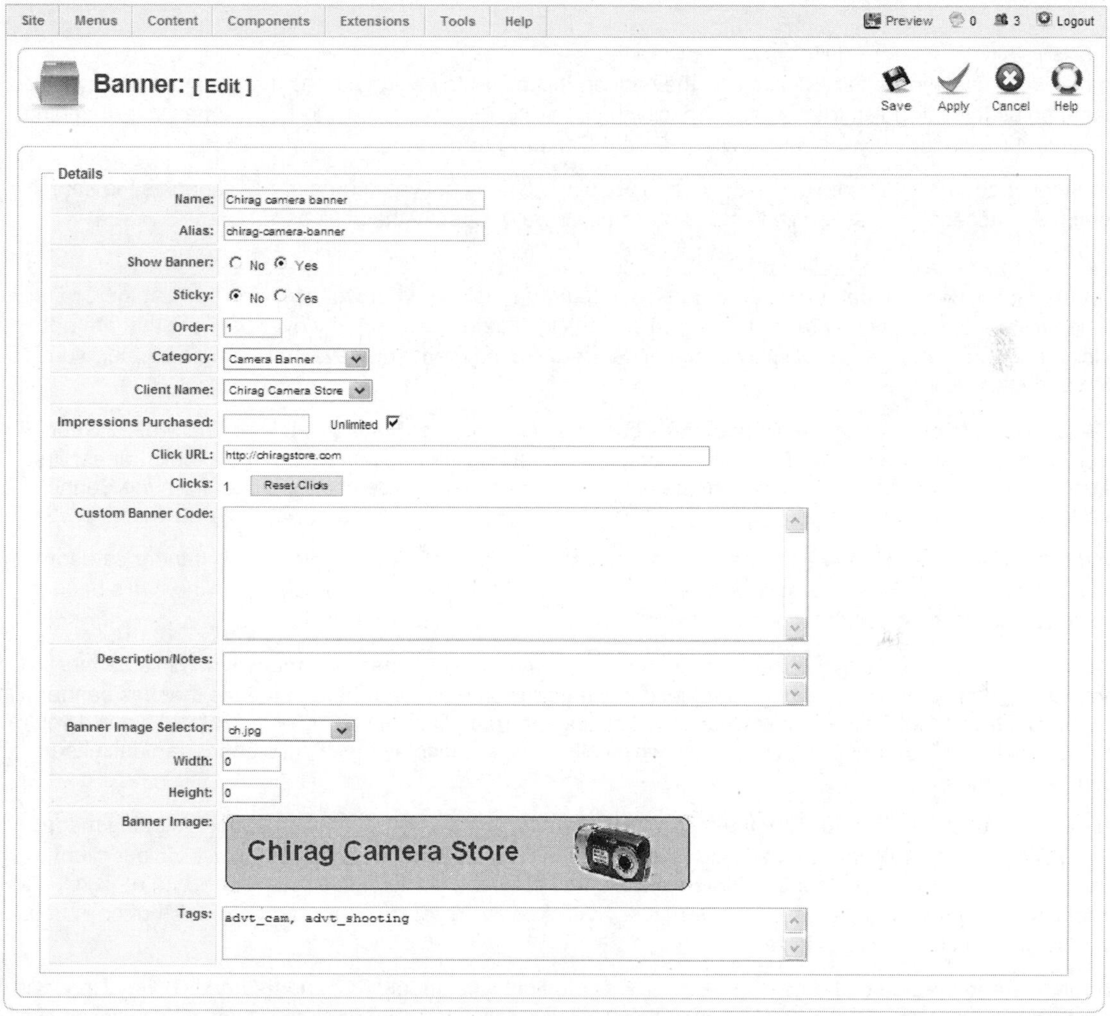

Figure 4-21. Adding a new banner

In the `Name` field, you enter the name of the banner. It is better to assign names that resemble their client's name so as to distinguish them easily. Specify the name as `Chirag camera banner`, as you are going to make this banner for your banner client, Chirag Camera Store.

As mentioned, the `Alias` field is used in the URL when SEF is activated (again, SEF enables the search engines to access the desired content in an optimized way). Specify the alias as `chirag-camera-banner`.

Set the `Show Banner` option to `Yes` to make the banner visible on your website. You can set the `Sticky` option to `Yes` to specify that the banner be sticky. Sticky banners take priority over banners that are not sticky, and their frequency of display is higher. Since at the moment you have just a single banner, you can keep this option set to `No`.

The `Order` field decides the sequence of the banners in the Banner Manager. It is normally used when there is more than one banner for a client/category and you want to decide which one should appear first. If you leave it blank, Joomla displays the default order. The order can be changed later from the Banner Manager.

In the `Category` field, you select the category to which the banner belongs. Select the banner category you just created: `Camera Banner`. In the `Client Name` field, you select the client to whom this banner belongs. Select the client that you just created: `Chirag Camera Store`.

In the `Impressions Purchased` field, you enter a number that defines how many times this banner will be displayed on your website. For example, if you enter a value of 1,000 here, it means that this banner will be displayed 1,000 times, after which it will disappear from your website. Leave this field blank if you're going to select the `Unlimited` check box, which allows you to display the client's banner an unlimited number of times.

In the `Click URL` field, you enter the URL of the client for whom this advertising banner is being made. The visitor will be navigated to this URL if the banner is clicked. Assume that the website of your client, `Chirag Camera Store`, is http://chiragstore.com, and enter the same in this field. The `Clicks` field displays the number of times this banner has been clicked by visitors. The `Reset Clicks` button is used to reset the number of clicks to zero.

To understand the use of the `Custom Banner Code` field, you should first understand two ways in which banners are used. One popular and conventional way is to display a banner image that, when clicked by the visitor, sends them to the client's URL. For this method, you need to specify the banner client's URL in the `Click URL` field. This method is preferred when only one banner of a particular client is being displayed. However, you may want to place banners supplied by advertising companies like TradeDoubler, Commission Junction, or Google's AdSense. If so, you should know that these companies provide the HTML code that contains the banner images and the URLs of the respective clients. You just need to copy and paste the HTML code provided by them into the `Customer Banner Code` field, and several small banner images will appear on your website, each pointing to its respective client. In that case, you have to leave the `Click URL` field blank.

The `Description/Notes` box is used to enter a small description for the banner. This description is not displayed on the web page.

From the `Banner Image Selector` field, you select the image file to be displayed as the banner. The image is loaded from the joomla_root/images/banners folder, so the client's banner image must be preloaded into this folder using the Media Manager. For this example, specify the client banner image file, ch.jpg, which you uploaded into the Media Manager at the beginning of this chapter. The `Banner Image` box displays the preview of the selected client's banner image file.

The `Tags` field is an optional field used for displaying specific banners based on the content of the article being viewed. Since you have defined `Tag Prefix` (refer to Figure 4-20) as `advt_`, you have to define the tags in this field with the prefix `advt_`. These tags will be matched with the keywords of the articles being viewed by the visitor, and the banner whose `Tags` field matches the keywords of the article will be automatically displayed on the screen. For this exercise, specify the tags as `advt_cam` and `advt_shooting`. Usually tags refer to important features of the product, and you can have any number of tags separated by commas. (I'll show you how these tags work soon.)

After entering the information for the banner, click the `Save` icon to save it. You'll see a message that reads `Item saved`, and a `Chirag camera banner` entry will appear in the Banner Manager, as shown in Figure 4-22.

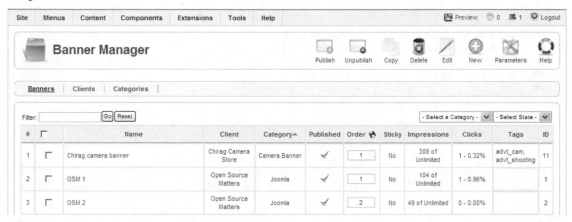

Figure 4-22. New banner added

The `Chirag camera banner` entry in the Banner Manager confirms that your banner has been made.

The columns in the Banner Manager display the information of the existing banners of your Joomla website. The `Name` column displays the name of the banner. The `Client` column displays the name of the client (organization or company name) to whom the banner belongs. The `Category` column displays the category in which this banner is placed. The `Published` column specifies whether the banner is in the published or unpublished state. The check mark signifies that the banner is in the published state, and the red *X* signifies that the banner is in the unpublished state. The `Order` column shows the display order (sequence) of the banners. You can change the order number of any banner being displayed from this column. The `Sticky` column specifies whether the banner is set to sticky mode (the frequency of appearance of sticky banners is greater than nonsticky ones). Setting this column to `No` signifies that the banner is in nonsticky mode. The `Impressions` field displays the number of times the banner has appeared on the website since it was created. In Figure 4-22, it's displaying `308 of Unlimited`, which means that the banner has appeared 308 times out of the unlimited number of times assigned to it. The `Clicks` column displays the percentage of clicks that were made on a banner in relation to the number of impressions (appearances on the website) that have taken place. The `Tags` column displays the tags of the banner, if any. The `ID` column displays the unique banner identification number that Joomla has assigned for internal maintenance.

The concept of an article **keyword** may be new to you. Keywords are comprised of a few words that briefly highlight the important information of an article. Recall Figure 3-16 in Chapter 3, when you created the article "Latest Cameras." At that time, you didn't use keywords, as there was no need for it. The same figure is shown in Figure 4-23, but this time including the `Keywords` field in the `Metadata Information` section. In Figure 4-23, the following keywords have been specified: `Night vision, 10 MB storage, Light weight, and advt_shooting`.

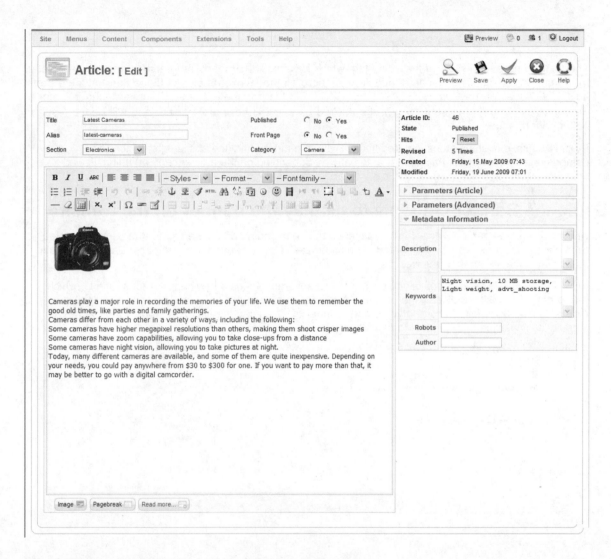

Figure 4-23. Article: [Edit] screen with the Keywords field populated

The thing to note is the use of the advt_ tag, which is particularly meant for searching the banner related to the current article. The Banners module will ignore all the keywords except those that have the prefix advt_ (because you have set `Tag Prefix` to `advt_` in the parameters of the Banner Manager—refer to Figure 4-20). That is, the searching of the desired banner will be more efficient and will hence result in better performance.

Next, I'll show you all the steps required in displaying a banner on your website, after which I'll demonstrate how a banner can appear automatically depending on the article (content) being viewed on your website.

Using the Banners module to display the banner on the website

Until now, you've been dealing with the Banner component: you made a category for the banner, created clients for the banner, and finally created the banner itself. Now you need the help of the Banners module for displaying the banner on the website.

By using the the Banners module, you can configure several settings of the banner—for example, which pages of your website to display the banner on, its position, its access level, and so on. The Banners module is also used for selecting which client's banner of which category is to be visible. The Banners module is accessible through the Module Manager.

From the menu bar, select `Extensions` ➤ `Module Manager`, and you'll see a list of modules, as shown in Figure 4-24.

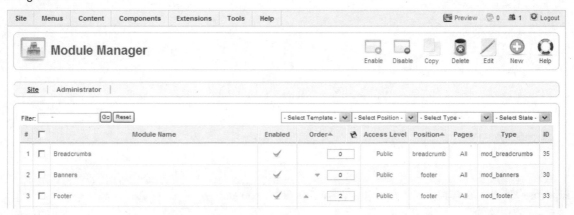

Figure 4-24. Module Manager

Let us see what information the columns of the Module Manager display. The `Module Name` column displays the name of the module. Joomla provides 20 standard modules and a facility to install more. Selecting a module name opens it in edit mode.

The `Enabled` column informs whether the module is enabled or disabled. A check mark signifies that the module is enabled and can be used in the website, and a red *X* signifies that the module is disabled (temporarily suspended) and won't be visible on the website.

The `Order` column shows the order in which the modules in a particular **position** will be displayed. The templates that you use to give a dynamic look to your website consist of styles and positions. A template internally divides a web page into different positions, including `left`, `right`, `header`, `footer`, and so on. If the `Order` column displays the value 2 for a particular module and the `Position` column displays `Left`, the module will appear at the left position on the web page, after the module whose order number is 1. You can change the display order of modules in a position by selecting a position in the `Select Position` drop-down and then clicking the up or down arrow in the `Order` column, or by entering the sequence number and clicking the `Save Order` icon in the column heading.

The `Access Level` column specifies the category of user that can access the module. The options are `Public`, `Registered`, and `Special`.

The `Position` column displays the position on the page where this module will be displayed (e.g., left or right).

The `Pages` column displays the menu items in which the module will be displayed. The options are `All` for all menu items, `None` for no menu items, and `Varies` for selected menu items.

The `Type` column displays the system name of the module. Recall that Joomla installs 20 standard modules and each has a unique system name.

The `ID` column displays a unique identification number for the module, assigned automatically by Joomla to identify the module internally.

The toolbar icons in the Module Manager are fairly self-explanatory. For instance, the `Enable` icon is used to enable a module (if the module was disabled earlier). Just select a module's check box and click this icon to enable it. Similarly, the `Disable` icon is used to disable a module. Disabled modules don't appear on the website.

> You can also toggle between enabled and disabled by clicking the icon in the `Enabled` column.

The `Copy` icon is used to make a copy of an existing module. Select the check box of the module to be copied and click this icon. The new module created will have the name "Copy of" plus the original module name, and will initially be disabled. You can edit the module, assign the new name to it, and enable it later.

Recall that you made a banner named Chirag camera banner and assigned it to the category Camera Banner for the client named Chirag Camera Store. To make it appear on the website, you opened the Module Manager. To activate the banner, you need to edit the Banners module from the Module Manager. Select the Banners module and click the `Edit` icon, or just click the module name. You'll see a screen for editing the Banners module, as shown in Figure 4-25. Here you'll configure the banner, but most important, you'll select the client whose banner you want and the category of banners to be displayed.

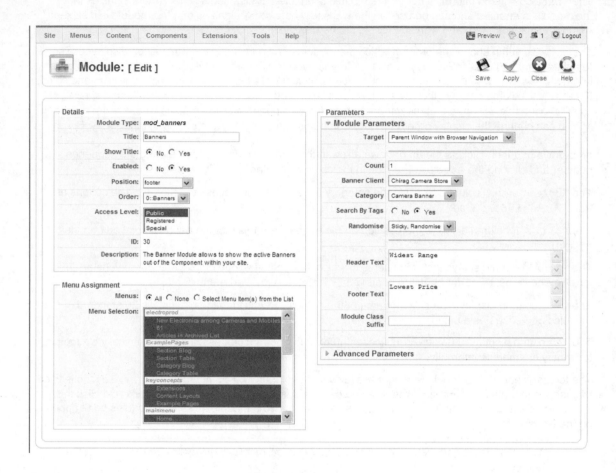

Figure 4-25. Configuring the Banners module to display the client's banner

This screen contains three sections: Details, Menu Assignment, and Parameters. I'll describe those now.

Details section

The Module Type field displays the system name of the module, which for the Banners module is mod_banners. The Title field displays the title name of the module, Banners. Set the Show Title option to No as you don't want to display the title of the banner along with the banner on the website. Set the Enabled field to Yes to make the banner visible on your website. In the Position field, you set the position where you want the banner to appear on your website—that is, left, right, footer, and so on. These positons are predefined in the template that you apply to your website. Set the position to footer to display the banner at the bottom of the web page. The `Order` field is used for setting the sequence of the module to appear when there is more than one module at the same position. Choose `0::Banners` to make the banner appear first in the footer position. The `Access Level` field specifies the level of users that can access the module. Select `Public` to make the banner visible to all visitors of your website. The `ID` field displays the ID of the module. This is a noneditable ID assigned by Joomla for internal use (for quick retrieval from database). The `Description` field displays a short description of the module.

Menu Assignment section

In the `Menu Assignment` section, the `Menus` option allows you select the menus in which you want this banner to appear. The options are `All`, to show the banners in all menus and pages; `None`, to not show the banner at all; and `Select Menu Item(s) from the List`, which is used to display the banners when certain menu items appear. For example, if you select the `Extensions` item of the `Key Concepts` menu from the `Menu Selection` box, the banner will appear only when the selected menu item is invoked. You can select multiple menu items by using Shift-click, Ctrl-click, or Cmd-click.

Parameters section

From the `Target` drop-down, you select the window in which you want the banner to appear (either the parent window or a new window). Select the `Parent Window with Browser Navigation` option to display the banner in the same window.

The `Count` field is used to specify the number of banners to be displayed simultaneously. Since you want to display just one banner at a time, enter `1` here.

From the `Banner Client` drop-down, select the client whose banners you want to display. Select the banner client `Chirag Camera Store` to display its banner.

From the `Category` drop-down, you select the category whose banners you want to display. Select the `Camera Banner` category created earlier.

Set the value of the `Search By Tags` option to `Yes`, as you want only the banners to appear whose tags match the keywords of the article being viewed. If you set this option to `No`, then the banners will be displayed randomly and won't relate to the content being viewed.

In the `Randomise` drop-down, you decide whether you want the banners to appear according to their order number (if more than one banner exists in the selected client and category), or in random order. The options are `Sticky, Ordering` and `Sticky, Randomise`. Select the `Sticky, Randomise` option to randomly display banners.

Any text you enter in the `Header Text` field is displayed before the group of banners. You can also leave this field blank. For this exercise, enter the text `Widest Range` in this box. Similarly, the content of the `Footer Text` field will appear after the group of banners. This can be left blank as well. For this exercise, enter `Lowest Price` in this field.

The `Module Class Suffix` field is used for applying styles to the module. Leave this field blank, as you don't have the suffix to be applied to the CSS class of the module.

Displaying the banner

After entering this information, save the Banners module by clicking the `Save` icon in the toolbar. You can now see the banner of your client on your Joomla website. Open the browser window displaying your website and click the `Refresh` button. The banner of your client should appear on the website, as shown in Figure 4-26.

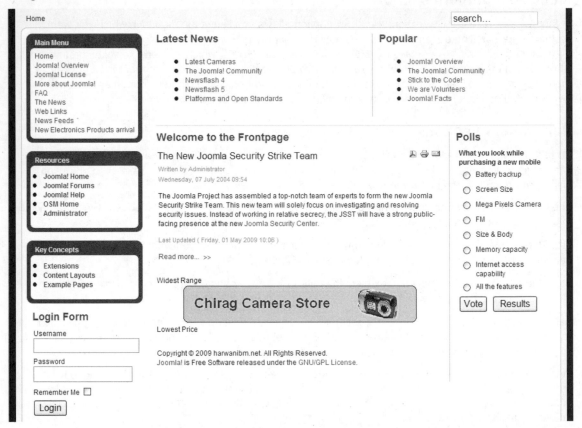

Figure 4-26. Client banner being displayed

Displaying banners on the basis of content

To demonstrate how a banner can automatically change according to an article being opened on your website, you need to have at least two articles and two banners in your Banner category. You already have one article, "Latest Cameras," and one banner, Chirag camera banner, in the Camera Banner category of your banner client, Chirag Camera Store. For simplicity, instead of making another article and banner from scratch, you will use the existing article and banner provided by Joomla in the default website. If you refer back to Figure 4-22, you'll see the list of banners that exist in your website. Below the `Chirag camera banner` entry is `OSM 1`. Select this to edit the OSM 1 banner. The OSM 1 banner should look something like Figure 4-27.

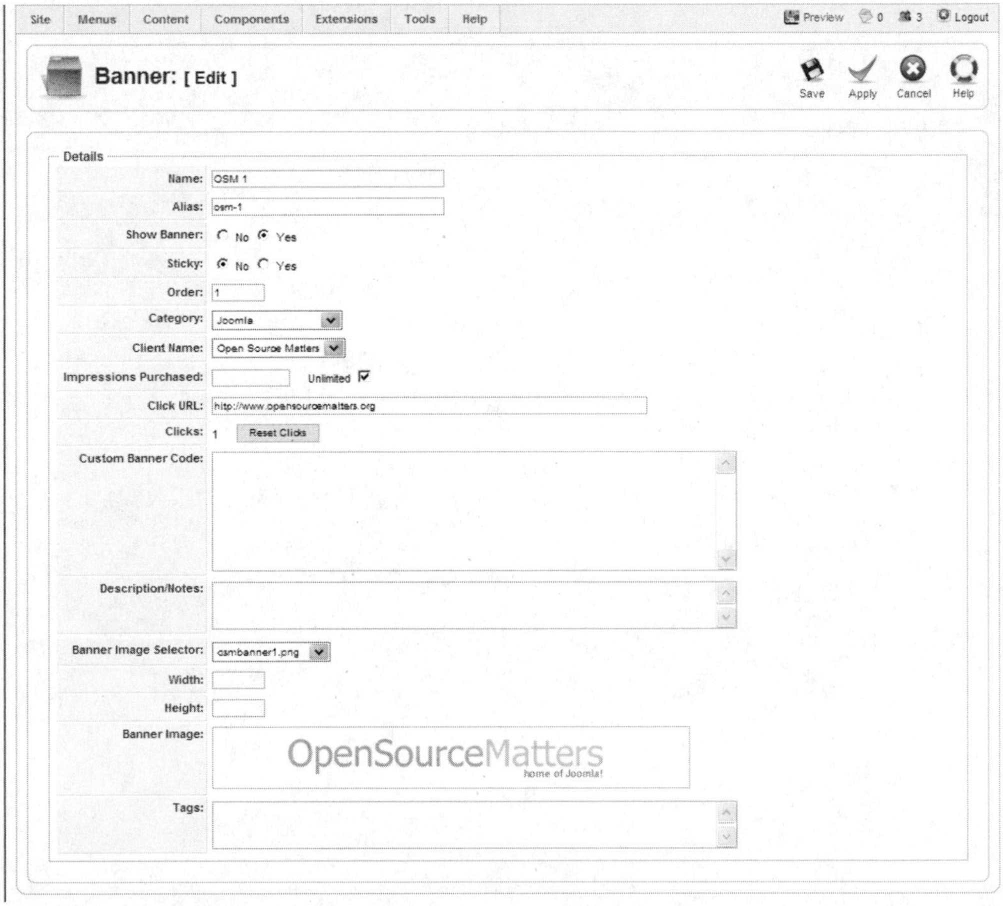

Figure 4-27. OSM 1 banner in edit mode

You just need to select `Camera Banner` and `Chirag Camera Store` from the `Category` and `Client Name` drop-downs, respectively. Then, in the `Tags` field, enter, `advt_open, advt_licensefree`, as shown in Figure 4-28. After making these changes, save the banner by clicking the `Save` icon in the toolbar.

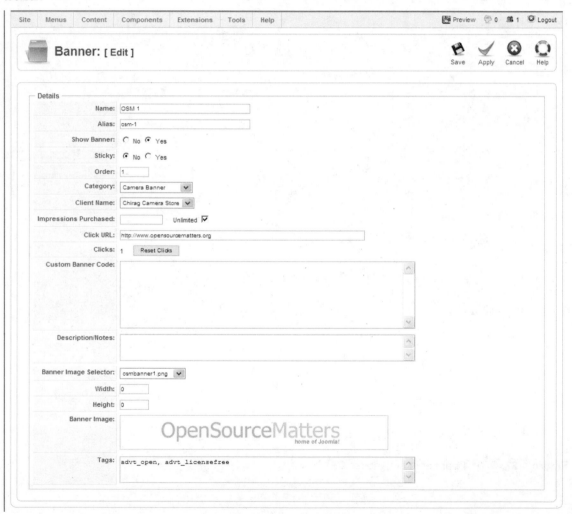

Figure 4-28. Editing the category, client name, and tags of the OSM 1 banner

The article that you will be using (provided by Joomla in the default website) is "Joomla! Overview." Select `Joomla! Overview` from the `Main Menu`, as shown in Figure 4-29.

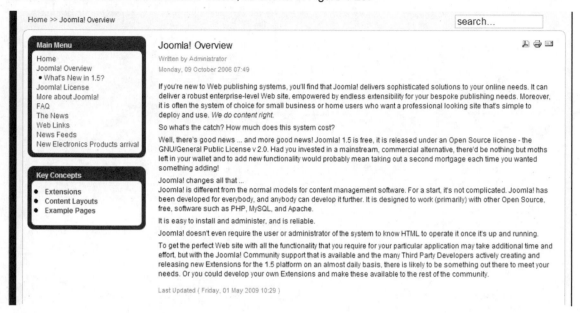

Figure 4-29. Display of the "Joomla! Overview" article

First, you'll edit "Joomla! Overview" to insert tags into it—this is going to play a major role in when the banner is displayed. Open the Article Manager by clicking on its icon in the control panel. The Article Manager will display a list of articles under different categories and sections. Select the "Joomla! Overview" article from the Article Manager, and it will open in edit mode. Then add the following keywords to it: advt_open, GPL, and community (or anything that highlights the main points of the article if you're using a different article), as shown in Figure 4-30. After entering the keywords, save the article by clicking the `Save` icon in the toolbar.

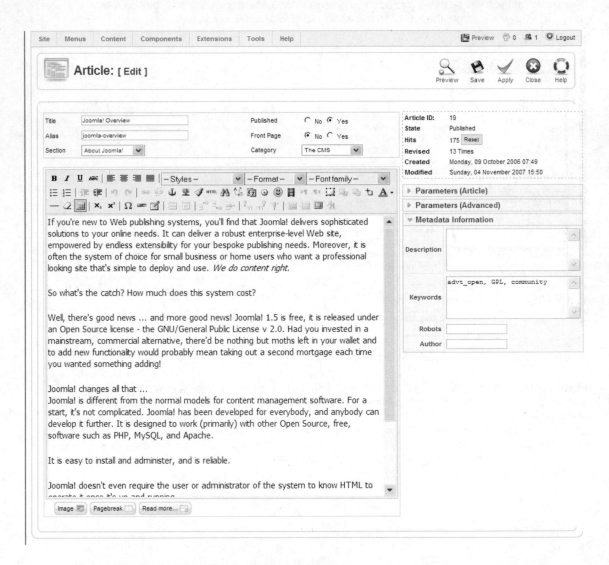

Figure 4-30. Adding keywords for the "Joomla! Overview" article

Now, if you compare the OSM 1 banner's tag with the keywords of the "Joomla! Overview" article, you'll find that *advt_open* is a common word between them. Similarly, the common word between the tags of Chirag camera banner and the keywords of the "Latest Cameras" article is *advt_shooting*. At least one word must be matching for the desired banner to appear (on the basis of the article being viewed).

Open the front end of your Joomla website to see the impact. Open your browser, point it to http://localhost/joomlasite, and invoke the "Latest Cameras" article by selecting the menu item New Electronics Products arrival. You'll find that the Chirag camera banner appears at the footer of the website (as shown in Figure 4-31), because both have advt_shooting in common.

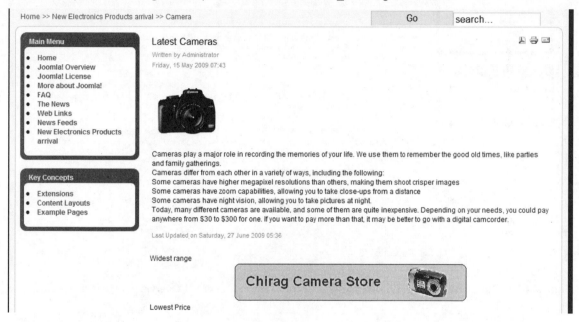

Figure 4-31. Chirag camera banner automatically appears when the "Latest Cameras" article is selected.

Similarly, when you open the "Joomla! Overview" article by selecting the Joomla! Overview menu item from the Main Menu, the OSM 1 banner will appear at the footer of the website (as shown in Figure 4-32), because they have advt_open in common among their respective keywords and tags.

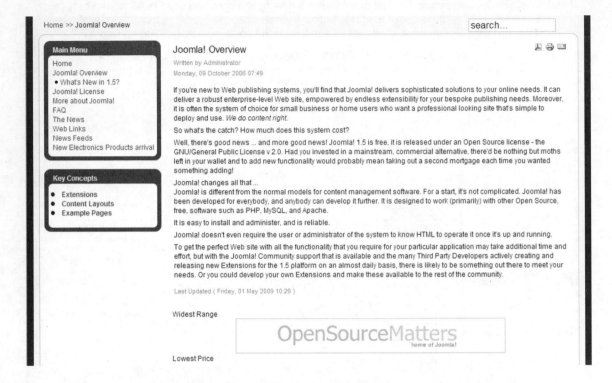

Figure 4-32. The OSM 1 banner automatically appears when the "Joomla! Overview" article is selected.

> *If you don't use tags, or if there are no matching words among the keywords of articles and tags of the banners, all the banners of the selected banner client and category will be displayed randomly one by one.*

Summary

In this chapter, you learned how to upload images to the Media Manager. You saw step by step how to create a category and a client for the banners, and also how to create banners. Finally, you learned how to edit the Banners module to display the banners of the specific client and category. In the next chapter, you'll see how users are created for your website. You'll also explore the different categories of users and their roles in website maintenance. Additionally, you'll learn to create contact forms to allow the visitors of your website to contact you (i.e., the website owner or any authorized person in the respective department of your organization).

Chapter 5

Creating Users and Contacts

In the previous chapter, you saw the role that the Media Manager plays in managing images in the articles, banners, and other contents of your website. You also saw how to create a category and clients for the banners. Finally, you created the banner for a specific client and used the Banners module to activate it. In this chapter, you'll create different types of users for your website. Users for a website can be of various types. One type comprises general visitors to your website; they can generally only view the content of your site, and don't have permission to edit information or upload their own content. Another type of user can contribute to your website by writing articles, but cannot edit existing content. There may also be users who cannot only contribute articles, but can edit and even publish them on your website. So, you will see how these different types of users can be created for your Joomla website, and what rights each has. You'll also create a **contact form** and allow visitors to your website to contact the authorized person in a selected department to get desired information. Contact forms are the forms you usually see when you select the Contact Us link on any website—blank forms with text boxes for you to enter your query and submit it. The information typed by the visitors in these contact forms is e-mailed to the concerned person or department (which I will be referring to from now onward as the **contact**). If the contact is a department, then it will be linked with a person who is authorized to receive information on behalf of the department and can take necessary action. In this chapter, you'll learn about the following:

- The User Manager

- Different types of user groups

- How to create users

- How to create a Contact category

- How to create contacts

- How to create menu items to link to contacts

What is a contact?

The main agenda in this chapter is to create a contact form on your website, which a visitor can fill in and click a button to send to you. On a standard website, the main contact will either be

- The concerned person of the organization (in case of smaller organizations).

- The department of an organization. The department contact is usually linked with an authorized person who is forwarded queries for the necessary action. In large organizations, each department has its own contacts, and each of them is linked with an authorized person.

Remember that if the contact is some department of an organization, it has to be linked to a user who is responsible for receiving the e-mails sent to it. Consequently, I'll first show you how users are created for a website.

> If the e-mail address of the department or contact item is not specified, all the e-mails sent to the department or contact Item will be sent to the e-mail address of the user to which it is linked.

If you specify the person as a contact, you don't need to link the contact to any user, since all the e-mails will be sent to that person directly.

Working with the User Manager

The User Manager provides tools for creating, viewing, editing, and deleting users for your website. Users play a major role in managing contents of a website. You can perform several functions with the User Manager, including

- Watching whether a user is logged in or not

- Blocking a user from logging into your site

- Seeing the last time a particular user visited your site

- Changing the state of a user from Logged In to Logged Out

Different types of user groups

The users you create can be assigned a to group, depending on what you want them to be able to do on your website. A newly created user is assigned a group to designate the user's access level. The user groups in Joomla are predefined, and you cannot create your own groups. Table 5-1 describes all the available groups.

Table 5-1. List of user groups

Group	Description
Registered User	Visitors who have registered on your site. They can view menu items that are assigned the Registered access level, but they cannot submit or edit articles.
Author	Users who can submit articles for approval (from the front end only). These articles must be approved by a member of the Publisher group or higher. Users in the Author group cannot edit existing articles.
Editor	Users who can submit articles and edit existing articles (from the front end only). These articles must be approved by a member of the Publisher group or higher.
Publisher	Users who can submit, edit, and publish articles (from the front end only).
Manager, Administrator, and Super Administrator	Users who can do all of the above plus log into the back end with increasing rights.

Creating users

Now that you know what kind of groups can be assigned to a user, let's create a user for your website. To do this, you need to open the User Manager. Open a browser window and enter your Administrator interface address—that is, http://localhost/joomlasite/administrator. Then, from the menu bar, select Site ➤ User Manager. You'll see a screen like that shown in Figure 5-1. It displays the list of all registered users of your website. The user named Administrator belongs to the Super Administrator group, and is automatically created by Joomla.

Figure 5-1. User Manager

The `Logout` icon in the User Manager toolbar is used for changing the state of the selected user from Logged In to Logged Out. Any user that is currently logged in can be logged out by the administrator. The rest of the icons in the toolbar have the usual meanings that you've learned so far.

You don't have to create a user account for everyone who visits your website, but you do need to create accounts for users who want to maintain your website. These users need extra privileges to contribute articles, edit existing articles, publish articles, and so on. Each user that the administrator creates for website maintenance is assigned a group depending on his role in website administration. Visitors of your website can also create their own accounts from the front end by selecting the link `Create an account`. These self-registered users are assigned the Registered User group by Joomla.

Now let's create a new user. Click the `New` icon in the toolbar, and you'll see a screen that lets you enter information for the new user. We'll create a user named sanjay. Fill in the information for the new user as shown in Figure 5-2.

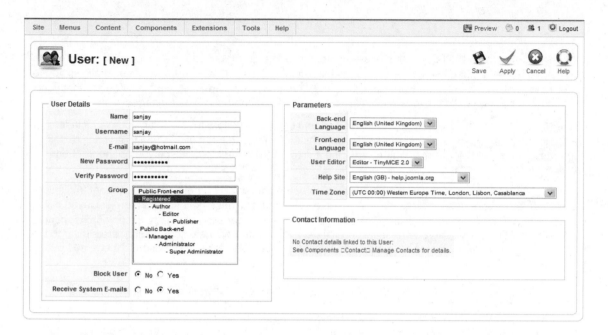

Figure 5-2. Creating new user sanjay

The `Name` field is for specifying the complete name of the user (unlike the `Username` field, it can include spaces). Enter `sanjay` for the name of the user here. The `Username` field is for the user ID for logging into the website. As mentioned, the username cannot contain spaces, and it must be unique for each user. Since we want our new user to log in by entering the name `sanjay`, type that name here. In the `E-mail` field, enter the e-mail address of the user: `sanjay@hotmail.com`. In the `New Password` and `Verify Password` fields, enter a password for the user (make sure the passwords entered in both boxes are exactly the same).

In the `Group` field, select the group to which the user will belong. The available choices are `Registered`, `Author`, `Editor`, `Publisher`, `Manager`, `Administrator`, and `Super Administrator`. Select `Registered` for `sanjay`, as we only want him to be able to view the website, not edit or add anything to it.

Set the `Block User` option to `No` when you want the user to be able to log into your website. If you want to disable a user from logging into your website, set this option to `Yes`. Only members of the Administrator and Super Administrator groups can set this option. Set the `Receive System E-mails` option to `Yes` if you want the user to receive system e-mails. This option too is visible only to administrators and super administrators. An example of a system e-mail is the e-mail sent by Joomla to a new user when they create an account. The `Register Date` field displays the date on which the user is registered. This date is displayed only when you are editing the information of an existing user.

Joomla allows you to administer the website in one language and access the website in some other language. In the `Back-end Language` field, you select the language to be used at the back end (i.e., for administering the website). For this exercise, set the language to English (United Kingdom). The default is the language set in the Language Manager. The Front-end Language field allows you to specify the language to be used while accessing the Joomla website. Select the same language that you chose for the back end. Again, the default is the language set in the Language Manager.

In the User Editor field, you select the front-end and back-end editors for the user. Joomla includes two editors: TinyMCE and XStandard Lite. TinyMCE is the default editor; it allows you to edit rich text. It supports various styles for formatting the text, and it allows the content to be displayed on the front end just like it does in the editor.

The Help Site field is for specifying the location of the help server. The **help server** is meant to display the help screens when a user clicks the Help icon on the toolbar. These help screens are displayed by default from a remote server: http:// help.joomla.org. However, you can also set the help server to display help screens from a local server. The local Joomla help server displays help screens that are similar to the remote server, with the advantage that you can customize them, add extra information to them, and even translate them to the language of your choice.

> *The local help server must be periodically updated to reflect the latest changes.*

You can easily set up your local help server by downloading the help screens from the Joomla website. Set the value of the Help Site field to English (GB) - help.joomla.org to access the remote help server.

In the Time Zone field, you can set the time zone for the user. The default is the time zone set in the Global Configuration section. The Contact Information section is for displaying the contact information if the user is linked to a contact (which you'll learn about next); otherwise, this field displays the message: No Contact details linked to this User.

After entering the information for the user sanjay, click the Save icon to save it. The user sanjay will appear in the User Manager list, as shown in Figure 5-3.

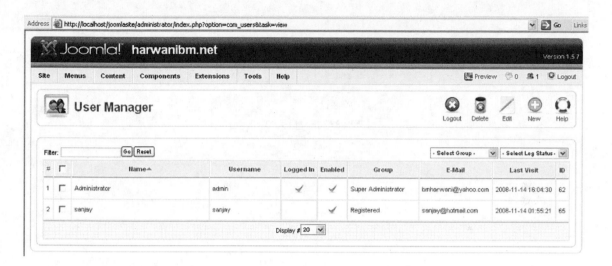

Figure 5-3. User Manager—user sanjay created

The User Manager displays the user information, including their complete name, their username (used to log into the website), whether they are currently logged in (a check mark means that they're currently logged in and a blank cell means that they're logged out), and whether a user is enabled or disabled (a check mark means they're enabled and a red *X* means they're disabled). You can click the icon to toggle between the two states. A disabled user can neither activate his account nor log into your website. When a user registers at your website, Joomla sends him a system e-mail carrying an activation link that has to be selected by the user in order to activate his account. But a disabled user cannot activate his account even by clicking at the activation link sent to him by e-mail. If the administrator or super administrator blocks a user, that user is disabled. The User Manager also displays the group to which users belong. Additionally, the users' e-mail addresses and the date that each was last logged into the website are also displayed. The last column of the User Manager table displays the ID number of the user, which is a unique number automatically assigned by Joomla to each user (used for internal maintenance tasks).

To verify that your user sanjay has been created, refresh your Joomla website. A login form appears on the website (its location will depend on the template you've chosen). In the login form, you enter the username and password for sanjay, as shown in Figure 5-4.

Figure 5-4. Login form

If the username and password are correct, the login form will change to display a welcome message, as shown in Figure 5-5.

Figure 5-5. Welcome message on the login form

Also, a user menu will appear on your website, as shown in Figure 5-6.

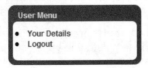

Figure 5-6. User menu that appears on successful login

Because the user sanjay is in the Registered User group, he can see his details but cannot submit an article (although he can view all the articles that are meant for registered users).

Now let's log out as user sanjay and, from the Administrator interface, try changing the group of this user. That is, open the User Manager by selecting `Site` ➤ `User Manager`, select the check box for user sanjay, and click the `Edit` icon in the toolbar. You'll get a screen to edit the settings of user sanjay (refer back to Figure 5-2). Change the group of this user to Manager, and save it. To see the effect, refresh your Joomla website. This time, when you log in as sanjay, you will see the screen shown in Figure 5-7.

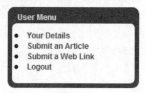

Figure 5-7. Options in the user menu when the user group is changed to Manager

Notice that sanjay, as a member of the Manager group, can now submit articles and web links.

Now that you've seen the impact of groups on a user, restore sanjay's user group to Registered, since you'll be using it later when dealing with contacts.

Creating a Contact category

Next, you need to link your new user, sanjay, to a contact; however, before creating a contact, you need to specify the category (or categories) for the contact. So, let's begin by creating a Contact category.

A Contact category simply categorizes different contacts. For example, you can create a category by the name of "suppliers" such that all the contacts (units within organization or user) dealing with suppliers are placed in that category. Similarly, a category might be named "technical" to group the contacts dealing with technical problems.

First, you need to open the Contact Category Manager. Open the Administrator interface and select `Components` ➤ `Contacts` ➤ `Categories`. You'll see a screen like the one shown in Figure 5-8. Notice that the Contact Category Manager list already contains a category by the name Contacts, which Joomla provides by default.

Figure 5-8. Contact Category Manager

Before creating our own Contact category, you should first understand the purpose of the icons in the toolbar. These are described in Table 5-2.

Table 5-2. Brief explanation of the Contact Category Manager toolbar icons

Icon	Description
Publish	Used to publish (make visible on the website) the selected Contact category.
Unpublish	Used to make the selected Contact category temporarily invisible from the website.
Delete	Used to permanently delete the selected Contact category. The user is asked for confirmation before it will be deleted.
Edit	Used to edit the information for the Contact category (such as its title, access level, image, and description).
New	Used to create a new Contact category. This icon provides a blank form for entering information about the new Contact category.
Help	Used to open the Joomla help website.

Click the New icon to create a new Contact category. You'll see a screen that lets you specify the information for the new Contact category. In this exercise, you'll be creating a Contact category by the name suppliers, so enter the information shown in Figure 5-9.

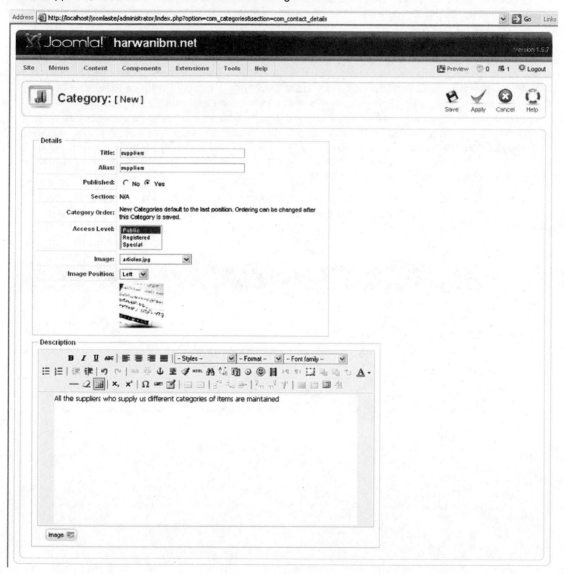

Figure 5-9. Creating the new Contact category, suppliers

In the `Title` field, you enter the name of the category as it should appear in the database. You're creating a category named suppliers, so you enter the same here. In the `Alias` field, you can enter the same text as for the title. The value of the `Published` field is `Yes` by default, so you can leave it as is. The `Section` field is noneditable and displays `N/A` for not applicable. This is because sections are not used for contacts. The `Category Order` displays the message that the new Contact category will appear last in the sequence in the Contact Category Manager list by default, but its order can be changed once it is saved. Set the value of `Access Level` to `Public`, as you want every visitor to your website to be able to access this Contact category. The `Image` field is used to select an image to be displayed next to the Contact category title on the website. You'll see a list of images stored in the Joomla_root/images/stories directory. Select an image—I'm using, articles.jpg in this example—to represent this Contact category. The preview of the image appears immediately. The value of `Image Position` is `Left` (by default). You can leave it like this to display the image on the left of the description text. In the `Description` field, you can enter a brief description of the Contact category in this box.

After entering the information for the suppliers Contact category, click the `Save` icon from the toolbar to save it. The suppliers Contact category will appear in the Contact Category Manager list, as shown in Figure 5-10.

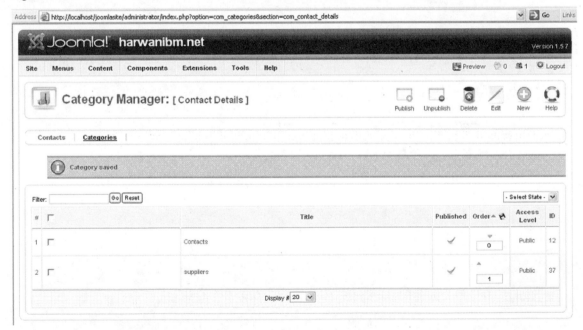

Figure 5-10. Contact Category Manager with suppliers added

Before proceeding to create contacts, take a look at Table 5-3, which describes the functions of the columns in the Contact Category Manager.

Table 5-3. Brief explanation of the columns in the Contact Category Manager

Column	Description
Title	Displays the name of the Contact category. Clicking the name will open the Contact category in edit mode.
Published	Displays whether the Contact category is in the published or unpublished state. The check mark means the Contact category is in the published state and will be visible on the website. If you click the check mark, it will toggle the state; that is, the Contact category will change to the unpublished state. A red *X* signifies that the Contact category is in the unpublished state; clicking this sign will again toggle the state.
Order	Used to change the order of the Contact category in the list. Click the up or down arrow to change its position in the list, or type in the new order number and click the Save Order icon in the heading of this column.
Access Level	Displays the level of users that can access this Contact category. The levels are Public, Registered, and Special. You can click the text link to change the access level. The three levels scroll in a continuous loop when clicked.
ID	Displays the category identification number automatically assigned by Joomla when the Contact category was first created.

Creating contacts

You're now ready to create a new contact for your suppliers Contact category. To do this, you need to open the Contact Manager. Either select the Contacts link from the Category Manager screen or select Components ➤ Contacts from the menu bar. The Contact Manager will open, as shown in Figure 5-11. It already contains a contact called Name in the Contacts category, which is provided in the default Joomla website.

> *Remember that you can always unpublish or delete the default items provided by Joomla if you don't want them.*

Figure 5-11. Contact Manager

We'll be creating two contacts:

- **John David**: The storekeeper in your organization

- **Purchases**: The department that you'll link to the sanjay user that you just created

The idea behind creating two contacts is that we want the queries made to John David to be e-mailed to him directly, but the queries to Purchases to be e-mailed to the user linked to it—that is, to the e-mail address for sanjay.

Before you create these contacts, take a look at Table 5-4, which briefly explains the toolbar icons in the Contact Manager.

Table 5-4. Brief explanation of the toolbar icons in the Contact Manager

Icon	Description
Publish	Makes the selected contact(s) visible on the website.
Unpublish	Makes the selected contact(s) not visible on the website.
Delete	Used to delete a contact permanently. The user is asked for confirmation before the contact is deleted.
Edit	Used to edit the information for the contact, such as the contact's category, linked users, e-mail address, and position.
New	Used to create a new contact.
Parameters	Opens the Global Configuration window (the Global Configuration settings are explained in detail in Chapter 10).
Help	Opens up the Joomla help website.

Click the New icon to create a new contact with the name John David. You'll be assigning him to the suppliers category. He isn't linked to any user, and he has an e-mail address to which all queries made via the contact form will be sent. Enter the information for the contact John David, as shown in Figure 5-12.

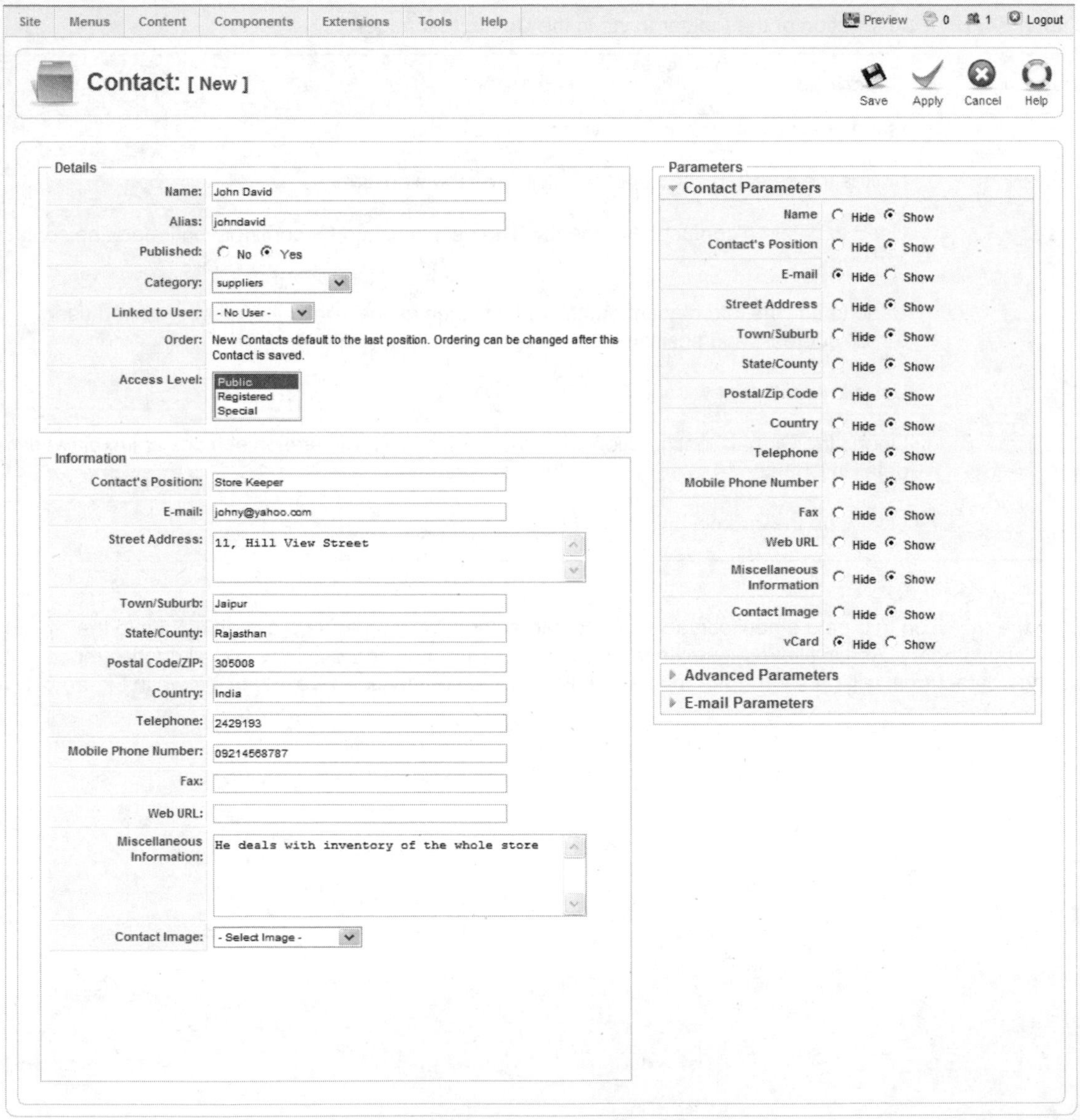

Figure 5-12. Creating the contact John David

Table 5-5 gives a brief description of each of the fields and the information you need to enter in them.

Table 5-5. Brief explanation of the fields of the Contact Manager

Fields	Description
Name	Enter `John David` for the name of the contact here.
Alias	This field designates the secondary name for the contact used in the URL when SEF is activated. It can be left blank, but if provided, it must be in lowercase and without spaces (use hyphens instead).
Published	Select `Yes` to make the contact visible on the website.
Category	Select the category with which this contact is to be associated. In this case, select the contact category that you created: suppliers.
Linked to User	From the drop-down list, select the registered user that you want the contact person to be associated with. Since John David himself is the responsible person for his department, select `No User`.
Order	By default, the added contact will appear at the end of the list, but you can change its order once it is saved.
Access Level	Select the level of users that can access this contact. The available options are `Public`, `Registered`, and `Special`. In this case, select `Public` to make the contact publicly accessible.
Contact's Position	Enter the position that the contact person holds within the website or organization.
E-mail	Enter the e-mail address of the contact.

Street Address	Enter the street address for the contact.
Town/Suburb	Enter the name of the town or suburb for the contact.
State/County	Enter the state or county name for the contact.
Postal Code/ZIP	Enter the postal or ZIP code for the contact.
Country	Enter the country for the contact.
Telephone	Enter the telephone number of the contact.
Fax	Enter the fax number of the contact.
Web URL	Enter the URL that provides information about the contact. Visitors who click the contact name will be taken to this URL. (You can leave this field blank if you don't know the contact's URL.)
Miscellaneous Information	You can enter additional information about the contact here.
Contact Image	Select an image to represent the contact.
Contact Parameters	Select the appropriate radio buttons to decide whether to show or hide the contact's information from the front end of the website.

After entering the information for the contact John David, click the Save icon to save it.

Now let's create one more contact, Purchases, and link it to the user sanjay. Again, click the New icon on the toolbar of the Contact Manager, and you'll see the form for entering information for a new contact again. Enter the information shown in Figure 5-13.

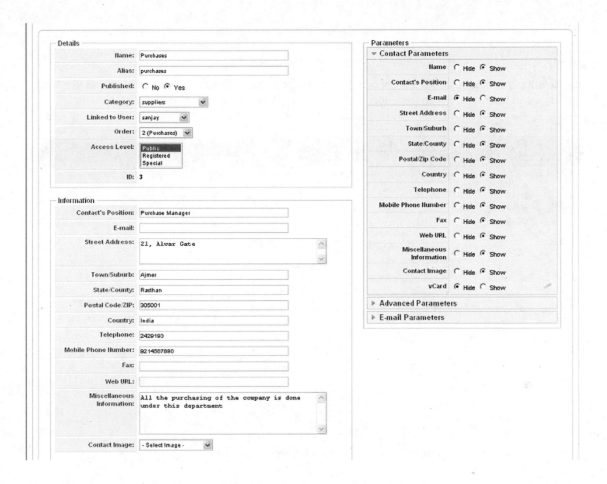

Figure 5-13. Creating the contact Purchases

Name the new contact Purchases, and assign it the position Purchase Manager and the category suppliers. The main things to note regarding this contact are

- It's linked to the user sanjay.

- The e-mail address is left blank, because it will use the e-mail address of the user sanjay.

Everything else is almost the same as for the contact John David.

After entering the information for the contact Purchases, click the `Save` icon to save it. You'll find that both contacts, John David and Purchases, appear in the Contact Manager list, as shown in Figure 5-14.

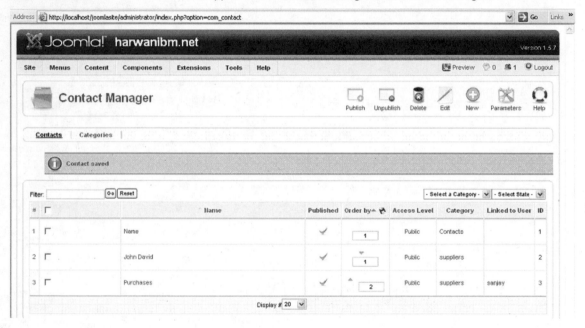

Figure 5-14. Two contacts added: John David and Purchases

Before continuing, Table 5-6 will give a brief description of the meaning of the columns in the Contact Manager list.

Table 5-6. Brief explanation of the columns of the Contact Manager

Column	Description
Name	Shows the name of the new contact. It can be a person, department, or anything else.
Published	Designates whether the contact is in the published or unpublished state.
Order by	Used to change the order in which the contact is displayed. Click the up or down icons to increase or decrease the position, and click the Save icon in the column header to save the order.

Access Level	Displays the level of users that can acces this contact. The access levels are: Public: Everybody can access this contact. Registered: Only registered users can access this contact. Special: Only users with Author or higher status can access this contact.
Category	Displays the category to which this contact belongs.
Linked to User	Displays the name of the registered user with whom the contact is linked. You can edit the information for the user by selecting this name. A registered user can be linked to more than one contact, but one contact Item cannot be linked directly to more than one registered user.

The Filter text box is used to display only the desired contacts. You can enter a keyword that is searched for in the contact names, and only the names having that keyword as part of it are displayed. For example, if you typed john in here, it would only show John David in the list. Click the Reset button to view the full list again. This is handy when you have a great many contacts.

Now that you've linked your Purchases contact to the user sanjay, if you open the user sanjay in edit mode from the User Manager, you'll find that the Contact Information section (which was blank when you created this user—refer to Figure 5-2) is filled in with the information for the contact Purchases, as shown in Figure 5-15.

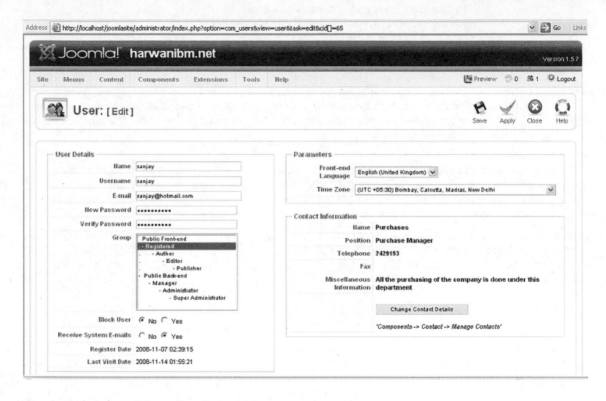

Figure 5-15. Contact information displayed for user sanjay

So, you've created a user, sanjay; a contact category, suppliers; and two contacts, John David and Purchases (linked to the user sanjay). Now it's time to create menu items to link to the contacts you've made. As mentioned in Chapter 4, a menu item is a text link in a menu that when clicked either invokes the module linked to it or displays the assigned information. The visitor of your website needs some link to click in order to open the contact forms of the two contacts that you have created. We'll create this in the next section.

Creating menu items to link to contacts

To access the contacts from your website, you'll create two menu items in the `Main Menu` of your website. Open the Administrator interface and, from the menu bar, select `Menus` ➤ `Menu Manager`. You'll see a list of all the menus. Click the `Edit Menu Items` icon in the `Main Menu` row, and you'll see a list of all the menu items in the `Main Menu`.

Click the New icon to create a new menu item. You'll see a screen for selecting the menu item type. Recall that you used the Articles node in Chapter 3 for creating menu items to point to the articles. Here, you'll use the Contacts node and select Standard Contact Layout, as shown in Figure 5-16.

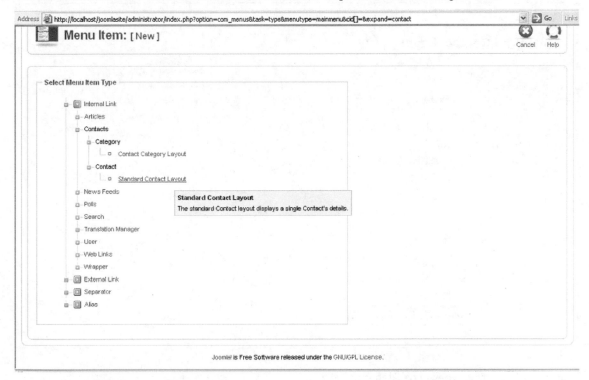

Figure 5-16. Different menu item types

The menu item type Standard Contact Layout will activate the contact form directly when the menu item is selected. The Contact Category Layout menu item type will instead first display the category of the contact; all the contacts in that category will be displayed, and the contact can be selected to send a query.

After selecting the menu item type, you'll see a screen that lets you enter the information for the Standard Contact Layout. Enter the information shown in Figure 5-17.

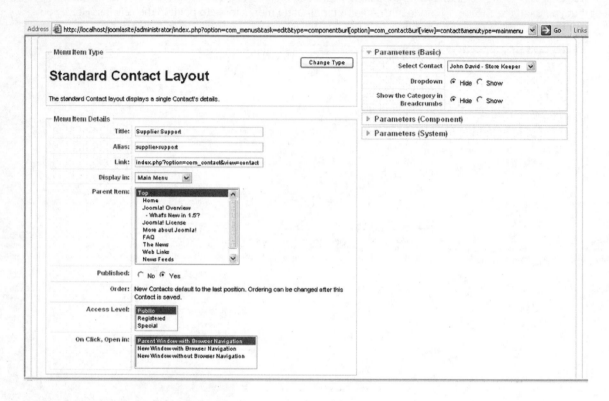

Address http://localhost/joomlasite/administrator/index.php?option=com_menus&task=edit&type=component&url[option]=com_contact&url[view]=contact&menutype=mainmenu ⯆ Go Links

Menu Item Type

Change Type

Standard Contact Layout

The standard Contact layout displays a single Contact's details.

Menu Item Details

Title: Supplier Support

Alias: supplier-support

Link: index.php?option=com_contact&view=contact

Display in: Main Menu ⯆

Parent Item: Top
 Home
 Joomla! Overview
  - What's New in 1.5?
 Joomla! License
 More about Joomla!
 FAQ
 The News
 Web Links
 News Feeds

Published: ○ No ● Yes

Order: New Contacts default to the last position. Ordering can be changed after this Contact is saved.

Access Level: Public
 Registered
 Special

On Click, Open in: Parent Window with Browser Navigation
 New Window with Browser Navigation
 New Window without Browser Navigation

⯆ **Parameters (Basic)**

Select Contact: John David - Store Keeper ⯆

Dropdown: ● Hide ○ Show

Show the Category in Breadcrumbs: ● Hide ○ Show

▶ **Parameters (Component)**

▶ **Parameters (System)**

Figure 5-17. Creating a new menu item

The title we want to appear for the menu item is Supplier Support, so enter that in the Title field. The Link field will be automatically filled in, depending on the menu item type selected. The link field informs Joomla whether to open the contact form directly or to display the category of the contact when the menu item is selected. The Display in field is used to decide which menu you want this menu item to appear in. Select Main Menu from the drop-down list.

The main thing to note is that the `Select Contact` field in the `Parameters (Basic)` section is set to `John David - Store Keeper` so that the query sent via the contact form will be e-mailed to this contact.

After entering the information for the menu item `Supplier Support`, click the `Save` icon to save it.

Similarly, create another menu item with the name Purchase Support, entering the information shown in Figure 5-18. This time, set the `Select Contact` field in the `Parameters (Basic)` section to the contact `Purchases - Purchase Manager`. Since this contact is linked to the user sanjay, a query sent to the contact via the contact form will be sent to the e-mail address for sanjay.

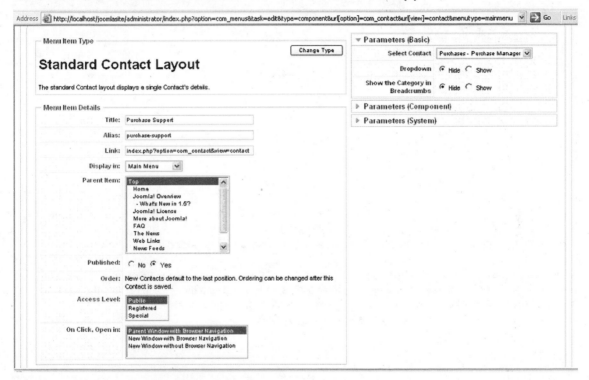

Figure 5-18. Menu item Purchase Support created

After entering the information for the menu item Purchase Support, click the `Save` icon to save it.

You'll find that both Supplier Support and Purchase Support appear in the list of menu items in the `Main Menu`, as shown in Figure 5-19.

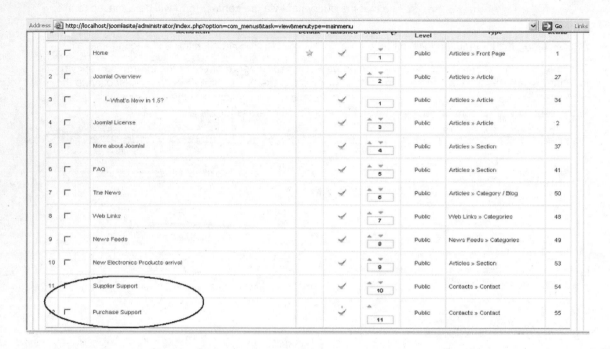

Figure 5-19. Two menu items, Supplier Support and Purchase Support, added in the Menu Manager

Now you're ready to run your website and see the impact of the various items we've created. Open the browser window pointing at your Joomla website—that is, at the address http://localhost/Joomlasite—and click the `Refresh` button. You'll find that two menu items, `Supplier Support` and `Purchase Support`, appear in the `Main Menu`, as shown in Figure 5-20.

Figure 5-20. Query to contact John David

When you select the `Supplier Support` menu item, which is connected to the contact John David, his detailed information—address, phone numbers, and so on—will appear at the top of the contact form, as shown in Figure 5-20, and the query entered will be e-mailed to him.

Similarly, if you select the menu item `Purchase Support`, which is connected to the contact Purchases, the information for this contact will appear in the contact form, as shown in Figure 5-21.

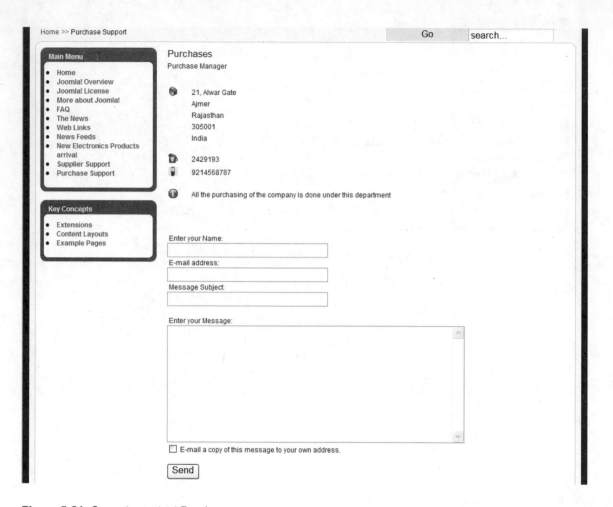

Figure 5-21. Query to contact Purchases

In this case, the query entered is sent to the contact Purchases. The sample shown in Figure 5-22 will be sent to the e-mail address for the user sanjay since the contact Purchases is linked to that user.

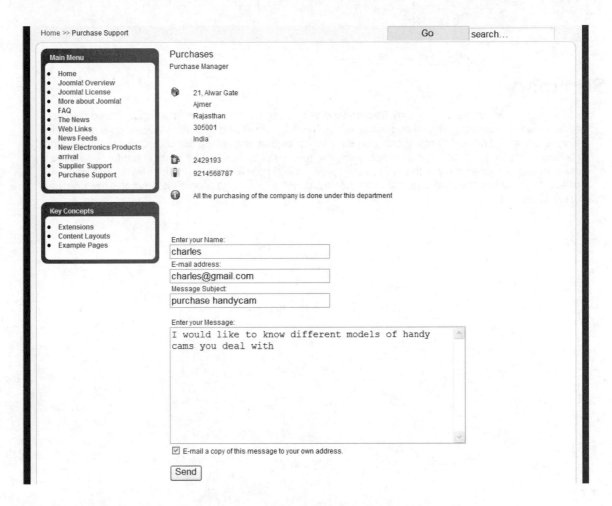

Figure 5-22. The query being sent to the e-mail address of user sanjay

The mail function must be configured from the Global Configuration section for e-mail to function properly; this will be explained in Chapter 10.

Summary

In this chapter, you've seen a step-by-step method of creating users of different groups. You've also seen how to create a Contact category and contacts. Contacts by name and department were both created to help you understand the difference between them when a query is sent via the contact form. Finally, you saw how to create the menu items for accessing the respective contacts. In the next chapter, you will learn how to develop interaction with the visitors of your website. The interaction with the visitors can be developed using several methods, including displaying news feeds and prompting them to select desired options from polls.

Chapter 6

Creating Interaction

In the previous chapter, you saw how to create users, contacts, and categories of contacts so that a visitor to the website can directly contact the authorized person of the department he is interested in. The purpose of that chapter was to define the interaction of visitors with the authorized person in an organization. In this chapter, you will increase the interaction, first with other data providers by using news feeds, and then with visitors by using polls on a particular subject. You'll learn

- How to create categories for news feeds

- How to create news feeds

- How to create polls

News feeds

News feeds are basically for sharing data from other providers. Before creating a news feed, you have to create a category to which the news feed will belong. The idea is to categorize similar news feeds under the same category.

Creating categories for news feeds

To create a category for a news feed, you need to open the News Feed Category Manager. In the administrator window, from the menu bar, select Components ➤ News Feeds ➤ Categories, and the News Feed Category Manager will open, as shown in Figure 6-1. It displays the news feed categories provided by default (which you can unpublish if you don't want them to appear on your website).

Figure 6-1. News Feed Category Manager

The tools in the News Feed Category Manager toolbar are fairly self-explanatory. As usual, you use `Publish` to make the selected categories visible on the website, and `Unpublish` to make the selected categories temporarily invisible from the website. The unpublished categories can be published again any time via the `Publish` icon. The `Delete` icon is for permanently deleting a category. The `Edit` icon is used to edit the information of the category that was entered while creating the category. This information includes the category's title, access level, image, and description. The `New` icon is for creating a new category of news feeds, and the `Help` icon is for displaying the help screen from the specified help server (in the global configuration settings).

The columns of the News Feed Category Manager display the respective information. For example, the `Title` column displays the name of the category. Clicking the name opens the category in edit mode. The `Published` column shows whether the category is visible on the website. A check mark signifies that the category is visible and a red *X* signifies that the category is invisible on the website. The `Order` column displays the order in which the category will be displayed. You can change the order by clicking the arrows, or entering the sequence number and clicking the `Save Order` icon in the column heading. The `Access Level` column displays which level of users can access the category. The options are `Public`, `Registered`, and `Special`. The `ID` column displays the category's unique identification number assigned automatically by Joomla for identifying it internally.

To create a category for your news feeds, click the `New` icon in the toolbar. You'll see a screen that lets you enter information for the new category. Enter the information shown in Figure 6-2.

Figure 6-2. Adding a new category

In the `Title` field, you specify the name for the new category. In this case, enter `Cell Phones`. The `Alias` field, as mentioned previously, is for SEF purposes, and you can leave it blank (Joomla will generate an alias for you from the title by lowercasing it and using hyphens in place of spaces). Set the `Published` option to `Yes` to make the category appear on the website. The `Section` field displays `N/A` (for "not applicable") because sections are not used for news feed categories—so nothing needs to be entered here. The `Category Order` field displays the sequence number of the category (usually it is the last place in the Category Manager list by default). You can always change the display order from the Category Manager later. In the `Access Level` field, you specify which level of users can access this category: `Public`, `Registered`, or `Special`. Set it to `Public` to make this category publicly accessible. From the `Image` drop-down list, select an image to represent the category. All the images available in the Media Manager (from the joomla_root/images/stories folder) will be displayed. Select the image cell.jpg (assuming you've already loaded it into the stories folder of the Media Manager). The image's preview will appear immediately. The `Image Position` field is for specifying the location of the image when displayed; the image has to appear to the left or right of the category title. The default is `Left`, and you can leave it as such. In the `Description` section, you can enter an introductory description of the category, and you can use the tools in the editor to format the text. You can even insert images in the description box with the help of the `Image` icon provided in the toolbar.

After entering the information for the category, save it by clicking the `Save` icon. You'll see the message `Category saved`, and your Cell Phones category will appear in the list, as shown in Figure 6-3.

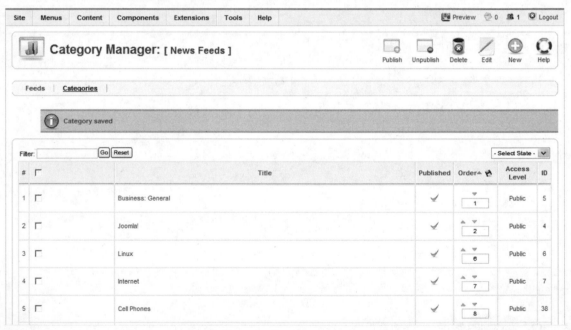

Figure 6-3. News Feed Category Manager with the Cell Phones category added

Creating news feeds

With the news feed category created, it's now time to create a news feed for that category. To create a news feed, either click the Feeds link (to the left of the Categories link) or, from the menu bar, select Components ➤ News Feeds ➤ Feeds. The News Feed Manager will open, displaying a list of several news feeds provided by default in your Joomla website, as shown in Figure 6-4 (you can unpublish them as you wish).

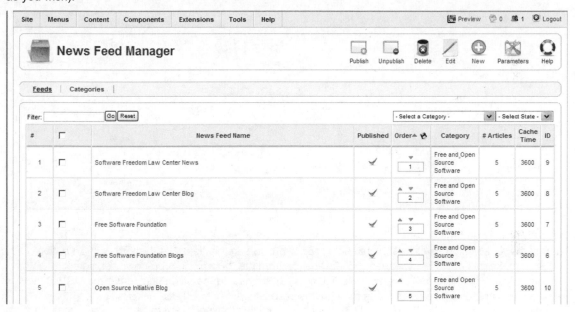

Figure 6-4. News Feed Manager displaying list of existing news feeds

Now click the New icon in the toolbar, and you'll see a screen that lets you enter information for the news feed. Enter the information shown in Figure 6-5.

Figure 6-5. Creating a news feed

In the `Name` field, enter the name of the news feed: `Cell Phones - fastest communication`. Though the `Alias` field can be left blank, enter `cell-phones` in this field. Set the `Published` option to `Yes` to make this news feed appear on the website. From the `Category` drop-down list, select the category to which this news feed should belong: Cell Phones. In the `Link` field, enter the URL of the website you want to get the news feeds from (in this case http://www.mobiledia.com/rss/news/). In the `Number of Articles` box, you specify the number of articles that you want to be accessed from the news feed website and displayed on your website for your visitors (you can leave it at the default of `5`). In the `Cache Time` field, you specify the number of seconds the news feed will be saved on your server before being downloaded again from the remote news feed website. The default time is 3600 seconds (1 hour). You can increase this time to reduce the network traffic, but this will make your news feeds less up to date. The `Order` field displays a message telling you that new news feeds default to the last position in the News Feed Manager, but the order can be changed from there. The `RTL Feed` field is used to specify the direction of the news feed content. RTL stands for "right to left." The three options are as follows:

- Site Language Direction: The direction of news feed text will be based on the language in which your website content is being displayed. (In Chapter 10, you will see how your website content can be viewed in different languages by using the translation mechanism). For example, if your website content is being viewed in English, the news feed content will move from left to right, and if it's being viewed in Hebrew or Arabic, it will move from right to left.

- Left to Right Direction: The news feed content will flow from left to right regardless of the language your website's being displayed in.

- Right to Left Direction: The news feed content will flow from right to left regardless of the language your website's being displayed in.

After entering the information for the news feed, click the Save icon to save it. You'll see the message News Feed saved, and the news feed "Cell Phones - fastest communication" will appear in the News Feed Manager list, as shown in Figure 6-6.

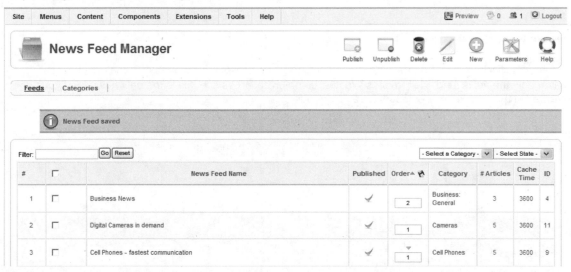

Figure 6-6. Your new news feed displayed in the News Feed Manager list

You can now check whether your news feed is visible on your website. Open the browser window, point to your Joomla website, http://localhost/joomlasite, and click the `Refresh` button. In the `Main Menu`, select the `News Feeds` menu item, and you'll see a screen that displays the news feed category you just created, as shown in Figure 6-7.

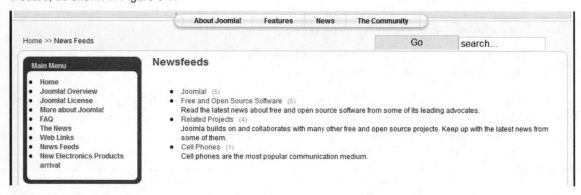

Figure 6-7. List of news feed categories on your website

When you click the `Cell Phones` news feed category, it will display all the news feeds under it—in this case, only the news feed "Cell Phones - fastest communication," since this is the only news feed you've created in the Cell Phones category (see Figure 6-8).

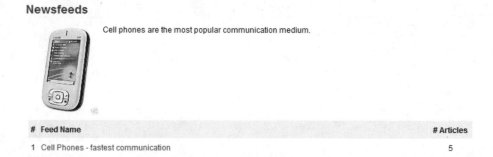

Figure 6-8. News feed "Cell Phones - fastest communication" displayed upon selecting the Cell Phones category

Click the `Cell Phones - fastest communication` link to get the news feed from the specified URL: http://www.mobiledia.com/rss/news/. You'll get a list of five articles from the remote news feed website, as shown in Figure 6-9.

Newsfeeds

Mobiledia: Cell Phone News

Find breaking news, reviews, and opinion on the latest cell phones and mobile devices worldwide.

- WiGig to Push for Fast Wireless in the Home
  Computer, handset and home entertainment titans plan to promote an even faster wireless technology to transfer large files, such as high-definition video, to consumer electronics like laptops, mobile phones and home television sets.

- T-Mobile G1 Software Update Coming Next Week
  T-Mobile said it will roll out a software update for the G1 smartphone at the end of next week, adding new features such as an on-screen QWERTY keyboard, video recording and playback and stereo Bluetooth technology.

- Nokia E52 Smartphone Offers Long Battery Life
  Nokia, the world's top mobile phone maker, today unveiled the E52 smartphone, an Eseries business device that claims eight hours of talk time and 23 days of standby time.

- Palm Pre Costs $170 to Make, Expects to Retail for $200
  Palm's highly-anticipated Pre smartphone costs $170 to make and is expected to be priced around $200 after a carrier subsidy from Sprint, according to market researchers at iSuppli.

- BlackBerry Curve Outsold Apple iPhone in Q1
  Research in Motion's BlackBerry Curve moved past Apple's iPhone in the first quarter to become the best-selling phone in the U.S., according to market researchers at The NPD Group.

Figure 6-9. Five articles related to cell phones displayed

Creating polls

Polling is a popular technique for getting feedback from website visitors on a particular subject. It helps you to better understand your visitors' choices and tastes. It also helps with understanding the reason behind the popularity of an item, as well as end users' requirements.

To begin, open the Administrator interface and select `Components ➤ Polls` from the menu bar. The Poll Manager will open, as shown in Figure 6-10. As usual, it already contains a poll—"Joomla! is used for?"—provided in the website by default.

Figure 6-10. Poll Manager

Click the `New` icon in the toolbar to add a new poll. You'll see a screen that lets you enter information and options for the poll. Enter the information for the poll shown in Figure 6-11. The title of the poll you're creating is "What you look for when purchasing a new cell phone."

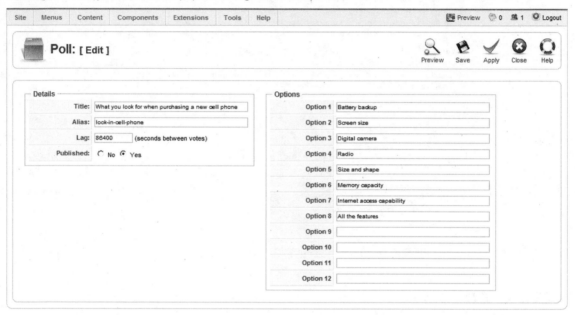

Figure 6-11. Creating a new poll

Click the `Save` icon to save your new poll. You'll see it in the Poll Manager list, as shown in Figure 6-12.

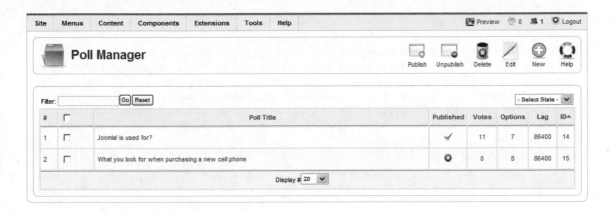

Figure 6-12. Your new poll in the Poll Manager list

Initially, your new poll may be in the unpublished state (usually all newly added polls are in the unpublished state by default). In that case, publish it by selecting its check box and clicking the `Publish` icon. The check mark in the Publish column, as shown in Figure 6-13, indicates that the poll will appear on the website.

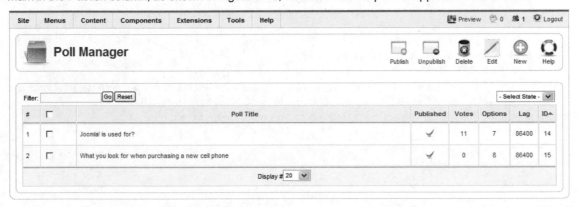

Figure 6-13. Your new poll in the published state

To view the poll on the Joomla website, open the site by pointing your browser to http://localhost/joomlasite, and click the Refresh button. [0]Alternatively, you can click the Preview link at the top right of the Administrator interface. This will open the home page in a new window (or tab, depending on the browser). Surprisingly, your new poll, "What you look for when purchasing a new cell phone," won't appear; instead, the poll "Joomla! is used for?" will appear, as shown in Figure 6-14. This happens because, although two polls are present on your website, only one poll can be active at a time.

Figure 6-14. Default poll provided by Joomla

If you click the Results button, you'll see a screen that displays the results of the poll with the percentage of each option selected by the visitors, as shown in Figure 6-15. This screen also has a Select Poll drop-down list where you can select the poll for which you want to see the results.

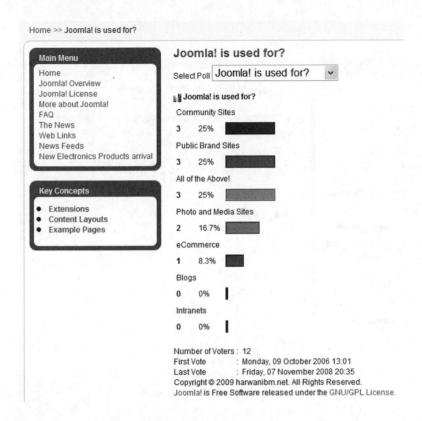

Figure 6-15. Results of the "Joomla! is used for?" poll

If you select the poll "What you look for when purchasing a new cell phone" from the drop-down list, you'll see the results of that poll, as shown in Figure 6-16.

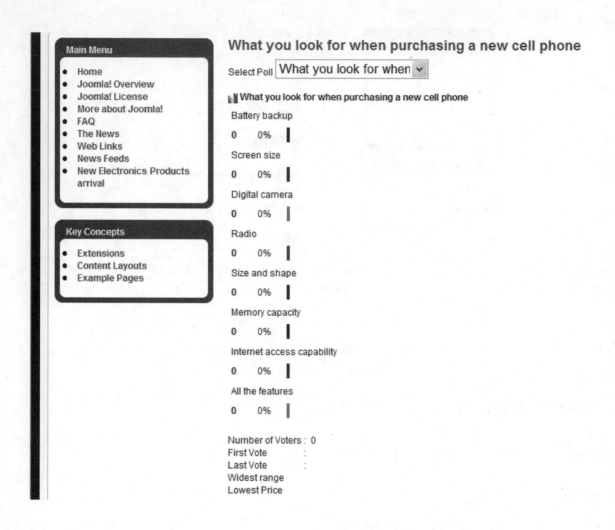

Figure 6-16. Results of the poll "What you look for when purchasing a new cell phone"

Now open the Poll Manager again, select the check box of the poll "Joomla! is used for?," and click the Unpublish icon in the toolbar to make it temporarily invisible from the website, as shown in Figure 6-17.

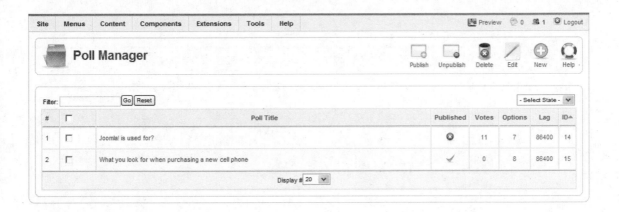

Figure 6-17. Unpublishing the "Joomla! is used for?" poll

Instead of unpublishing the poll that you don't want to see, there's another method to see only the desired poll: open the Polls module from the Module Manager and configure it to show the desired poll. That is, select `Extensions` ➤ `Module Manager`, select the Polls module, as shown in Figure 6-18, and click the `Edit` icon at the top.

> *Another method to open a module in edit mode is to just select its name in the Module Manager.*

Figure 6-18. Selecting the Polls module in the Module Manager

You'll see a screen for editing the Polls module. Keep the values of all the fields as they are, except in the `Parameters` section; there, use the `Poll` drop-down list to select the poll "What you look for when purchasing a new cell phone," as shown in Figure 6-19. Click the `Save` icon to save the changes. This will make the selected poll active, and only that poll will appear on the website.

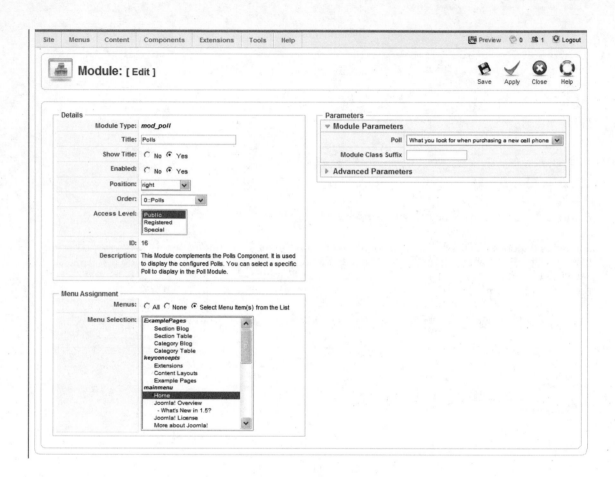

Figure 6-19. Editing the Polls module in the Module Manager

Refresh the browser window displaying your Joomla website, and only the poll "What you look for when purchasing a new cell phone" will appear there, as shown in Figure 6-20.

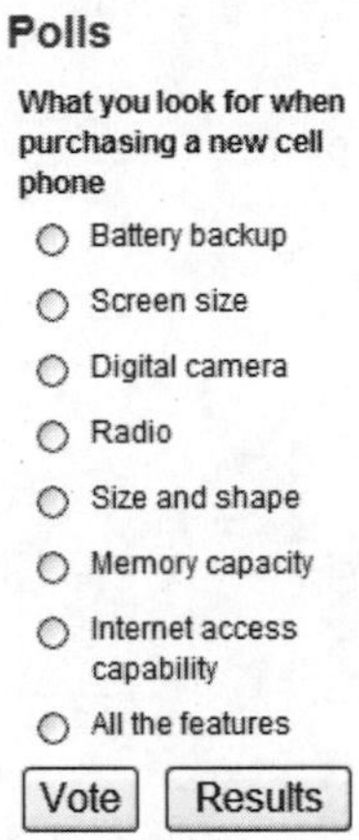

Polls

What you look for when purchasing a new cell phone

- ○ Battery backup
- ○ Screen size
- ○ Digital camera
- ○ Radio
- ○ Size and shape
- ○ Memory capacity
- ○ Internet access capability
- ○ All the features

[Vote] [Results]

Figure 6-20. Displaying the poll "What you look for when purchasing a new cell phone"

Summary

In this chapter, you learned how to create news feeds for sharing content from other data providers. You also learned how to create polls to get feedback from website visitors. In the next chapter, you will learn how to create menus, which are the mode of interface between visitors and the website. Menus display different options in the form of menu items that a visitor may select to see the desired information.

Chapter 7

Dealing with Menus

In the previous chapter, you saw how to create interaction with the user and with other data providers. You used news feeds to get updated information from other data providers, and used polls to learn visitors' views on a subject. Also, you learned how to provide related topics from other websites in the form of web links to enable data sharing. In this chapter, you'll learn how to create menus, and how to create menu items of different types so that they can be set to display articles, section categories, contacts, web links, news feeds, polls, login forms, and more.

There are four predefined menus in Joomla:

- The `Top Menu`, which runs horizontally across the top of the screen and appears as shown in Figure 7-1

Figure 7-1. Top Menu

- The `Main Menu`, a vertical menu that appears on the left side of the screen and contains the menu items that display the most frequently used contents of the website (see Figure 7-2)

Figure 7-2. Main Menu

- The `Other Menu`, which appears at the bottom left of the screen and includes links to external websites (see Figure 7-3)

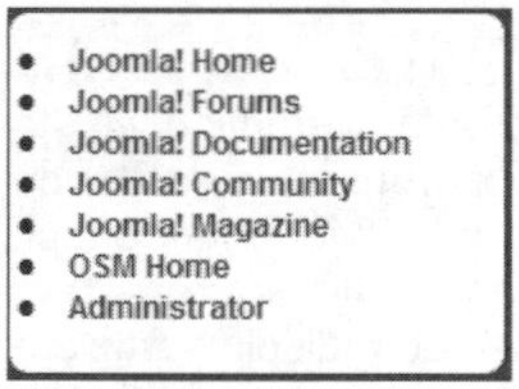

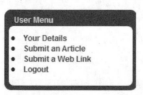

Figure 7-3. Other Menu

- The `User Menu`, which doesn't appear on the screen until a user has logged into the website, and contains links such as `Your Details` and `Logout`, as shown in Figure 7-4

Figure 7-4. User Menu

> *The position of these menus is not fixed, and is completely dependent upon the template. For example, the* `Top Menu` *doesn't necessary have to be at the top of the screen; its location is totally based on the settings defined in the template.*

When you create a menu item, you assign a menu item type to it, which defines what it is supposed to display. The menu item types are broadly classified into four categories:

- **Internal link**: This menu item type can access the articles or modules that are the part of the same website (i.e., located on the same domain).
- **External link**: This type is used to access web pages of an external website. For example, to access Google from your website, you would use this type.
- **Separator**: This is meant for creating a separator (in the form of a horizontal line or a blank line) within a menu. It is used for breaking up long menus. Usually, we see a separator in the form of a horizontal line in the `File` menu (in most word processing packages) between `Save`, `Print`, and other options.
- **Alias**: This menu item type category creates a link to an existing menu item. That is, it can access and display information that is already displayed in an existing menu item. Suppose you have a menu item by the name of `Making Films` that displays the information of the "Latest Cameras" article, and you want another menu item, `Shooting Accessories`, to display the same information. You can set the menu item type of `Shooting Accessories` to `Alias`, and this will make it refer to the same article.

In this chapter, you'll learn about the following menu item types:

- Articles
- Contacts
- News Feeds
- Polls
- Search
- User
- Web Links
- Wrapper
- External Link
- Separator
- Alias

Though you can create menu items in any of the existing menus provided in the default Joomla website, to keep the things separate and clean, we will create a new menu of our own for testing. So, let's start with creating a menu.

Creating a menu

To add a new menu, you need to open the Menu Manager. Open the Administrator interface (by pointing the browser window to `http://localhost/joomlasite/administrator`). Then, from the menu bar, select `Menus` ➤ `Menu Manager`. When the Menu Manager opens, click the `New` icon in the toolbar to create a new menu. You'll see a screen for entering information about the new menu, as shown in Figure 7-5. We want the menu title to be Electronic Products on our website, so enter that text in the `Title` field. The menu has to be activated via the Module Manager, and we have to specify the title by which it will appear in the Module Manager. Enter `Latest Electronic Range` in the `Module Title` field, since we want the menu to appear with the same name in the Module Manager. After entering the information for the new menu, click the `Save` icon.

Figure 7-5. Entering information for your new menu

For reference, Table 7-1 gives a brief description of the fields on the `Menu: [New]` screen.

Table 7-1. Brief description of the Menu: [New] options

Field	Description
Unique Name	The name used by Joomla to identify the menu. It must be unique and must not include spaces. In this exercise, it's specified as `ElectroProd` (though it could be any name).
Title	The name of the menu as displayed on the web page. In this exercise, it's specified as `Electronic Products`.
Description	A brief description of the menu.
Module Title	The name by which this menu will appear in the Module Manager, from which it is enabled to appear on the web page. If the title is left blank, a module will not be created, and this menu will not appear on the front end (i.e., the website). In this exercise, the module title is specified as `Latest Electronic Range`.

Table 7-2 gives a brief description of the icons on the `Menu: [New]` screen's toolbar.

Table 7-2. Brief description of the icons in the toolbar

Icon	Description

Save	Saves the menu and returns to the Menu Manager
Cancel	Cancels any modifications made
Help	Opens the Joomla help website

Upon saving the menu, you'll find it listed in the Menu Manager, as shown in Figure 7-6.

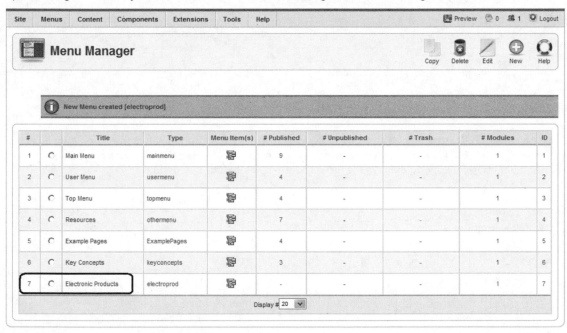

Figure 7-6. The new menu, Electronic Products, displayed in the Menu Manager

Creating menu items

We can now add menu items to our Electronic Products menu. Click the Edit Menu Item(s) icon in the Menu Item(s) column in the Electronic Products row. You'll get a Menu Item Manager: [electroprod] page that will contain a listing of all the menu items created in this menu, as shown in Figure 7-7. At the moment, it is empty, as we have not yet created any menu items in this menu.

Figure 7-7. The Menu Item Manager of the Electronic Products menu

Click the New icon to create menu items in this menu. You'll see a screen to select the menu item type, as shown in Figure 7-8. This menu item type decides the type of content that the menu item will display. As shown in the figure, the menu item type is broadly classified into four categories:

- Internal Link
- External Link
- Separator
- Alias

Figure 7-8. Categories of menu item types

The `Internal Link` category of menu item types consists of several options—`Articles`, `Contacts`, `News Feeds`, `Polls`, `Search`, and so on—where each option specifies the type of contents the menu item will display. Let's start with the first option, `Articles`.

Articles

When the `Articles` link is selected, it expands to display the options shown in Figure 7-9.

Figure 7-9. Menu item types in the Articles node

Table 7-3 briefly describes the options in the `Articles` node.

Table 7-3. The options of the Articles node

Option	Description
Archived Article List	Displays the articles that have been archived (in stored format and not currently visible)
Article Layout	Displays a single article
Article Submission Layout	Displays a form enabling users to submit their own articles
Category Blog Layout	Displays the contents of the articles in the selected category in blog layout
Category List Layout	Displays a list of the articles in the selected category
Front Page Blog Layout	Displays all the articles on the front page (only those articles that are set to be published on the front page) in blog layout

Section Blog Layout	Displays the contents of all the articles in the selected section in blog layout
Section Layout	Displays a list of the categories in the selected section

Let's look at each option in detail. In order to see what each menu item type does, we don't have to create a new menu item for each one. Instead, we can create a menu item of one menu item type, observe its impact from the front end, edit it to set it to the next menu item type in the option list, and so on. Before creating a menu item of any type, however, we need to do a little groundwork. For example, the Archived Article List menu item type is meant to display the articles that are archived (temporarily removed) from our website. So, until we archive some articles from our website, this menu item type is not going to show any effect. So, click the Cancel button from the toolbar to cancel the creation of a menu item at this stage.

Archived Article List

This menu item type is used to show the list of articles that have been archived. "Archived" means that the contents are not required currently and are in stored format. These articles can be searched by date. To try it out, let's open the Article Manager (Content ➤ Article Manager). In the Article Manager, we see a list of articles, some provided by Joomla and others created by us. Select a few articles in the list and click the Archive icon in the toolbar to change the status of the articles from the published state to the archived state. Let's select the three articles shown in Figure 7-10 and archive them.

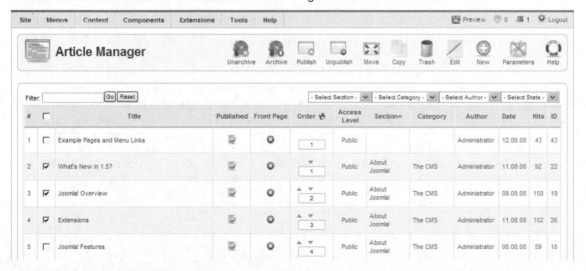

Figure 7-10. Changing the state of three articles from published to archived

Note the change in the state of the articles in the Published column (shown marked in Figure 7-11), signifying that the selected articles will not be displayed on the website (by default) and are in the archived state.

213

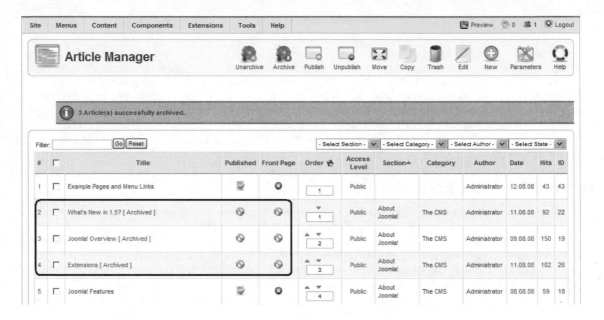

Figure 7-11. The three articles converted to the archived state

These archived articles can be seen from the front end when a menu item of type Archived Article List is selected by the visitor. Let's create a menu item of this type in the `Electronic Products` menu we created earlier. Open the Menu Manager by selecting the `Menu ➤ Manager` option. Click the `Edit Menu Item(s)` icon in the `Menu Item(s)` column in the `Electronic Products` row to open the `Menu Item Manager: [electroprod]` page. Click the `New` icon to create a new menu item in this menu. You'll get a screen to select the menu item type. From the list of menu item types, select the `Articles` node to expand it, and you'll get all the menu item types in it (refer to Figure 7-9). Upon selecting the Archived Article List menu item type, you'll see a screen for specifying certain information, as shown in Figure 7-12.

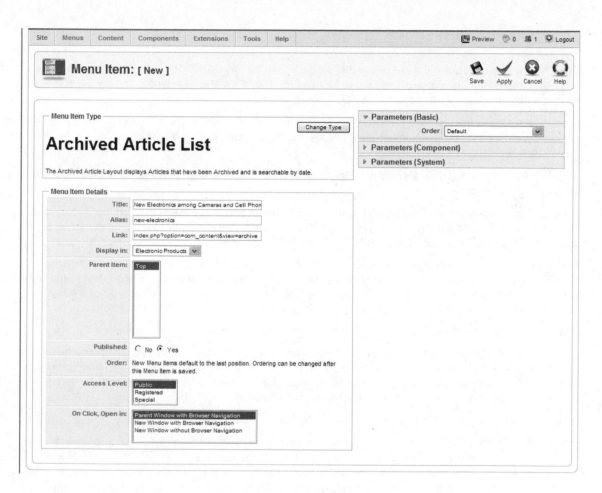

Figure 7-12. Creating a menu item of type Archived Article List

In the `Title` field, you enter the title of the menu item. It can be any text. Since you will be creating one menu item and editing the same menu item to be used for different menu item types, specify the title of this menu item as `New Electronics among Cameras and Cell Phones`.

As usual, the `Alias` field specifies a sort of secondary name for the title, and can be left blank. If it is specified, it must be lowercase and use hyphens instead of spaces. Let's specify the alias as `new-electronics`.

The `Link` field is automatically filled to point to the type of contents we want to display via this menu item. This field cannot be edited.

The `Display in` field is used to specify the menu name under which this menu item will be displayed (the current menu name we are dealing with appears by default). Since we want the menu item to appear under the `Electronic Products` menu, set the `Display in` field to `Electronic Products`.

In the `Parent Item` field, you specify whether the menu item is a top-level menu item or a submenu of an existing menu item. Since there is no other menu item present in this menu and it is the first menu item of this menu, there is only one option: `Top` (meaning that the current menu item will appear at the top of hierarchy, not as a submenu).

Set the `Published` field to `Yes` (the default) to make this menu item visible on the website.

The `Order` field is used for specifying the position of the menu item in the menu. Usually, the menu item is added to the end of the menu, but since there are no other items in the `Electronic Products` menu, our menu item is assigned the sequence number 1, meaning that it will be the first item in the menu. (As expected, you can change the order from the Menu Manager later).

Set the `Access Level` field to `Public` to allow all visitors to access the menu item.

The `On Click, Open in` field is used to specify where the contents of the articles are supposed to appear. The available options are `Parent Window with Browser Navigation`, `New Window with Browser Navigation`, and `New Window without Browser Navigation`. If the option `Parent Window with Browser Navigation` is selected, the selected information will be displayed in the current window; if `New Window with Browser Navigation` is selected, the desired contents will be displayed in a new browser window containing navigation controls to move among the web pages. If `New Window without Browser Navigation` is selected, the contents will be displayed in a new browser window without navigation controls. Let's select the `Parent Window with Browser Navigation` option.

After entering the information, click the `Save` icon to save the menu item. Your new menu item `New Electronics among Cameras and Cell Phones` will appear in the Menu Item Manager list, as shown in Figure 7-13.

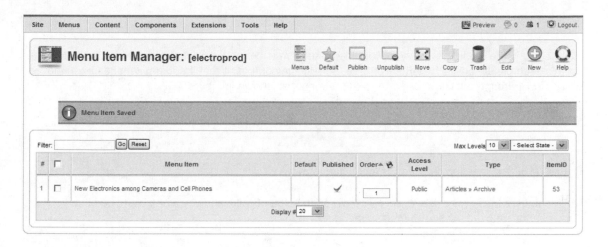

Figure 7-13. The new menu item

Moving menu items

While the menu item that you just created is part of the `Electronic Products menu`, you can move it to another menu easily. Just select the check box of the menu item that you want to move and click the `Move` icon. You'll see a list of all the menus under `Move to Menu`, as shown in Figure 7-14.

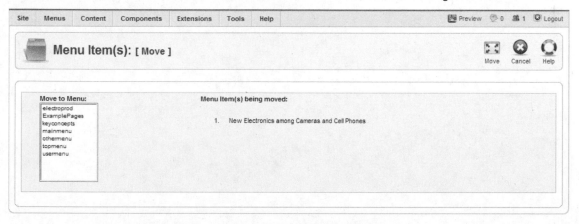

Figure 7-14. List of menus to where the selected menu item can be moved

After selecting the menu to which you want the menu item to be moved, click the Move icon in the toolbar. For this example, select mainmenu. You'll get a message confirming that the menu item has been moved to mainmenu from the Electronic Products menu, as shown in Figure 7-15.

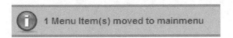

Figure 7-15. Confirmation message of menu item movement

The Menu Item Manager of the Main Menu will open automatically, and you'll be able to see that your menu item has moved, as shown marked in Figure 7-16.

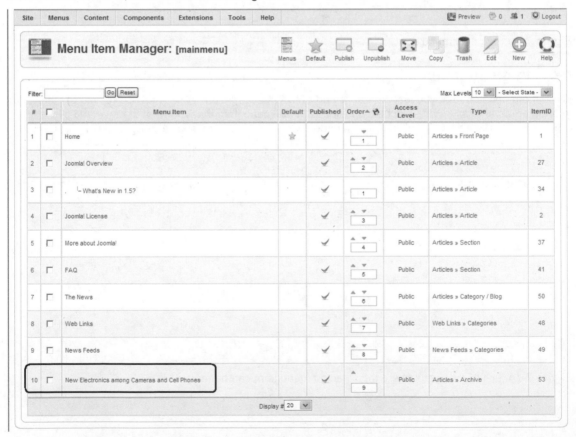

Figure 7-16. New Electronics among Cameras and Cell Phones menu item moved to the Main Menu

Now move the menu item back to the `Electronic Products` menu using the same procedure.

Making menu items visible

To display the menu item from the front end, we need to activate it via the Module Manager. Let's open the Module Manager by selecting `Extensions ➤ Module Manager`. You'll find a module named `Latest Electronic Range` (which was the module title given for the new menu earlier in the chapter), but it won't be enabled, as shown in Figure 7-17.

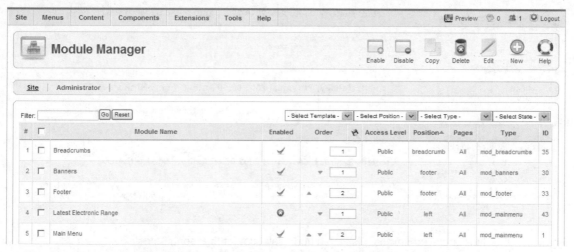

Figure 7-17. The Latest Electronic Range module in the disabled state

To enable the menu so that it will be visible from the website, select the check box in the `Latest Electronic Range` row, and click the `Enable` icon. To see whether the menu and its item appear on the website, open the browser window pointing to the Joomla website (`http://localhost/joomlasite`). A new menu, `Latest Electronic Range`, will appear with the menu item `New Electronics` among `Cameras` and `Cell Phones`.

When selected, the menu item will display a list of all the articles that have been archived (because the menu item type chosen was `Archived Article List`), as shown in Figure 7-18.

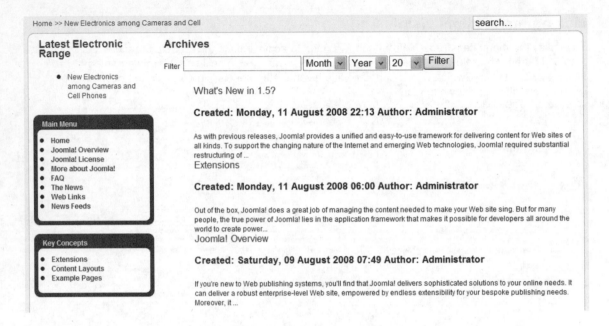

Figure 7-18. All the archived articles, displayed upon selection of the menu item

You can also see all the archived articles from a particular date by using the drop-down boxes. Selecting the title of any archived article displays the article's contents, as shown in Figure 7-19.

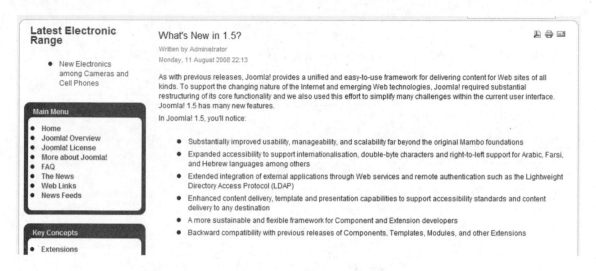

Figure 7-19. The contents of the article displayed upon selecting its title

Doing the groundwork for the other menu item types

In order to understand how the other menu item types (Article, Category, Section, etc.) work, it will help to do some preparation. Recall that we created a section named Electronics with a category called Camera in Chapter 3. We also created an article in that category called "Latest Cameras." For this exercise, we need to create one more category in the Electronics section: Cell Phone. Also, we'll create three articles in each category. The titles of the three articles created in the Camera category will be as follows:

- "Latest Cameras" (already created in Chapter 3)
- "Web Cams - Video chatting"
- "Cameras for Safari"

Each article will contain some short text and an image (an example is shown in Figure 7-20).

> *The dotted line in the article shown in the figure designates the page break.*

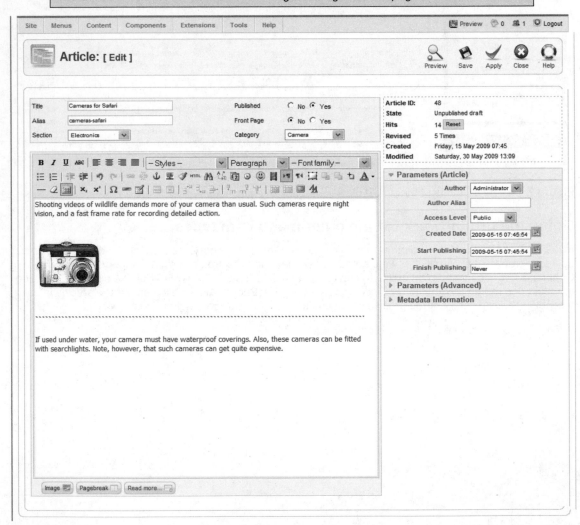

Figure 7-20. The contents of the "Cameras for Safari" article

You can write any text and insert any image, just don't forget to load the images into the Media Manager first. There are two ways to insert images into the article: one way is using the `Image` icon in the tools provided at the top, and the other is using the `Image` button at the bottom left. The `Image` icon in the toolbar, when selected, displays the screen shown in Figure 7-21.

Figure 7-21. Dialog box to insert/edit image from a URL

In the `Image URL` field, you can specify the URL of an image on the Internet, or the URL of an image already uploaded to the Media Manager of your website. Let's say we wanted to insert an image called `cam4.jpg` that already exists in the Media Manager. In this case, we specify it's URL as `c:\xampp\htdocs\joomlasite\images/stories/cam4.jpg`, and then click the `Insert` button.

If you click the `Image` button at the bottom, you'll get the screen shown in Figure 7-22. This dialog box helps with uploading new images to the Media Manager and inserting the selected image into the article.

Figure 7-22. Inserting an image from the Media Manager

Select the `cam4.jpg` image and click the `Insert` link to insert the image into your article. You can also click the `Browse` button to select an image on your local disk drive and click `Start Upload` to upload the image to the Media Manager. Additionally, if you like, you can insert a page break by clicking the Insert `Page Break` icon at the bottom (refer to Figure 7-20). If you do this, you'll get a dialog box like the one shown in Figure 7-23. You can specify the page title for the second page and also the alias to be used for SEF URLs.

Figure 7-23. Inserting a page break

After entering this information, click the `Insert Page Break` button to insert a page break into your article. Assuming that you've created the three articles mentioned previously, if you open the Article Manager (`Content ➤ Article Manager`) and select the Camera category from the drop-down list, you will see the list of three articles shown in Figure 7-24.

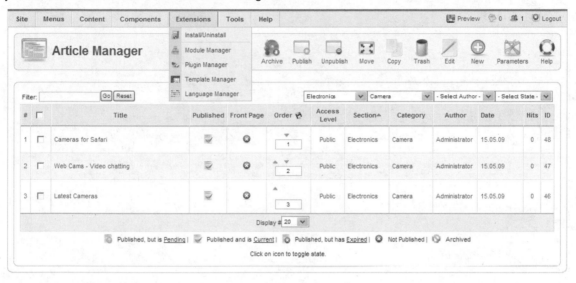

Figure 7-24. The three articles of the Camera category

Next, create three articles in the Cell Phone category, with the following titles:

- "CDMA Cell Phones"
- "Java Supported Cell Phone"
- "Autotracking Cell Phones"

For example, the article "CDMA Cell Phones" might contain the information shown in Figure 7-25.

Figure 7-25. The contents of the article "CDMA Cell Phones"

If you open the Article Manager (Content ➤ Article Manager), you'll find that there are three articles in the Cell Phone category, as shown in Figure 7-26.

Figure 7-26. The three articles in the Cell Phone category

Now we have two article categories—Camera and Cell Phone—in the Electronics section, and each category has three articles in it, so we can go ahead and test the next menu item type: Article Layout.

Article Layout

This menu item type is used for displaying a single article. Upon selecting this menu item type, you'll see a form for specifying information, including the title, menu name, parent menu item, and so on. You can leave all the information the same as that shown in Figure 7-12. The only thing you need to specify for this menu item type is the article name to be displayed. To do so, click the Select button at the top right, which will display a list of all available articles on your website. Select the article "Latest Cameras" from the list, as shown marked in Figure 7-27. Then click the Save icon to save the changes.

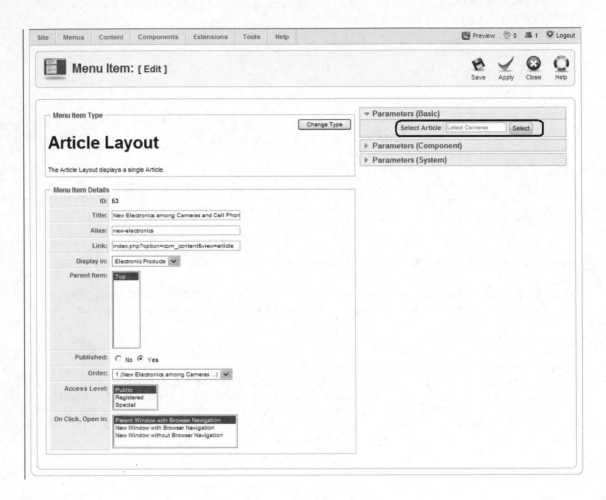

Figure 7-27. Entering information for the menu item type Article Layout

Open the browser window pointing at your Joomla website and click the `Refresh` button. This time when you select the menu item `New Electronics among Cameras and Cell Phones`, you'll see the contents of the article "Latest Cameras," as shown in Figure 7-28.

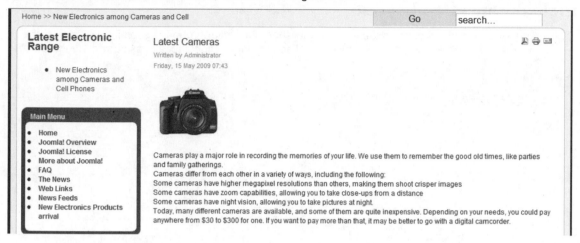

Figure 7-28. The contents of the "Latest Cameras" article, displayed upon selection of the menu item New Electronics among Cameras and Cell Phones

> *To see the usage of the different menu item types, we will be using the menu item just created: `New Electronics among Cameras and Cell Phones`. After looking at the impact of each menu item type from the front end, we will open the same menu item (from the back end) in edit mode. That is, we will open the Menu Manager by selecting the `Menu` ➤ `Manager` option, click the `Edit Menu Item(s)` icon in the `Menu Item(s)` column in the `Electronic Products` row to open the `Menu Item Manager: [electroprod]` page, select the `Electronics among Cameras and Cell Phones` menu item to open it in `Edit` mode, click the `Change Type` button to display the list of all menu item types available, and finally select the menu item type that we want to apply.*

Article Submission Layout

This menu item type allows users in the Author, Publisher, and Editor groups to submit an article. When you move the mouse over the menu item type, you'll see an informational tooltip, as shown in Figure 7-29.

Figure 7-29. Selecting the menu item type Article Submission Layout

Members of the Registered or Public groups will not be able to submit articles, and will see an error message when they select a menu item of this type. The error message will be like the one shown in Figure 7-30.

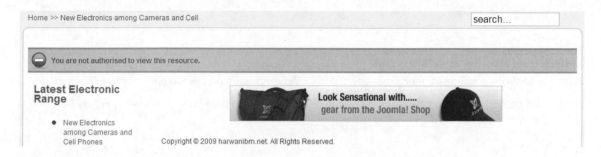

Figure 7-30. Error message that appears if members of the Registered or Public groups access a menu item of type Article Submission Layout

To understand this better, let's create a user that belongs to the Author group with the help of the User Manager. The User Manager can be invoked by either selecting the `Site` ➤ `User Manager` option or clicking the `User Manager` icon from the control panel. In the User Manager, click the `New` icon from the toolbar to create a new user. You'll see a screen like the one shown in Figure 7-31.

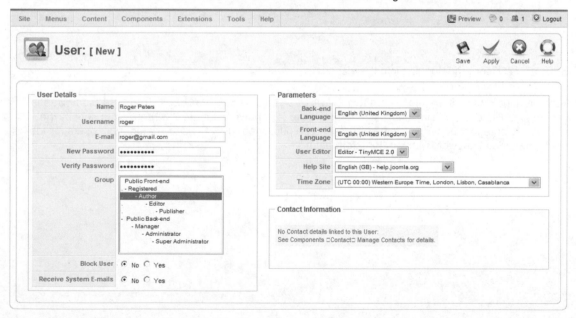

Figure 7-31. Creating a new user of the Author group

For `Name`, enter `Roger Peters`, and for `Username` (by which your user will be logging onto your website), enter `roger`. Enter any e-mail address and password. Assign this user to the Author group. Keep the rest of the values at their defaults, and click the `Save` icon on the toolbar to create this user.

Let the new user log in into your website by entering the username and password, as shown in Figure 7-32.

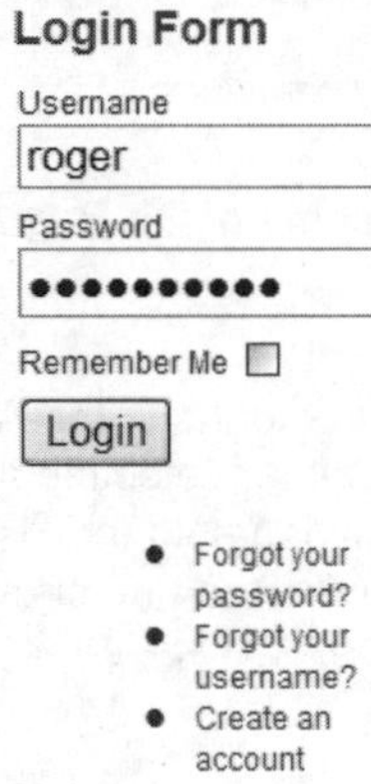

Login Form

Username

    roger

Password

    ••••••••••

Remember Me ☐

[Login]

- Forgot your password?
- Forgot your username?
- Create an account

Figure 7-32. User roger logging into the website

After the user logs in, if the menu item `New Electronics among Cameras and Cell Phones` is selected, you'll get an article submission form to fill in (as shown in Figure 7-33). You can specify the section and category under which the article is to be published, as well as the category of users for the article, metadata, keywords, and other information.

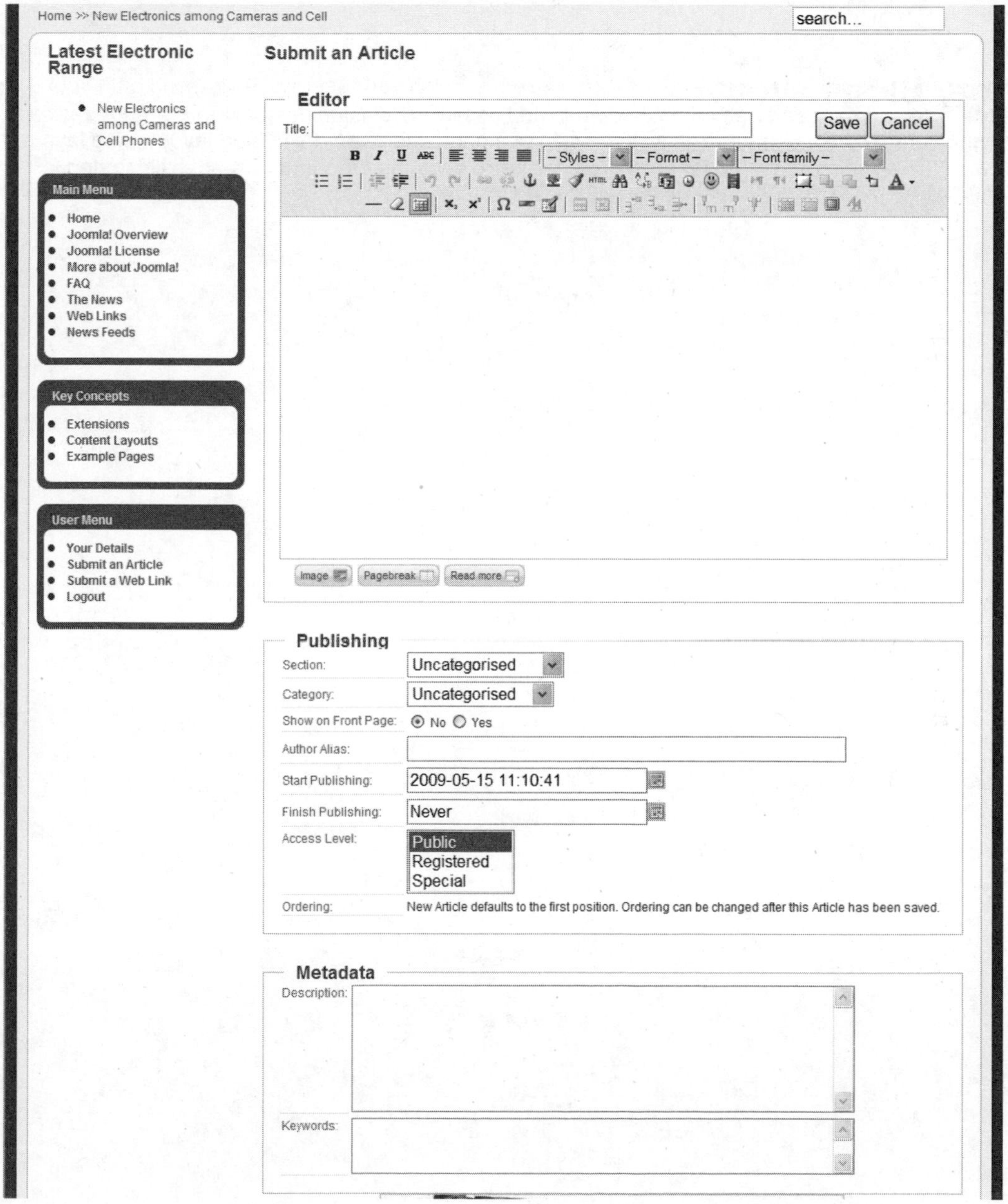

Home >> New Electronics among Cameras and Cell   search...

Latest Electronic Range

- New Electronics among Cameras and Cell Phones

Main Menu

- Home
- Joomla! Overview
- Joomla! License
- More about Joomla!
- FAQ
- The News
- Web Links
- News Feeds

Key Concepts

- Extensions
- Content Layouts
- Example Pages

User Menu

- Your Details
- Submit an Article
- Submit a Web Link
- Logout

Submit an Article

Editor

Title: Save   Cancel

B *I* U ABC | ≡ ≡ ≡ ≡ | – Styles – ⌄ | – Format – ⌄ | – Font family – ⌄

Image 🖼   Pagebreak ⬚   Read more 📖

Publishing

Section: Uncategorised ⌄

Category: Uncategorised ⌄

Show on Front Page: ⦿ No ○ Yes

Author Alias: [   ]

Start Publishing: [2009-05-15 11:10:41   ]

Finish Publishing: [Never   ]

Access Level: Public
                  Registered
                  Special

Ordering: New Article defaults to the first position. Ordering can be changed after this Article has been saved.

Metadata

Description: [   ]

Keywords: [   ]

Figure 7-33. Article submission form

Category Blog Layout

This menu item type is used for displaying articles of a particular category in blog layout. Blog layout consists of three main areas: the **leading area**, the **intro area**, and the **links area**, as illustrated in Figure 7-34.

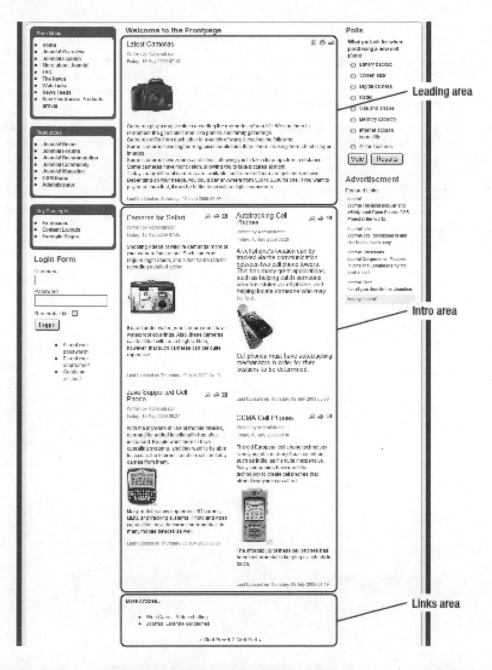

Figure 7-34. The three main areas of a blog layout: leading, intro, and links

Articles displayed in the leading area use full display width and are shown in one column. Articles displayed in the intro area may appear in one, two, or three columns, depending on the `Columns` settings specified in the `Parameters (Basic)` section, as shown in Figure 7-35. The links area is used for displaying links to articles that couldn't be displayed on the first page.

Select the menu item type Category Blog Layout, and you'll get the screen shown in Figure 7-35. There is no need to make any changes in the `Menu Item Details` section. You just need to specify the `Category`, `# Leading`, `# Intro`, `Columns`, and `# Links` settings in the `Parameters (Basic)` section. Enter the information shown in Figure 7-35, and click the `Save` icon.

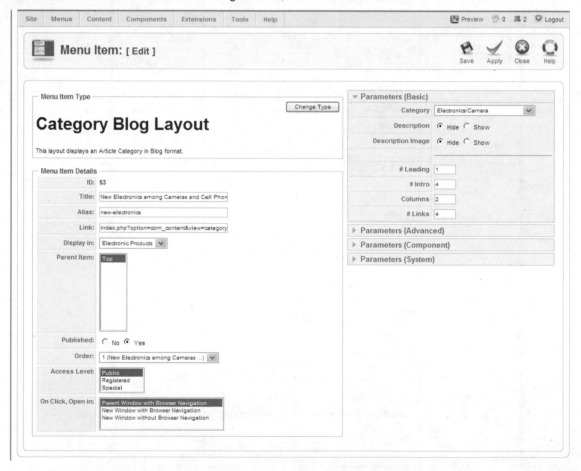

Figure 7-35. Specifying information for the Category Blog Layout menu item type

In the `Category` field, select `Electronics/Camera` to display the articles in the `Camera` category of the `Electronics` section.

Set the `Description` setting to `Hide`, since we don't want to display the description of the category and section. If you set this to `Show`, the description will be displayed above the first article, just below the page title. Also set the `Description Image` setting to `Hide`, since we are not interested in displaying the image of the description.

The `# Leading` field is for specifying the number of articles that you want to take up the full width of the main display area. Set it to `1` since we want one article to take up the full width. If you want all articles to appear in two or more columns, enter `0`.

In the `# Intro` field, you specify the number of articles to be displayed after the leading article(s). Set its value to `4` since we want four articles to appear after the leading article.

In the `Columns` field, you specify how many columns the number of articles specified in the `# Intro` field are to be displayed in. That is, if you enter `2` here, four articles will be displayed in two columns.

In the `# Links` field, you specify the number of links to be displayed in the links area of the page. This field is usually used when there are more articles than can fit on the first page of the blog layout. Set it to `4` so that if any of our four articles don't fit, they can appear as links.

After specifying the information, open your Joomla website and refresh it. You should find that the articles in the Camera category are displayed in category blog layout, as shown in Figure 7-36. In the figure, there are no entries in the links area because all three articles in the Camera category are visible in this layout (i.e., there are none that could not be displayed).

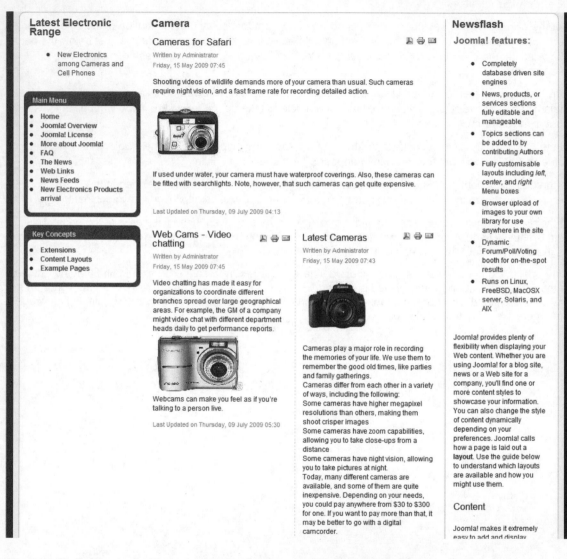

Figure 7-36. Articles in the Camera category displayed in category blog layout

Category List Layout

This menu item type is used for displaying articles in list layout format. In this format, all the articles in the category are displayed in a list from which a visitor can select any article title to see its contents.

After selecting this menu item type, you'll see a screen for specifying certain information. For this example, there is no need to make any changes in the `Menu Item Details` section. You only need to change the settings in the `Parameters (Basic)` section. Enter the information shown in Figure 7-37, and click the `Save` icon.

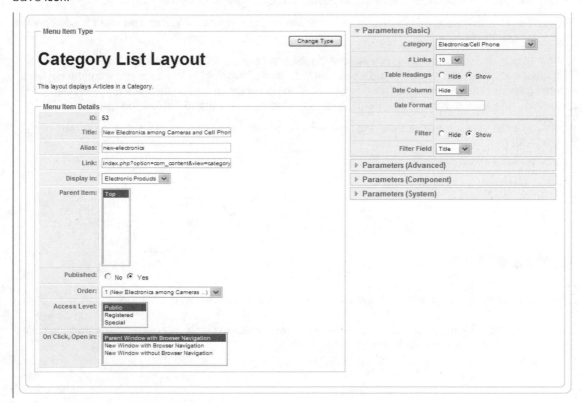

Figure 7-37. Specifying information for the menu item type Category List Layout

In the `Category` field, you specify the category whose articles you want to display. Since you want to display the articles in the Cell Phone category of the Electronics section, choose the value `Electronics/Cell Phone` from the drop-down list.

In the `# Links` field, you specify the number of article titles to be displayed as links. If a category has more articles than the number specified in the `# Links` field, the visitor can use the `Display #` drop-down list (shown in Figure 7-38) to see more links, or click the `Next` link to see the next page of articles.

Set `Table Headings` to `Show` to show the column headings in the article list table, as shown in Figure 7-38.

The `Date Column` drop-down is for displaying the date on which the article was created. Set it to `Hide` since we're not interested in showing the date.

In the `Date Format` field, you specify the format in which you want to see the creation date for articles. Usually this field is left blank, since the default date format is taken from the language file.

Set `Filter` to `Show` since we want to see the filter box on the website, which may be used to see only the desired articles.

In the `Filter Field` drop-down, you specify the field name you prefer to be used for filtering the articles. The options are `Title, Author,` and `Hits.` Set the value of this field to `Title` if you want the keyword entered in the `Title Filter` box (see Figure 7-29) to be searched among the titles of the articles (i.e., the articles with titles matching the keyword entered in the `Title Filter` box will be displayed).

When you open your Joomla website, the browser window will display the list of articles, as shown in Figure 7-38.

Figure 7-38. Displaying the articles in the Cell Phone category in list layout

You can see the contents of any article by selecting its title. If, for example, you select "Autotracking Cell Phones," you'll see the contents shown in Figure 7-39.

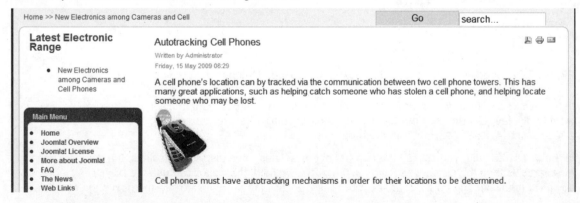

Figure 7-39. The information in an article displayed upon selecting its title

Front Page Blog Layout

This menu item type is used to display all articles set to be published on the front page in blog layout format. You have already seen blog layout in the discussion of the Category Blog Layout type, and you know that it consists of three main areas: leading, intro, and links.

When you select this menu item type, you'll see a screen for entering certain information, as shown in Figure 7-40. The meanings of the fields are the same as earlier—and here, too, you don't need to enter anything extra. Keep the default settings as they are, and click the `Save` icon to save the selected menu item type.

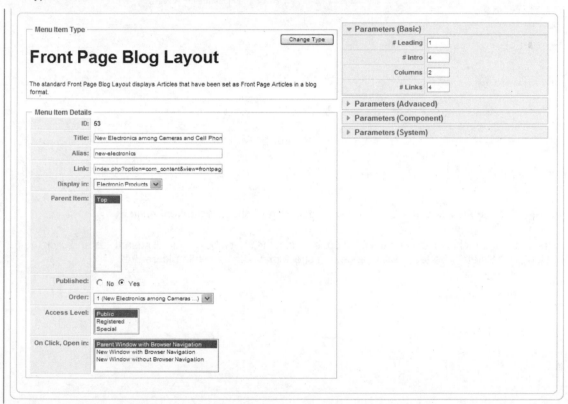

Figure 7-40. Specifying information for the Front Page Blog Layout menu item type

Before opening the Joomla website to see the effect of this menu item type, you need to set the articles in both the Camera and Cell Phone categories to be published on the front page. Open the Article Manager by selecting `Content ➤ Article Manager`, and you'll find that the articles in the Electronics section have a red *X* in the `Front Page` column (as shown in Figure 7-41), designating that these articles will not be displayed on the front page.

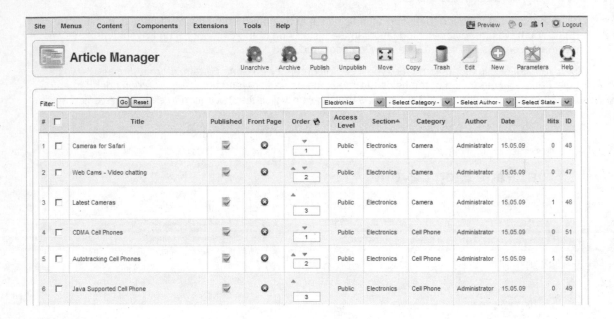

Figure 7-41. The articles of the Cell Phone category unpublished on the front page

To make these articles display on the front page, select the check boxes for all six articles and click the red *X* to toggle the state. The red *X* will change to a check mark, as shown in Figure 7-42.

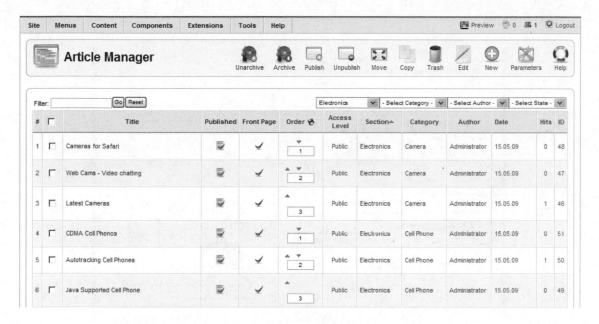

Figure 7-42. The articles of the Electronics section are now published on the front page.

Now open the browser window to see the Joomla website. You'll find that all the articles of the Camera and Cell Phone categories, along with any default articles (provided by Joomla) that are set to be published on the front page, are displayed in blog layout format, as shown in Figure 7-43.

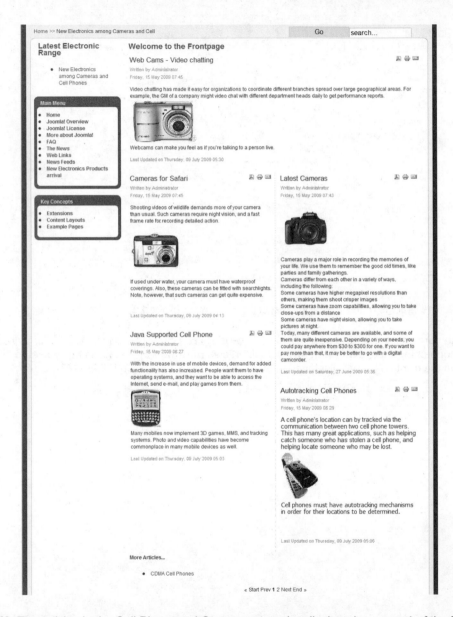

Figure 7-43. The articles in the Cell Phone and Camera categories displayed on page 1 of the front page in blog layout format

Since there are more articles than could be displayed on one page, we find that links appear at the end, each pointing to an article that couldn't be displayed. Also, the links `Start`, `Prev`, `1, 2, 3`, `Next`, and `End` appear at the bottom, for navigating to the desired page. For example, if you select the `2` link, you'll see the articles on page 2, as shown in Figure 7-44.

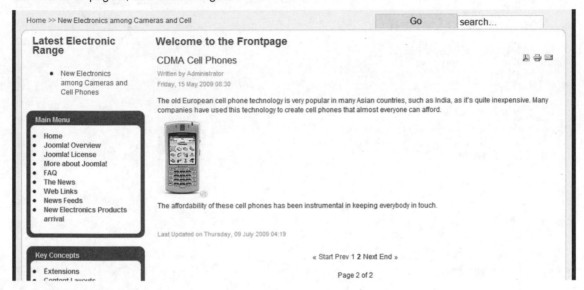

Figure 7-44. The article displayed on page 2 of the front page in blog layout format

Section Blog Layout

This menu item type displays all the articles in the specified section in blog layout. The screen for entering information is the same as in other blog layouts, with the small difference that you have to select the section whose articles you want to display. Since for this example we want to display the articles of the Electronics section, select that section from the `Section` drop-down, as shown marked in Figure 7-45.

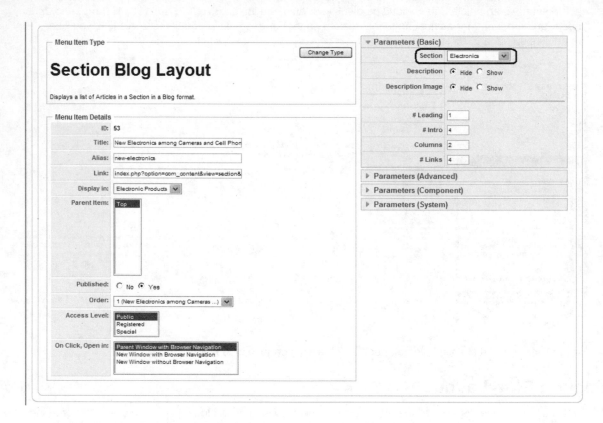

Figure 7-45. Entering information for the menu item type Section Blog Layout to display the articles of the Electronics section

Enter the information shown in Figure 7-45 and click the Save icon. From your Joomla website, when you select the menu item New Electronics among Cameras and Cell Phones from the menu Latest Electronic Range, the articles of the Electronics section (six in all) will be displayed in the format specified in the Parameters (Basic) section—that is, one article in the leading area to take up the whole display area, four articles in two columns in the intro area, and the article "Latest Cameras" in the links area. The output should be something like that shown in Figure 7-46.

Figure 7-46. Articles displayed in section blog layout

When you click the link `Latest Cameras`, it displays the contents of that article, as shown in Figure 7-47.

Figure 7-47. The contents of the article displayed upon selecting its title in the links area

Section Layout

This menu item type displays all the categories in the selected section. Each category, when selected, displays all the articles that belong to it in category list layout. Visitors can select any article title from the list to display its contents.

When you select this menu item type, you'll see a screen for entering information for the menu item. There is no need to make any changes except to select the section for which you want to see the categories. In this case, select the Electronics section, as shown in Figure 7-48.

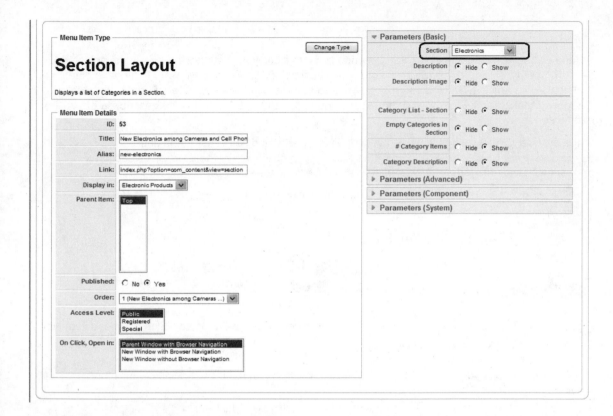

Figure 7-48. Entering information for the Section Layout menu item type

The Description option is used to display the description of the section at the top of the page, under the title. In this case, set it to Hide, since we are not interested in showing the description. The Description Image option is used for displaying the description image of the category or section. Set this to Hide as well since we don't want the image to be displayed.

Set the `Category List - Section` option to `Show` to display the list of categories in the selected section. Set the `Empty Categories in Section` option to `Hide` since we want to hide the categories that contain no articles. Set `# Category Items` to `Show` to display the number of articles in each category. Finally, set the `Category Description` option to `Show` to display the description of each category.

In the browser window, when you open your Joomla website and select the menu item `New Electronics among Cameras and Cell Phones`, you'll find that the Electronics section appears with two categories under it—Camera and Cell Phone—as shown in Figure 7-49.

Figure 7-49. The Electronics section with its two categories displayed upon selecting the menu item New Electronics among Cameras and Cell Phones

If you select the Camera category, you'll see the list of articles under it, as shown in Figure 7-50.

Figure 7-50. The articles of the Camera category displayed upon selecting its link

If you select the Cell Phone category, you'll likewise see all the articles under it, as shown in Figure 7-51.

Figure 7-51. The articles of the Cell Phone category displayed upon selecting its link

You can select the title of any article to see its contents. For example, if you select "CDMA Cell Phones," you'll see the contents displayed in Figure 7-52.

Figure 7-52. The contents of the article displayed upon selecting its title

Explanation of Parameters sections (Advanced, Component, and System)

In all the blog layouts, the parameters are specified under four headings:

- `Parameters (Basic)`
- `Parameters (Advanced)`
- `Parameters (Component)`
- `Parameters (System)`

We have already discussed `Parameters (Basic)`. Let's look at the fields in the remaining three `Parameters` sections. Let's edit the menu item `New Electronics among Cameras and Cell Phones` and change its menu item type to `Category Blog Layout`, and then select the `Parameters (Advanced)` section.

Parameters (Advanced)

The options in the `Parameters (Advanced)` section appear as shown in Figure 7-53.

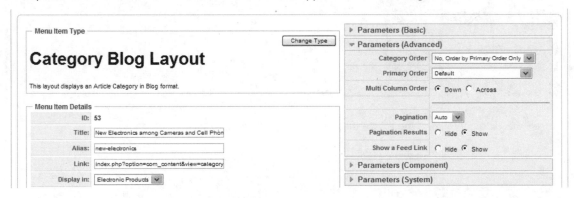

Figure 7-53. The options in the Parameters (Advanced) section

The `Category Order` drop-down is used to decide the order in which the categories will be displayed. The options are as follows (see Figure 7-54):

- `No, Order by Primary Order Only`: Displays articles ordered only by the primary order without regard to category (for this example, select this option).
- `Title (Alphabetical)`: Displays categories in alphabetical order.
- `Title (Reverse Alphabetical)`: Displays categories in reverse alphabetical order.
- `Order`: Displays categories according to the order specified in the `Order` column of the Category Manager.

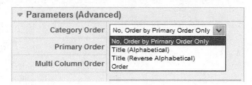

Figure 7-54. Category order options

The `Primary Order` drop-down is used to decide the order of articles within a category. The options are as follows (see Figure 7-55):

- `Default`: Displays articles according to the order specified in the `Order` column of the Front Page Manager (for this example, select this option).
- `Oldest first`: Displays articles starting with the oldest and ending with the most recent.
- `Most recent first`: Displays articles starting with the most recent and ending with the oldest.
- `Title (Alphabetical)`: Displays articles in alphabetical order of their title.
- `Title (Reverse Alphabetical)`: Displays articles in reverse alphabetical order of their title.
- `Author - Alphabetical`: Displays articles in alphabetical order according to author.
- `Author - Reverse Alphabetical`: Displays articles according to the reverse alphabetical order of their author.
- `Most Hits`: Displays articles according to the number of hits they've received. The articles with the most hits appear at the top.

- `Least Hits`: Displays articles according to the number of hits they've received. The articles with the least hits appear at the top.
- `Order`: Displays articles according to the order specified in the `Order` column of the Article Manager.

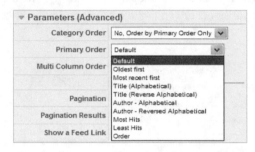

Figure 7-55. Primary order options

The `Multi Column Order` option is used to decide whether to order the articles down the column or across the columns (when articles are displayed in more than one column). For this example, select the `Down` option.

The `Pagination` drop-down is used to display page links when the number of articles is large (such that they can't all be displayed on a page).

The `Pagination Results` option is used to display which page number you are on and the total page count. For example, "Page 1 of 3" designates that there are three pages in all, and you are on page 1. For this example, set `Pagination Results` to `Show`.

The `Show a Feed Link` option determines whether to display an RSS feed link. That is, if you have set a news feed related to the contents being viewed, the feed link (to get the contents from the news feed site) will be displayed if the value of this option is set to `Yes`. Please refer to Chapters 6 and 9 for news feeds and RSS feeds, respectively.

Parameters (Component)

The options in the `Parameters (Component)` section appear as shown in Figure 7-56.

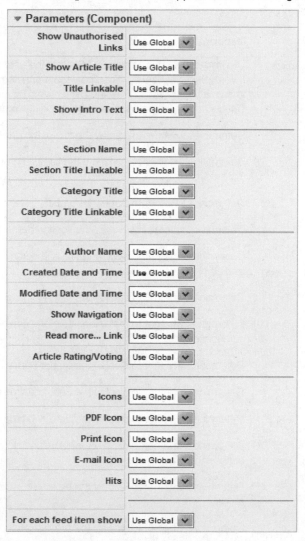

Figure 7-56. The Parameters (Component) section

Table 7-4 gives a brief description of the options in this section.

Table 7-4. The Parameters (Component) options

Field	Description
Show Unauthorised Links	Determines whether to display links that the user is not authorized to access. If you select No, users will see only the menu items that they are authorized to see. If you select Yes, all the menu items will be displayed, and if a user selects an unauthorized menu item, a login screen will be displayed.
Show Article Title	Determines whether to display the title of the article.
Title Linkable	Determines whether to the make the title of the article act as a hyperlink to the article.
Show Intro Text	Determines whether to display intro text.
Section Name	Determines whether to display the section name.
Section Title Linkable	Determines whether to make the title of the section act as a hyperlink to the section page.
Category Title	Determines whether to display the category title.
Category Title Linkable	Determines whether to make the title of the category act as a hyperlink to the category page.
Author Name	Determines whether to display the author name.
Created Date and Time	Determines whether to display the date and time the article was created.
Modified Date and Time	Determines whether to display the date and time the article was last modified.
Show Navigation	Determines whether to display a navigation link (e.g., Next or Previous) between articles.
Read more... Link	Determines whether to display the Read more link to display the rest of the article.
Article Rating/Voting	Determines whether to display the Article Rating/Voting module.
Icons	Determines whether to display the PDF, Print, and E-mail buttons for the article in the form of icons or text. If set to the Hide option, these buttons will be displayed as text. If set to the Show option, they will be displayed as icons.

PDF Icon	Determines whether to display a button that enables the article to be displayed in PDF format (enabling the user to view, print, or save the article as a PDF file).
Print Icon	Determines whether to display a button that enables the article to be printed.
E-mail Icon	Determines whether to display a button that enables a link to the article to be e-mailed. A form is displayed that allows the visitor to send an e-mail with a link to the current article.
Hits	Determines whether to display the number of hits for the article.
For each feed item show	Determines whether to display a small introduction or complete description of the feed item being displayed. The available options are Use Global, Intro Text, and Full Text. Use Global makes decisions on the basis of the global configuration settings. The Intro Text and Full Text options are for displaying the introductory or complete description of the feed item, respectively.

Parameters (System)

The options in the Parameters (System) section appear as shown in Figure 7-57.

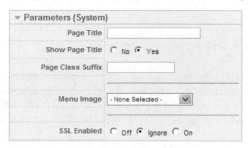

Figure 7-57. Options in the Parameters (System) section

In the Page Title field, you enter the title of the page that will be displayed in the title area. If it is left blank, the menu title is displayed—so let's leave it blank.

Set the Show Page Title option to Yes to display a page title above the first article.

The Page Class Suffix field is used to specify the CSS class suffix that has to be attached to all classes of this page (used for creating customized CSS styles). We would need to edit our template's template.css file to use this feature. Since we are not using any CSS styles, you can leave this field blank.

The Menu Image drop-down is used to display an image from the images/stories folder. We don't select any image since we don't want one to appear. If we select an image, it will appear on the left side of the title by default.

257

The SSL Enabled option determines whether this page should support the secure HTTPS protocol or not. That is, if this option is set to On, the contents will be displayed as a secure page (encrypted transaction). If the value of this option is set to Off, it will display the contents as a standard page (anybody can view it). The Ignore option ignores the secure site URL and displays the contents as a standard page. It is better to enable this option if you are transferring some sensitive or confidential material between the server and the client's browser. However, for that, you need to configure certain settings in Global Configuration, as explained in Chapter 10.

Contacts

With this menu item type, you decide whether to display contact categories or contacts for submitting queries. It has two subtypes, Category and Contact, as shown in Figure 7-58.

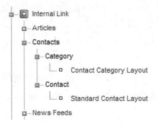

Figure 7-58. The subtypes of the Contacts menu item type

The Standard Contact Layout type is used to display all the published contacts of a given category. Recall that in Chapter 5 you created two contacts, John David and Purchases, under the suppliers category. You saw how the menu item type Standard Contact Layout was linked to the specified contact and how a contact form was displayed when the menu item was selected. The query entered in the contact form was e-mailed to the linked contact.

Also in Chapter 5, we used the menu item type Contact Category Layout to display the suppliers category, which when selected displayed the contacts John David and Purchases for contacting individually.

News Feeds

News feeds are used for receiving updates from certain websites. If you regularly require access to information from certain websites, it would be difficult to visit those websites continually to look for updates. News feeds help by merging the feeds from other pages into one page. This menu item type has three options in it, as shown in Figure 7-59:

- All Categories
- Category
- Individual Feed

Figure 7-59. The options in the News Feeds menu item type

To understand these options, you need to create one more news feed inside the Cell Phones news feed category created in Chapter 6. Recall that in Chapter 6 you created a news feed category by the name of Cell Phones with one feed in it: "Cell Phones - fastest communication." Let's create a news feed with the name "Cell Phones - basic commodity" in the same Cell Phones news feed category. Select Components ➤ News Feeds ➤ Feeds; then click the New icon and enter the information shown in Figure 7-60 to create a news feed. In the Link field, the RSS feed URL specified in this news feed is www.cellaz.com/news-rss2.php.

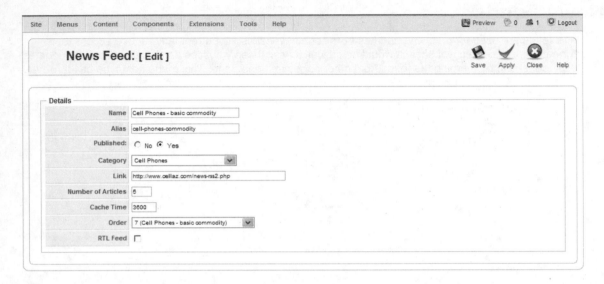

Figure 7-60. Entering information for the news feed "Cell Phones – basic commodity" in the Cell Phones category

After entering the information, click the Save icon to save the news feed. There will now be two news feeds in the Cell Phones category, as shown in Figure 7-61.

Figure 7-61. The two news feeds in the Cell Phones category, as listed in the News Feed Manager

Next, let's look at the impact of each menu item type.

Category List Layout

The menu item type Category List Layout, as shown in Figure 7-62, displays a list of all news feed categories.

Select Menu Item Type
Internal Link
Articles
Contacts
News Feeds
All Categories
Category List Layout
Category
Category Layout
Individual Feed
Single Feed Layout
Category List Layout
This layout shows a list of all News Feed Categories.

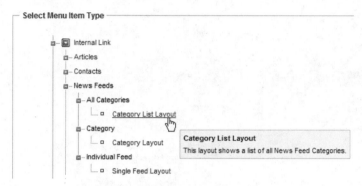

Figure 7-62. The menu item type Category List Layout

If you open the browser window pointing to your Joomla website, you'll find that besides the default news feed categories provided by Joomla, there is a Cell Phones category, as shown in Figure 7-63. The number 2 in parentheses after `Cell Phones` indicates that it contains two news feeds.

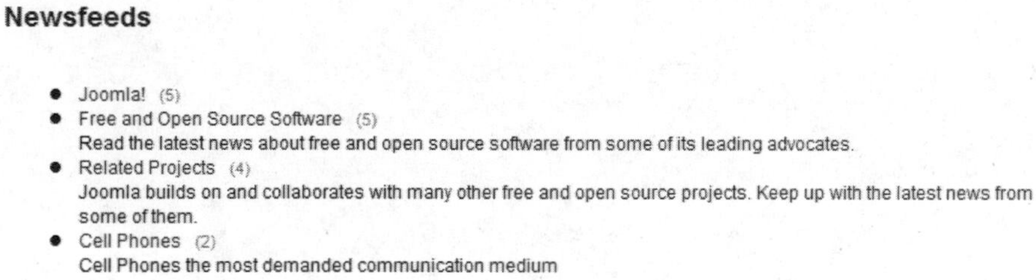

Newsfeeds
Joomla! (5)
Free and Open Source Software (5)
Read the latest news about free and open source software from some of its leading advocates.
Related Projects (4)
Joomla builds on and collaborates with many other free and open source projects. Keep up with the latest news from some of them.
Cell Phones (2)
Cell Phones the most demanded communication medium

Figure 7-63. The Cell Phones news feed category displayed along with the default categories provided by Joomla

If you select the Cell Phones news feed category, both the news feeds in that category are displayed, as shown in Figure 7-64.

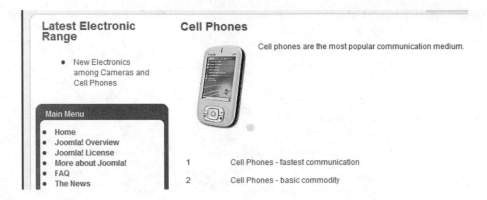

Figure 7-64. The news feeds in the Cell Phones category displayed

You can select either of the links shown in Figure 7-64 to get updates from the specified website (the website with which these news feeds are linked).

Similarly, if you select the Joomla category, the news feeds in that category will be displayed, as shown in Figure 7-65.

Newsfeeds

#	Feed Name	# Articles
1	Joomla! Announcements	5
2	Joomla! Core Team Blog	5
3	Joomla! Community Magazine	20
4	Joomla! Developer News	5
5	Joomla! Security News	5

Figure 7-65. The news feeds in the Joomla category displayed

Select the news feed "Cell Phones - fastest communication" from the Cell Phone category to see the information supplied by that news feed. You will get the list of five articles shown in Figure 7-66.

Newsfeeds

Mobiledia: Cell Phone News

Find breaking news, reviews, and opinion on the latest cell phones and mobile devices worldwide.

- Samsung Jack to Arrive in ATT Stores Next Week
  AT&T, the second-largest U.S. wireless provider after Verizon, today announced the Samsung Jack, a new Windows Mobile 6.1 smartphone and successor to the award-winning BlackJack II, will hit store shelves next week.

- Motorola W7 Uses Body Movement to Perform Tasks
  Troubled U.S. phone maker Motorola today announced the W7 Active Edition, a motion-enabled slider that senses the body's motions to perform tasks such as launching its built-in pedometer, silencing incoming calls or controling the music player.

- Sprint Mobile Hotspot Offers Wi-Fi On-the-Go
  A week after rival Verizon Wireless announced plans to offer a compact Wi-Fi device, Sprint said that it would launch its own "Mobile Hotspot" gadget, a similar portable unit that creates a localized Wi-Fi cloud to share high-speed Internet with wireless electronics like laptops, netbooks, cameras and music players.

- Google Mobile App Locates Constellations in the Night Sky
  Internet search giant Google has rolled out an update to its "Sky Map" application to aid Android users figure out which constellations they are looking at in the night sky.

- SlingPlayer Mobile Arrives for iPhone, Wi-Fi Only
  The long-awaited SlingPlayer Mobile for iPhone application will be hitting Apple's App Store in the next 24 hours -- but it will only stream video over Wi-Fi, not AT&T's 3G data network.

Figure 7-66. List of articles in the "Cell Phones - fastest communication" news feed

Similarly, the list of articles that will be displayed on selecting the "Cell Phones - basic commodity" news feed will be as shown in Figure 7-67.

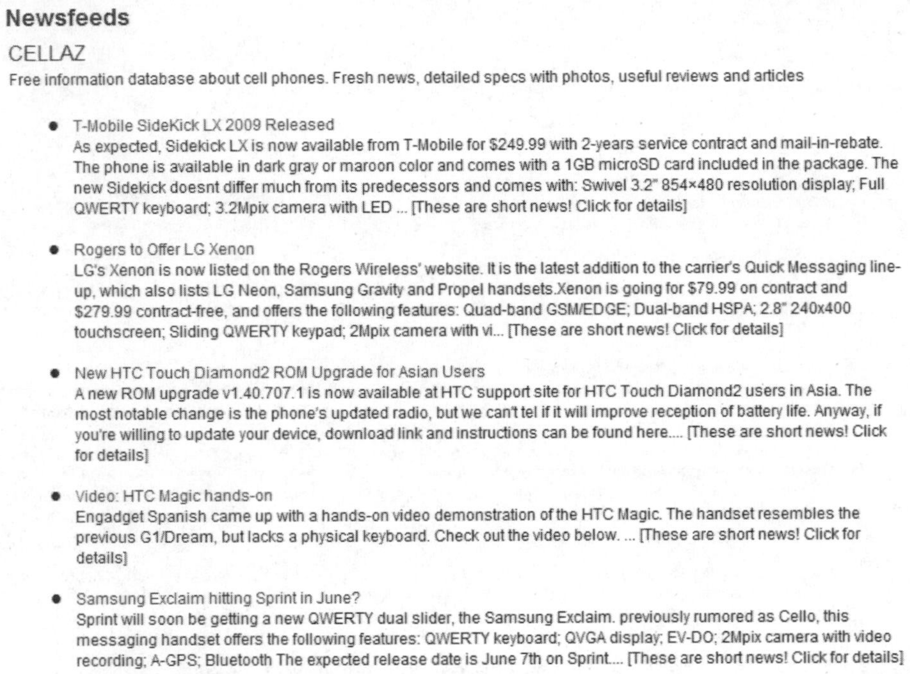

Newsfeeds

CELLAZ

Free information database about cell phones. Fresh news, detailed specs with photos, useful reviews and articles

- T-Mobile SideKick LX 2009 Released
  As expected, Sidekick LX is now available from T-Mobile for $249.99 with 2-years service contract and mail-in-rebate. The phone is available in dark gray or maroon color and comes with a 1GB microSD card included in the package. The new Sidekick doesnt differ much from its predecessors and comes with: Swivel 3.2" 854×480 resolution display; Full QWERTY keyboard; 3.2Mpix camera with LED ... [These are short news! Click for details]

- Rogers to Offer LG Xenon
  LG's Xenon is now listed on the Rogers Wireless' website. It is the latest addition to the carrier's Quick Messaging line-up, which also lists LG Neon, Samsung Gravity and Propel handsets.Xenon is going for $79.99 on contract and $279.99 contract-free, and offers the following features: Quad-band GSM/EDGE; Dual-band HSPA; 2.8" 240x400 touchscreen; Sliding QWERTY keypad; 2Mpix camera with vi ... [These are short news! Click for details]

- New HTC Touch Diamond2 ROM Upgrade for Asian Users
  A new ROM upgrade v1.40.707.1 is now available at HTC support site for HTC Touch Diamond2 users in Asia. The most notable change is the phone's updated radio, but we can't tel if it will improve reception of battery life. Anyway, if you're willing to update your device, download link and instructions can be found here.... [These are short news! Click for details]

- Video: HTC Magic hands-on
  Engadget Spanish came up with a hands-on video demonstration of the HTC Magic. The handset resembles the previous G1/Dream, but lacks a physical keyboard. Check out the video below. ... [These are short news! Click for details]

- Samsung Exclaim hitting Sprint in June?
  Sprint will soon be getting a new QWERTY dual slider, the Samsung Exclaim. previously rumored as Cello, this messaging handset offers the following features: QWERTY keyboard; QVGA display; EV-DO; 2Mpix camera with video recording; A-GPS; Bluetooth The expected release date is June 7th on Sprint.... [These are short news! Click for details]

Figure 7-67. List of articles in the "Cell Phones - basic commodity" news feed

Category Layout

This menu item type displays the list of all news feeds in the selected category. For this menu item type, you only have to select the news feed category whose news feeds you want to display. Let's select the Cell Phones news feed category, as shown in Figure 7-68.

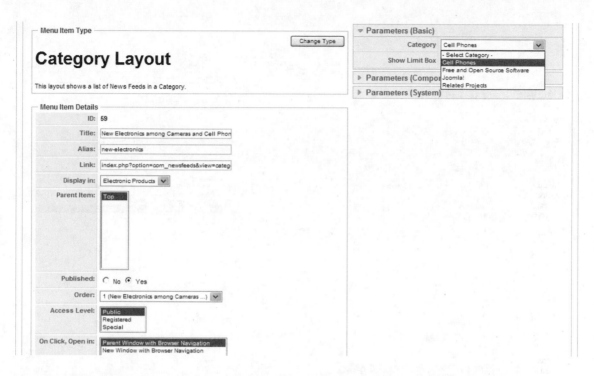

Figure 7-68. Selecting the Category Layout menu item type to represent the Cell Phone category

The Joomla website will display the news feeds in the Cell Phone category, as shown previously in Figure 7-64.

Single Feed Layout

As the name suggests, this menu item type is used to show the articles from a single news feed. After selecting this menu item type, you need to select the news feed from which the updates have to be merged. You use the `Feed` drop-down (Figure 7-69) to specify the news feed from which you want to get updates upon selecting the menu item. Let's select the news feed "Cell Phones-Cell Phones - fastest communication" from the drop-down list.

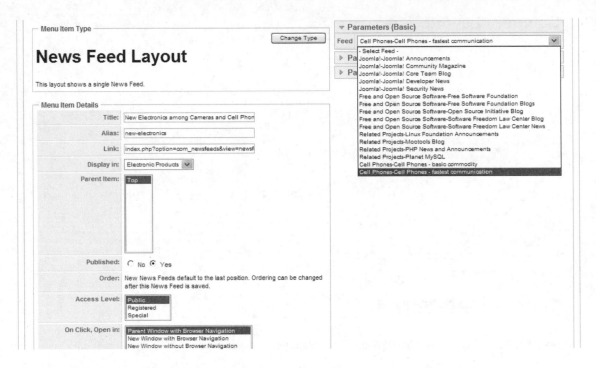

Figure 7-69. Specifying the news feed from which the updates are to be merged

Now this menu item will display the articles of the selected news feed, as shown previously in Figure 7-66.

Poll

This menu item type has an option called `Poll Layout` (as shown in Figure 7-70), used to show the results of the selected poll.

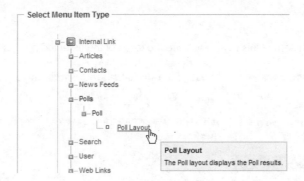

Figure 7-70. Selecting the menu item type Poll Layout

Select the desired poll from the `Poll` drop-down list, as shown in Figure 7-71. Recall that we created a poll entitled "What you look for when purchasing a new cell phone" in Chapter 6 using the Poll Manager. Let's select that poll. The `Poll` field is used for selecting the poll for which we want to see the results.

Figure 7-71. Selecting the poll

When you select the menu item of this type, you'll see the result of the selected poll, as shown in Figure 7-72.

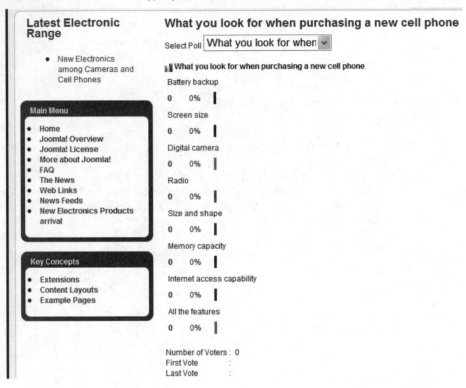

Figure 7-72. Result of the selected poll displayed

Search

This menu item type has a search layout option, as shown in Figure 7-73.

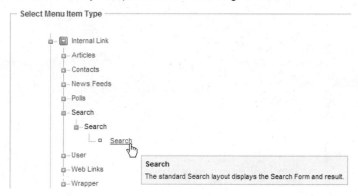

Figure 7-73. Selecting the menu item type Search

The search layout option is used for displaying a search form in which users can enter a keyword to be searched for in articles, contacts, categories, and so on, as shown in Figure 7-74.

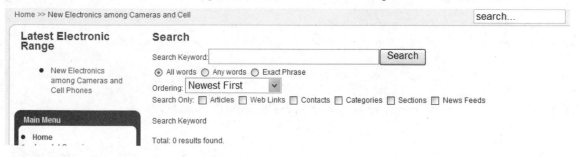

Figure 7-74. Search form for searching for a keyword

Let's search for the keyword Camera in `Articles`. Enter the keyword, select the items in which to search for the keyword (in this case, `Articles`), and then click the `Search` button. You'll see all the articles that have the keyword Camera in them, as shown in Figure 7-75.

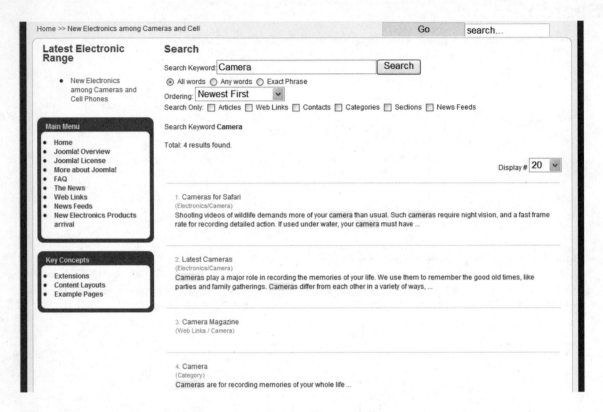

Figure 7-75. The output we see when we search for the keyword Camera in Articles

User

This menu item type has several options, as shown in Figure 7-76:

- `Default Login Layout`
- `Default Registration Layout`
- `Default Remind`
- `Default Reset Layout`
- `Default User Layout`
- `User Form Layout`

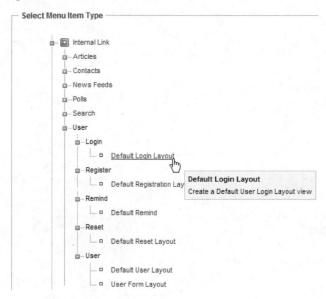

Figure 7-76. The User menu item type

Default Login Layout

This menu item type displays a login form so that a visitor can log into the site. If you click `Default Login Layout` from the `Select Menu Item Type` screen, you'll see a screen for entering certain information, as shown in Figure 7-77.

Figure 7-77. Entering information for login layout

Table 7-5 gives a brief description of the Default Login Layout options.

Table 7-5. The Default Login Layout options

Option	Description
Show Login Page Title	Select Show to display the title of this login page.
Login Page Title	Specify the title for the login page. If you leave this blank, the title of the menu item will be used. For this example, you can enter Sign In here.
Login Redirection URL	Specify the URL of the page to which the visitor is to be redirected after a successful login. If you leave this blank, the front page will be displayed.
Login JS Message	Select Show to display the JavaScript pop-up indicating a successful login.
Login Description	Select Show to display the login description text, which you enter in the following field.
Login Description Text	Enter the text to be displayed upon a successful login.
Login Image	Select the image from the images/stories folder to be displayed on the login page.
Login Image Align	Specify whether the login image is to be left-aligned or right-aligned.
Show Logout Page Title	Select Show to display the logout page title.
Logout Page Title	Specify the text to be displayed at the top of the logout page. If you leave this blank, the menu item title will be displayed.
Logout Redirection URL	Specify the URL of the page to which the visitor is to be redirected after a successful logout. If you don't specify any URL, the front page will be displayed.
Logout JS Message	Specify whether to hide or show the JavaScript pop-up that indicates a successful logout.
Logout Description	Select the Show option to display the logout description text, which you enter in the following field.
Logout Description Text	Enter the text to be displayed upon a successful logout.
Logout Image	Select the image from the images/stories folder to be displayed on the logout page.
Logout Image Align	Specify whether the logout image is to be left-aligned or right-aligned.

When you select the menu item from the website, you'll see a login form, as shown in Figure 7-78.

Figure 7-78. The login form that you'll see upon selecting the menu item

Default Registration Layout

This menu item type allows visitors to your website to register, as shown in Figure 7-79.

Figure 7-79. The registration form displayed for the menu item type Default Registration Layout

Default Remind

This menu item type is used to help visitors who have forgotten their username. It displays a layout asking the visitor to enter his or her e-mail address, as shown in Figure 7-80. The username will be e-mailed to the visitor.

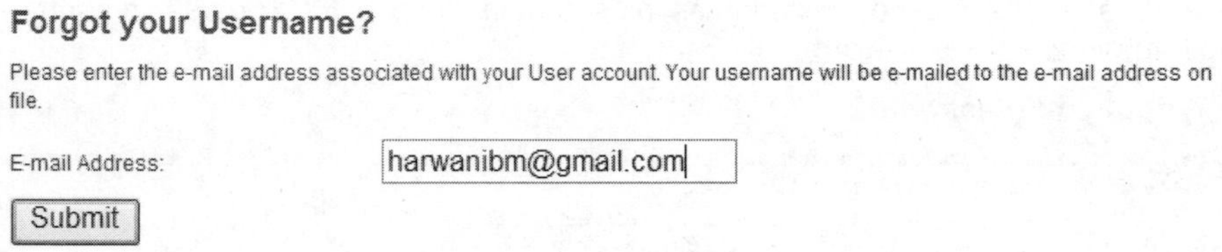

Forgot your Username?

Please enter the e-mail address associated with your User account. Your username will be e-mailed to the e-mail address on file.

E-mail Address: 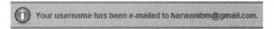 harwanibm@gmail.com

Submit

Figure 7-80. The form that assists visitors in getting their username, displayed when the menu item type is Default Remind

On submitting the e-mail address of an existing user (for this example, assume that `harwanibm@gmail.com` is the e-mail address of a user named peter), we get a message saying that the username will be e-mailed to the user, as shown in Figure 7-81.

Your username has been e-mailed to harwanibm@gmail.com.

Figure 7-81. Message showing that the e-mail has been sent

On opening the e-mail, the content that you'll see (automatically sent to the user by Joomla) will be something like that shown in Figure 7-82.

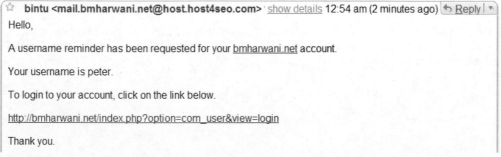

Your bmharwani.net username Inbox

☆ bintu <mail.bmharwani.net@host.host4seo.com> · show details 12:54 am (2 minutes ago) ↩ Reply ▼

Hello,

A username reminder has been requested for your bmharwani.net account.

Your username is peter.

To login to your account, click on the link below.

http://bmharwani.net/index.php?option=com_user&view=login

Thank you.

Figure 7-82. Content of the automatically sent e-mail

Notice that the username (peter) is supplied, as expected.

Default Reset Layout

This menu item type displays a default layout form for visitors who have forgotten their password. The visitor is asked to enter his or her e-mail address, as shown in Figure 7-83. The user is sent a verification token and can then reset the password.

Forgot your Password?

Please enter the e-mail address for your account. A verification token will be sent to you. Once you have received the token, you will be able to choose a new password for your account.

E-mail Address: `harwanibm@gmail.com`

Submit

Figure 7-83. The form that assists visitors in resetting their password, displayed when the menu item type is Default Reset Layout

On submitting the e-mail address, you get a dialog box to enter the verification token that is sent via e-mail, as shown in Figure 7-84.

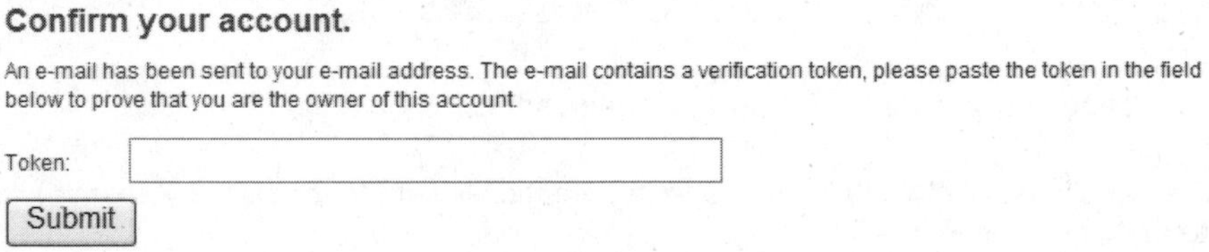

Confirm your account.

An e-mail has been sent to your e-mail address. The e-mail contains a verification token, please paste the token in the field below to prove that you are the owner of this account.

Token:

Submit

Figure 7-84. Dialog box to enter the token sent in the e-mail

On opening the e-mail, you'll notice that the token is a long string of numbers and characters, as shown in Figure 7-85. You need to copy this verification token and paste it into the Token field (from Figure 7-84), and then click the Submit button.

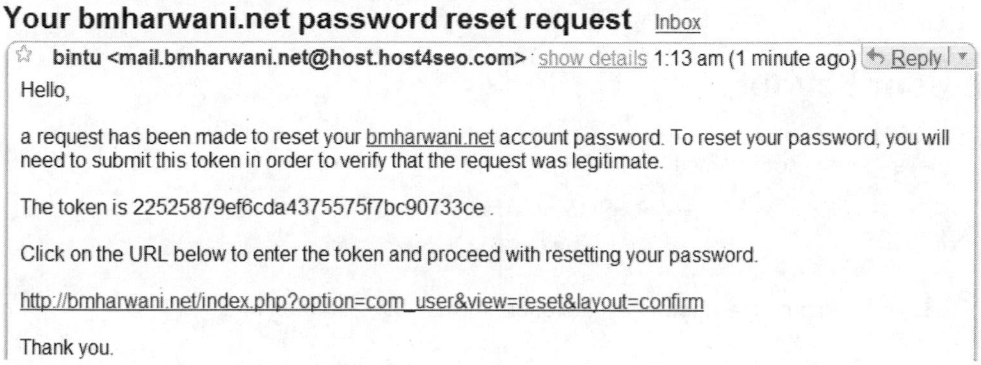

Your bmharwani.net password reset request Inbox

☆ bintu <mail.bmharwani.net@host.host4seo.com> · show details 1:13 am (1 minute ago) ↩ Reply ▾

Hello,

a request has been made to reset your bmharwani.net account password. To reset your password, you will need to submit this token in order to verify that the request was legitimate.

The token is 22525879ef6cda4375575f7bc90733ce .

Click on the URL below to enter the token and proceed with resetting your password.

http://bmharwani.net/index.php?option=com_user&view=reset&layout=confirm

Thank you.

Figure 7-85. Automatic e-mail sent to the user carrying a token

On sending the verification token, you'll get a screen for entering a new password, as shown in Figure 7-86.

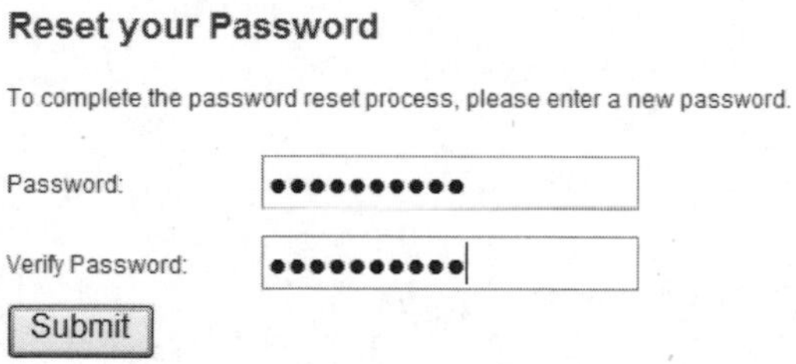

Reset your Password

To complete the password reset process, please enter a new password.

Password: ••••••••••

Verify Password: ••••••••••

[Submit]

Figure 7-86. Dialog box to enter a new password

Enter any password in the `Password` field, duplicate it in the `Verify Password` field, and then click the `Submit` button. The password will be reset and a confirmation message will be displayed, as shown in Figure 7-87.

Figure 7-87. Message showing that the password has been changed

Default User Layout

This menu item type displays a welcome message when the user enters the registered zone. The welcome message may look something like Figure 7-88.

Registered Area

Welcome to the registered user area of our site.

Figure 7-88. The welcome message when the user enters the registered zone

User Form Layout

This menu item type allows users to edit their account details, including the password, e-mail address, front-end language, and time zone, as shown in Figure 7-89. Users with publishing permissions may choose a text editor, and those with administrator permissions may choose the help site they want to use on the back end.

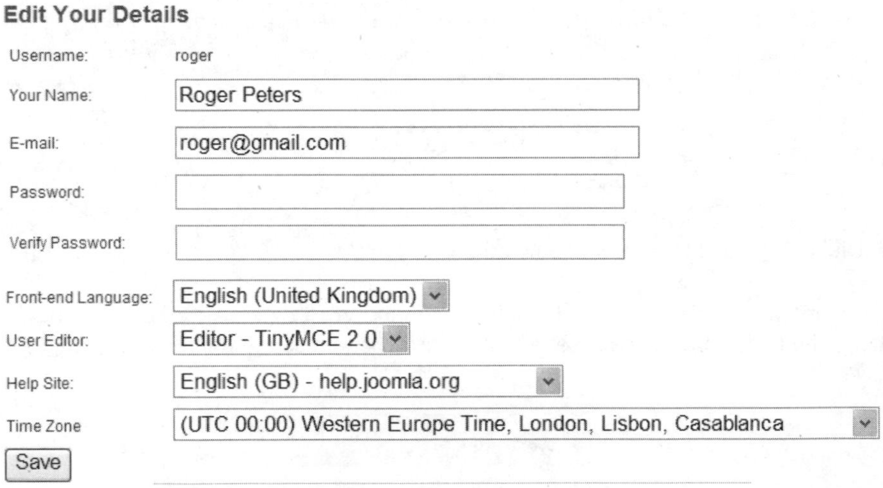

Edit Your Details

Username:	roger
Your Name:	Roger Peters
E-mail:	roger@gmail.com
Password:	
Verify Password:	
Front-end Language:	English (United Kingdom)
User Editor:	Editor - TinyMCE 2.0
Help Site:	English (GB) - help.joomla.org
Time Zone:	(UTC 00:00) Western Europe Time, London, Lisbon, Casablanca

Save

Figure 7-89. The form for editing user account details, displayed when the menu item type is User Form Layout

Web Links

This menu item type has the following options in it, as shown in Figure 7-90:

- `All Categories`
- `Category`
- `Web Link`

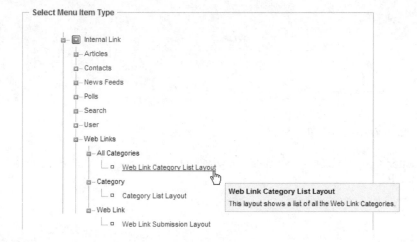

Figure 7-90. The options in the Web Links menu item type

To help you understand this menu item type, let's create a web link category called Camera, and a web link called `Camera Magazine` belonging to the Camera category. Open the Web Links Category Manager by selecting `Components` ➤ `Web Links` ➤ `Categories`. You'll find the default Web Links categories, as shown in Figure 7-91.

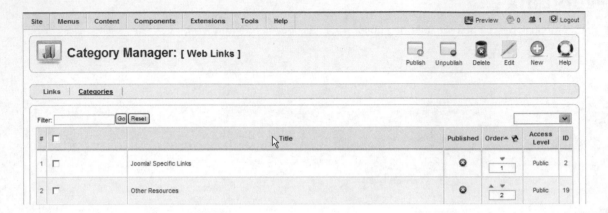

Figure 7-91. Default Web Links categories

Click the New button from the toolbar to create a new Web Links category. You'll get a screen like the one shown in Figure 7-92.

Figure 7-92. Creating a web link category

Let's specify the title as Camera and the alias as camera. Enter a short description in the Description field, keep all the other settings at their defaults, and click the Save icon to save it.

Next, we'll create a web link in this category. Let's select the Components ➤ Web Links ➤ Links option to open the Web Link Manager. In the Web Link Manager, click the New icon from the toolbar to create a new web link. Let's create a web link by the name Camera Magazine, which when selected will open the site www.digicamera.com (as shown in Figure 7-93).

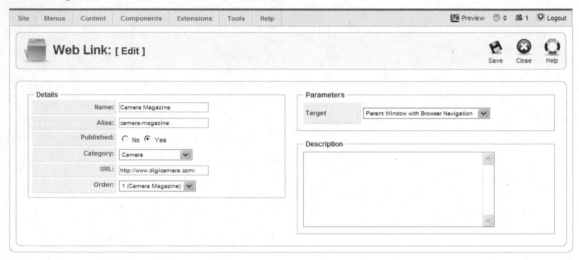

Figure 7-93. A web link by the name Camera Magazine created in the Camera category

In the Name field, enter the name Camera Magazine. In the Alias field (though it can be left blank), enter the alias as camera-magazine. Set the Published option to Yes to make it visible. Set the category of the web link to Camera, and in the URL field, specify any website or web page location that you want to open on selecting the menu item. Let's enter http://www.digicamera.com in this field. Keeping the rest of the options at their defaults, click the Save icon from the toolbar to save the web link.

Now that you have created a web link and a web link category, you are in a position to explore the Web Link menu item types.

Web Link Category List Layout

This menu item type displays a list of all the web link categories. The user may click a category to see the links for that category. The website will display output like that shown in Figure 7-94.

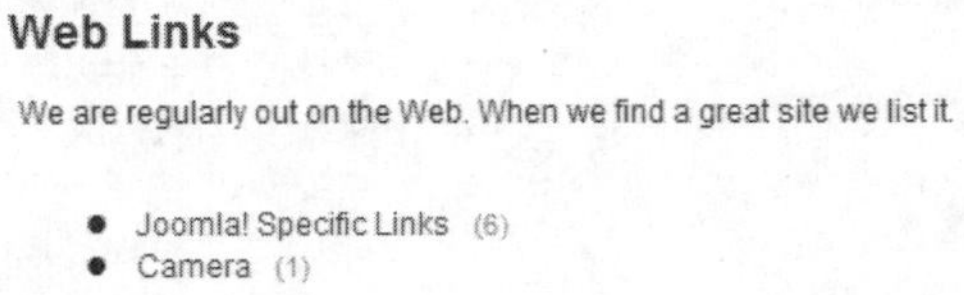

Web Links

We are regularly out on the Web. When we find a great site we list it.

- Joomla! Specific Links (6)
- Camera (1)

Figure 7-94. *The list of all the web link categories, displayed when the menu item type is Web Link Category List Layout*

Besides the default web link categories provided by Joomla, this menu item type displays our custom web link category, Camera. If you click the `Camera` link, you'll see the web links in it, as shown in Figure 7-95.

Camera

This is Web Link Category: Camera

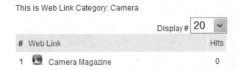

Figure 7-95. *The web links in the Camera category*

If you select the `Camera Magazine` web link, you will be navigated to the website `http://www.digicamera.com`, as it is the URL that we specified in this web link (refer to Figure 7-93).

Category List Layout

This menu item type displays a list of all the web links in the selected category. For example, if you select the Camera category, as shown in Figure 7-96, it will display all the web links in that category.

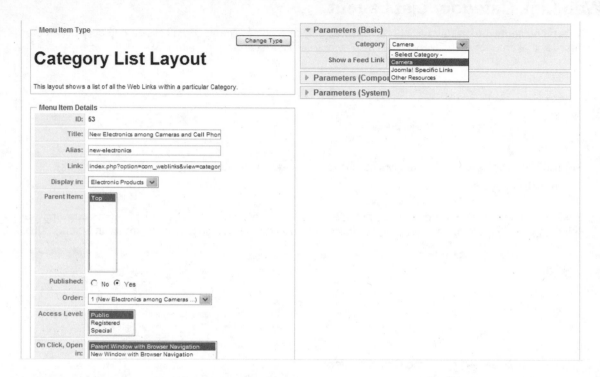

Figure 7-96. Web link category Camera selected in the Category List Layout menu item type

Web Link Submission Layout

This menu item type displays a form that allows users in the Author, Publisher, and Editor groups to submit a web link. It is a very nice option, as it allows the users to submit their web links from the front end also. If the logged-in user does not belong to the Author, Publisher, or Editor group, he will get the error shown in Figure 7-97 on selecting the menu item of this type.

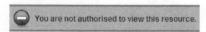

Figure 7-97. Message displayed to users of a group other than Author, Publisher, or Editor

If a user belonging to any of those groups logs in and the menu item is selected, a web link submission form will appear, as shown in Figure 7-98.

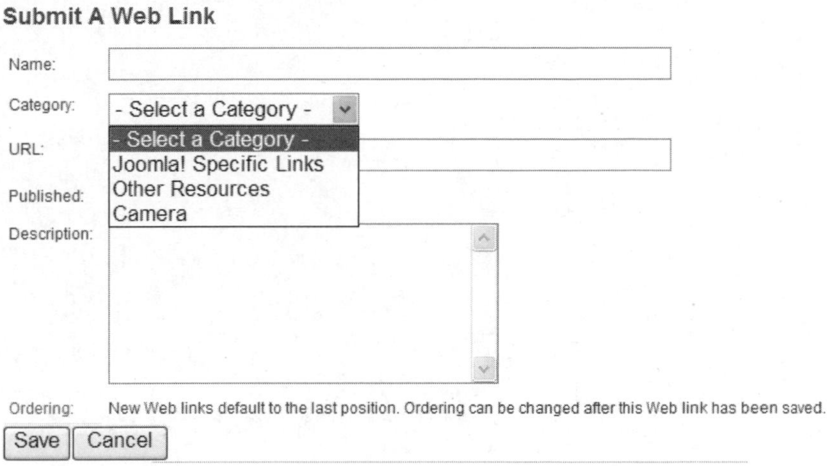

Submit A Web Link

Name:

Category: - Select a Category -

     - Select a Category -
     Joomla! Specific Links
URL: Other Resources
     Camera

Published:

Description:

Ordering: New Web links default to the last position. Ordering can be changed after this Web link has been saved.

Save   Cancel

Figure 7-98. Form that allows submission of a web link

The user has to specify the name of the web link, a category to which the web link will belong, the URL of the web page or website to be displayed (on selecting the menu item), and a small description of the web link. After entering the information, as shown in Figure 7-98, the user needs to click the Save button to submit the web link to the website.

Wrapper

This menu item type provides a layout that displays an external website inside a page of your website using an HTML frame. The external website is contained inside the wrapper. You can move around to any web page of the wrapped site, all inside the page of your website. When you move the mouse over this menu item type, you'll see a message to this effect, as shown in Figure 7-99.

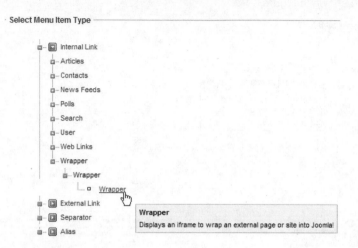

Figure 7-99. Selecting the Wrapper menu item type

If you select the Wrapper type from the `Select Menu Item Type` screen, you'll see, among other options, a field to specify the wrapper URL—that is, the URL of the website that you want to open in your web page. Let's enter the URL `http://www.bmharwani.com`, as shown in Figure 7-100.

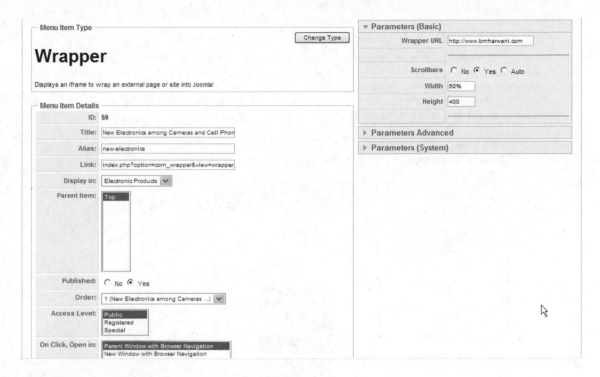

Figure 7-100. Entering the wrapper URL

There are some other options in the `Parameters (Basic)` section that I'll go over as well. The `Width` and `Height` are for assigning the desired width and height to the website that will be displayed. If the value of the `Scrollbars` option is set to `Auto`, then scrollbars will appear only when some part of the website is not visible. If you set the value of this option to `Yes`, then scrollbars will always be displayed.

Keep the rest of the settings at their defaults, and click the Save icon from the toolbar to save the Wrapper menu item. Upon selecting the menu item type from your Joomla website, you'll find that the website with the specified wrapper URL opens, as shown in Figure 7-101. You can navigate the pages of the external website and see the contents of your website simultaneously. The external website appears in a frame of the given width and height, along with scrollbars.

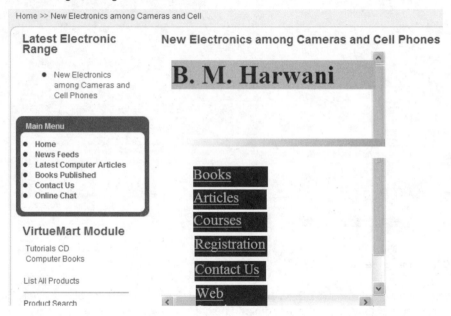

Figure 7-101. Another website displayed inside your website

External Link

This menu item type is used to create a menu item that links to an external website or page. When you select this menu item type, you'll see a screen like the one shown in Figure 7-102. For this example, you can leave all the settings as is, except for one field: Link.

For this field, you specify the URL of the web page to which you want the visitor to navigate when the menu item of this type is selected. Let's specify http://bmharwani.com/imagemap.htm. After entering the URL of the web page or website, click the Save icon.

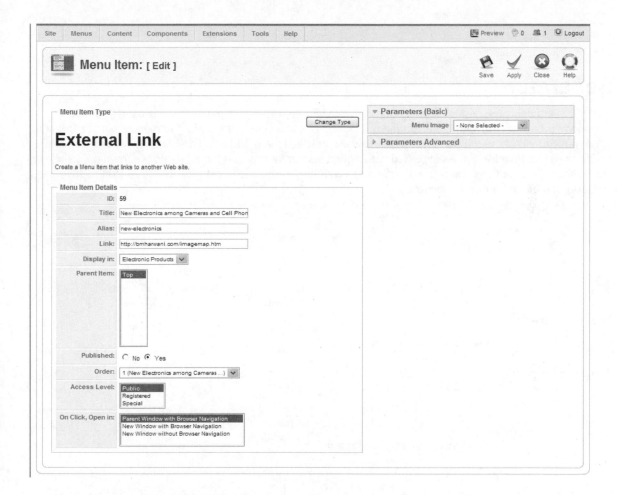

Figure 7-102. Specifying the Link setting to link to an external website

The main difference between the Web Link and External Link menu item types is that the Web Link type can refer to any web page, whether it is on the local domain or another place on the Internet; whereas the External Link type can refer only to web pages that are external to your domain, and hence must begin with http://.

Separator

This menu item type creates a menu **placeholder**, or **separator**, within a menu. It is used to break up a long menu. From the Menu Item Manager, select the New icon from the toolbar to make a blank separator. When you select the New icon, you'll get a screen to select the menu item type. On this screen, select Separator from the list. As expected, you'll get a screen for entering the separator information, as shown in Figure 7-103. In this case, you don't need to enter any information; just click the Save icon to save this separator in the form of a blank line.

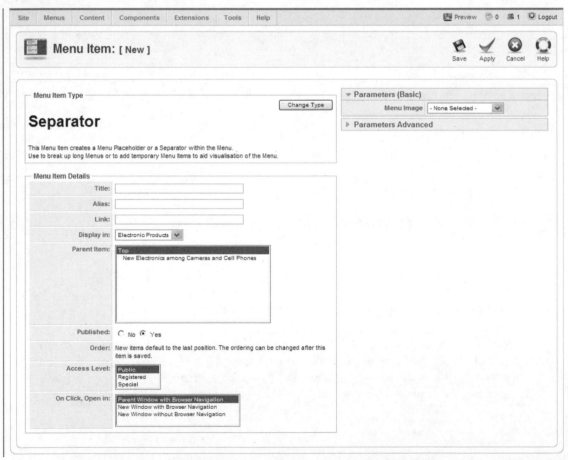

Figure 7-103. Leave the form blank in order to make a blank line as a separator.

To see the effect of this separator, we'll add one more menu item after this separator. Make a menu item of any type, with the title `Articles in Archived List`, and save it. You should now have two menu items with a separator in between, as shown in the Menu Item Manager in Figure 7-104.

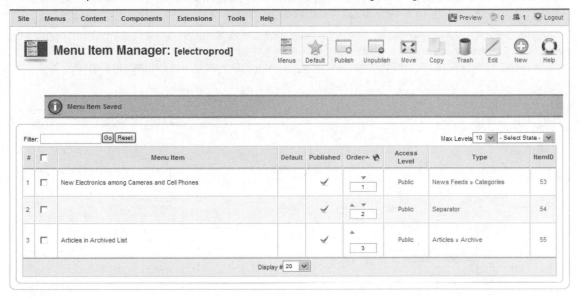

Figure 7-104. A separator between two menu items in the Menu Item Manager

When you open the browser window to open the Joomla website, you'll find that the two menu items are displayed with a separator in between, as shown in Figure 7-105.

Figure 7-105. A separator between two menu items upon execution of the website

Alias

This menu item type creates a link to an existing menu item. It enables you to have identical menu items in two or more menus without duplicating the settings. For example, suppose that you want the current menu item to point to the existing menu item `Joomla! Overview`. The idea is that you want the current menu item to display the same article to which the menu item `Joomla! Overview` is pointing.

When you select the Alias menu item type, you'll see a screen for entering certain information. Keep all the settings as is, except for the `Menu Item` drop-down, where you can select the menu item to which the current menu item is to point. Select the menu item `Joomla! Overview`, as shown in Figure 7-106.

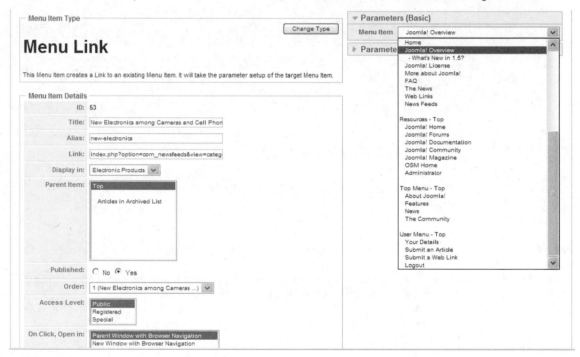

Figure 7-106. The menu item New Electronics among Cameras and Cell Phones set as an alias of Joomla! Overview

Now when you select the menu item, it will display the same article that was attached to the `Joomla! Overview` menu item, as shown in Figure 7-107.

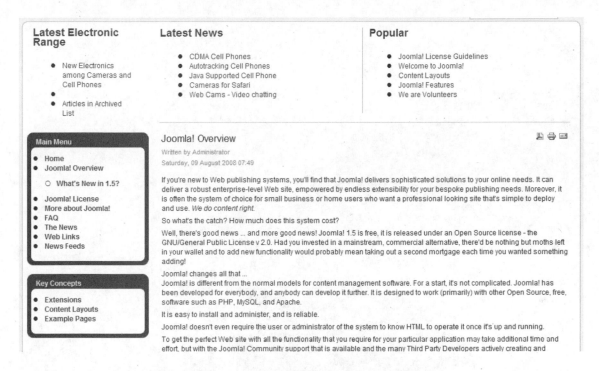

Figure 7-107. The "Joomla! Overview" article displayed upon selection of the menu item New Electronics among Cameras and Cell Phones

Summary

In this chapter, we've explored the four categories of menu item types that you can add to your Joomla menus: Internal Link, External Link, Separator, and Alias. The Internal Link type has several subtypes, and each is meant for displaying a specific type of content. You have tested out the different menu item types, and you have seen how to create menus and the items within them.

In the next chapter, you will learn about the 20 standard modules provided by Joomla, including Banner, Breadcrumbs, Feed Display, RSS, Poll, and Search. You'll see the methodology of using each module, and you'll discover their roles in increasing the functionality of a website.

Chapter 8

Modules

In the previous chapter, you learned about menus and their menu item types. In this chapter, you'll learn about different types of standard modules and their uses.

The Module Manager

So what is a module? Simply put, it is a collection of several related items. For example, a module can be a collection of any of the following:

- Menus

- Popular articles or related articles

- Advertisements, banners, or random images

The main benefit of collecting several related items in a module is to gain better control. For example, you could make a module become invisible on the website (which would be easier than unpublishing the individual items), apply a CSS style uniformly to all items in a module, change its access level or position, and so on.

By default, Joomla provides 20 built-in modules, and you can add more using the Module Manager. When you open the Module Manager (by selecting `Extensions` ➤ `Module Manager`), the list of modules present in it is displayed, as shown in Figure 8-1.

Figure 8-1. List of modules on page 1 of the Module Manager

These are the modules visible on the first page. On selecting the link 2, the modules on the second page are displayed, as shown in Figure 8-2.

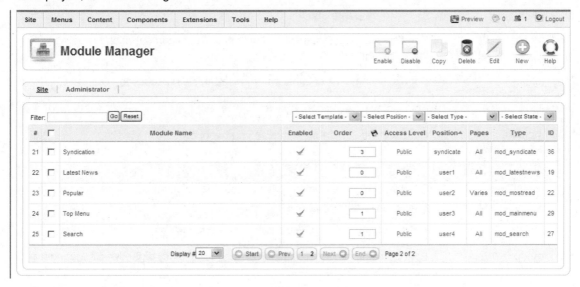

Figure 8-2. List of modules on page 2 of the Module Manager

There are 25 modules present in the Module Manager. However, if you look at the `Type` column that displays the type of module to which the module belongs, you'll observe that several modules belong to the same module type. For example, Main Menu, Resources, Key Concepts, User Menu, Example Pages, and so on are modules that belong to the same module type: mod_menu. In this way, we can say that Joomla has 20 built-in module types. You can also make your own modules belonging to an existing module type.

> *A module type name is a sort of system name for the module. You cannot edit the module type name of any module.*

Table 8-1 lists the different module types and their purposes.

Table 8-1. Different module types

Module Type	Purpose
mod_archive	For displaying archived articles
mod_banners	For displaying client banners
mod_breadcrumbs	For displaying breadcrumbs to show your position in the website

mod_feed	For displaying news feeds
mod_footer	For displaying the footer (often containing website information including owner, copyright, etc.)
mod_latest	For displaying a list of latest information (articles) accessed
mod_login	For displaying a login form
mod_mainmenu	For displaying different menus on your website
mod_mostread	For displaying popular articles
mod_newsflash	For displaying one or more articles from the selected category each time the page is refreshed
mod_poll	For displaying polls to the visitors to get feedback on a specific subject
mod_random_image	For displaying random images from a specific folder of the Media Manager (with every page refresh)
mod_related_items	For displaying the articles that having matching keywords in the metadata information
mod_search	For displaying the search box to help in searching for desired information
mod_sections	For displaying different sections that exist on the website
mod_stats	For displaying website statistics, such as information regarding the operating system, the PHP version, MySQL, the server time, caching, and so on
mod_syndicate	For creating an RSS feed link for the page
mod_whosonline	For displaying information about users currently browsing the website
mod_wrapper	For displaying an external website inside your website (using this module, you can browse an external website as well as your own site)

Note that all the modules that we're going to look at in this chapter have the same fields in the Details and Menu Assignment sections; however, they have different Parameters sections.

Open the Module Manager by selecting Extensions ➤ Module Manager. You'll see a list of modules, as shown previously in Figure 8-1. Using the Module Manager, you can add new modules, edit existing modules, delete undesired modules, and more.

If you click the name of any module, it will open in edit mode. For example, click the Archive module, and its edit page will open, as shown in Figure 8-3.

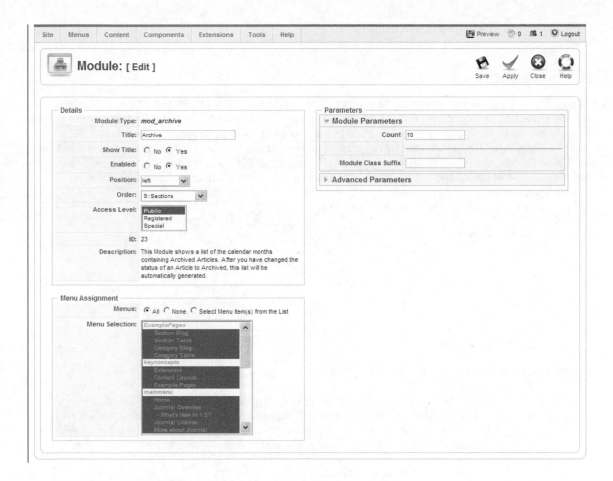

Figure 8-3. Module information divided into three sections

You'll find that the settings displayed are divided into three sections: Details, Menu Assignment, and Parameters. Again, all the module types have the same settings in the Details and Menu Assignment sections; the only difference is in the options of the Parameters section. Next, I'll briefly go over the options in the Details section.

Details section

The `Module Type` field shows the system name of the module. It cannot be edited. In the `Title` field, you enter the title of the module. For this example, enter `Archive`. This is the name that will appear in the Module Manager. Set the `Show Title` option to `Yes` to see the title displayed on the front end. Set the `Enabled` option to `Yes` to make the module visible on the website. The `Position` drop-down is used to specify the location of the module on the web page. The positions in the drop-down list are provided by the template we're using, and appear as shown in Figure 8-4. For this example, let's keep its default position, left.

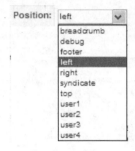

Figure 8-4. Possible positions for displaying the module

You can easily display all of the default positions provided by the current template on the web page by simply adding the text `?tp=1` to the end of any front-end Joomla URL. For example, our website URL is http://localhost/joomlasite/, so if we type the URL as `http://localhost/joomlasite/?tp=1`, we will see our web page displayed with labeled rectangles indicating the predefined positions for the current template, as shown in Figure 8-5.

Figure 8-5. Web page displayed with rectangles indicating predefined positions for the current template

The `Order` drop-down in the `Details` section is used to specify the display sequence if more than one module is assigned the same position. The module positions are decided by the template that you've applied to your website, and a template may specify the same position to several modules. For example, suppose the Main Menu and Login Form modules have the same position (defined in the current template). In this case, the value in the `Order` drop-down decides which will appear first on the front end. The drop-down list shows all modules being assigned the current position. You can select the module after which you want the current module to appear. The order can also be changed later from the Module Manager. For this example, let's keep the default order (i.e., keep the value of this field unchanged so that the modules are displayed in the default sequence).

The `Access Level` field is used to specify the level of user that's allowed to access this module. The access levels are as follows:

- **Public**: Everyone can access this module.

- **Registered**: Only registered users can access this module.

- **Special**: Only users with author status or higher can access this module.

For this example, set the `Access Level` to `Public`, as we want the module to be publicly viewed.

The `ID` is a unique identification number that Joomla assigns automatically for internal use. It cannot be changed. The `Description` field displays a description of the module being created. It's not editable.

Menu Assignment section

The `Menu Assignment` section is for deciding the web pages on which the current module is to be displayed. We can make a module appear or disappear upon selection of certain menu items.

The `Menus` option is for deciding the menus in which we want to display our module. The options are as follows:

- `All`: Displays the current module on all menu items of the web page. For this example, choose this option.

- `None`: Makes the module invisible (not displayed on any menu items).

- `Select Menu Item(s) from the List`: Displays the module on only selected menu items.

The `Menu Selection` list is used when `Select Menu Item(s) from the List` is selected. It helps in selecting individual menu items on which you want to display the module. You can Ctrl-click to select multiple menu items and Shift-click to select a range of menu items.

> The `Menus` option for a module is usually set to `None` by default. However, we will set it to `All` for all the modules that will be discussed in this chapter to make them appear on all menu items of the web page.

Now we'll look at each module in turn. Since all the module types have the same fields in the `Details` and `Menu Assignment` sections, we'll discuss only the fields of the `Parameters` section for each module. Likewise, we'll only discuss one example module per module type, since all the modules of a particular module type work according to the same concept.

Archive

This module shows articles that have been archived—that is, temporarily removed from active display and stored. This module will not display anything if no articles are archived. If an article is archived, it's stored by creation date, not by archive date, and the module displays the month and year of creation. This module and the menu item type Archived Article List Layout (discussed in Chapter 7) work in a similar fashion.

In the Module Manager, when we select the Archive module, it opens in edit mode. The fields in its `Parameters` section are as shown in Figure 8-6.

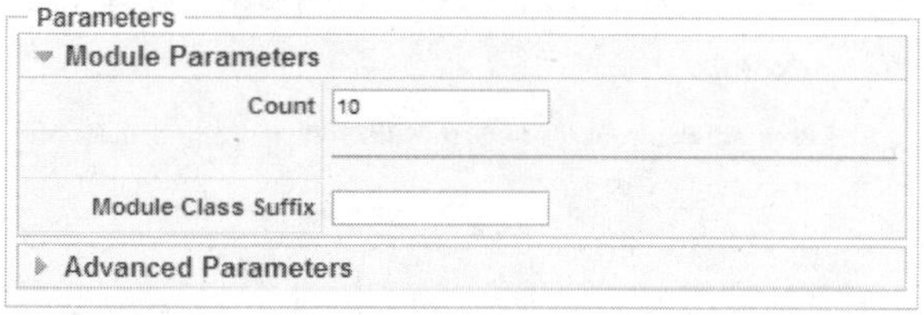

Figure 8-6. The parameters of the Archive module

The `Count` field is for specifying the number of articles to be displayed. The default value is 10, but you can set it to any value that you want.

The `Module Class Suffix` field is used when you want to apply your own CSS class to certain modules, independent of the site's default template CSS classes. **CSS classes** are for applying your own styles (font, color, etc.) to the modules of your website in a consistent manner. To do this, you need to create CSS classes in the template CSS file and specify its name in this field. Suppose the class name is module-archive; if we enter its suffix, `-archive`, in this field, its styles will be individually applied to the Archive module. Click the `Save` icon from the toolbar to save the changes made in the module.

Upon opening the front end of your Joomla website, you'll see a link with the title `Archive` (marked in Figure 8-7), indicating that some articles created in August 2008 have been archived. If you click the link, you'll see all the archived articles that were created in that month and year, as shown in the figure.

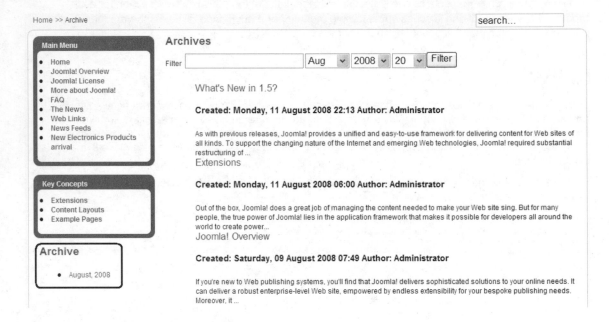

Figure 8-7. Clicking the Archive link displays all the archived articles

Banners

This module is used to activate the banner(s) created through the Banner component—that is, for displaying the banner on the website. When the Banners module is selected in the Module Manager, it's opened in edit mode. Using the options in its `Parameters` section (shown in Figure 8-8), you can activate the banner created earlier through the Banner component.

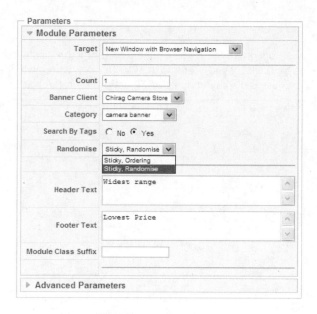

Figure 8-8. The parameters of the Banners module

The `Target` drop-down is used to specify whether to open the client's URL in the same window or in a separate window when the user clicks the banner. There are three options:

- `Parent Window with Browser Navigation` opens the client's URL in the current browser window with back and forward navigation facilities.

- `New Window with Browser Navigation` opens the client's URL in a new browser window with back and forward navigation facilities.

- `New Window without Browser Navigation` opens the client's URL in a new browser window without back and forward navigation facilities.

For this example, select the `Parent Window with Browser Navigation` option from the `Target` drop-down.

In the `Count` field, you specify the number of banners to be displayed. Let's set it to 1 (assuming we have only one banner for the client).

In the `Banner Client` drop-down, you select the client whose banner is to be displayed. As mentioned in Chapter 4, banner clients are created with the help of the Banner Client Manager. We created a banner client named Chirag Camera Store in Chapter 4, so let's select that client here.

In the `Category` drop-down, you select the category of the banners to be displayed. Banner categories are created with the help of the Banner Category Manager. We created a banner category named Camera Banner in Chapter 4, so select that category here.

You set the `Search By Tags` option to `Yes` if you want the banner to be displayed on the basis of the matching tags of the articles being displayed. Refer to the Figure 4-21, where we created a banner called Chirag camera banner. This figure is displayed again as Figure 8-9 for reference.

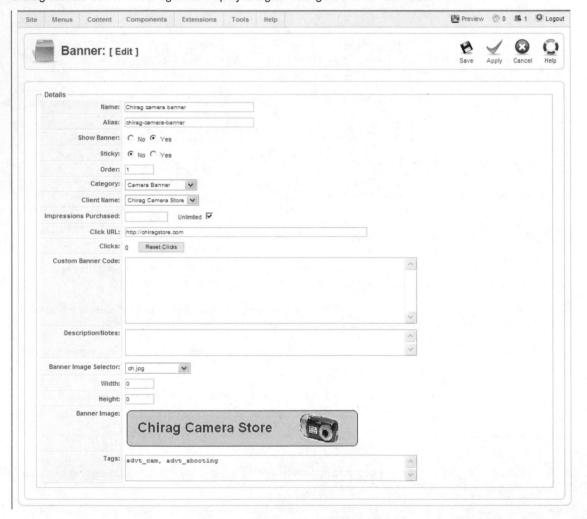

Figure 8-9. Adding a new banner

Notice that this screen contains a `Tags` field at the bottom. Suppose we remove the existing tags, advt_cam and advt_shooting, and enter some other keywords in this field—say, `cheapest` and `night` `vision`—in order to associate this banner with the article being viewed by the visitor. If the visitor opens an article having either of these keywords, the banner will also appear automatically. To try it practically, open the "Latest Cameras" article and enter the keywords `cheapest` and `night vision` in it. The keywords for an article can be entered in the `Keywords` field of the article's `Metadata Information` section, as shown in Figure 8-10. Now, if this article is displayed on the web page, the associated banner will be displayed (since their tags/keywords match).

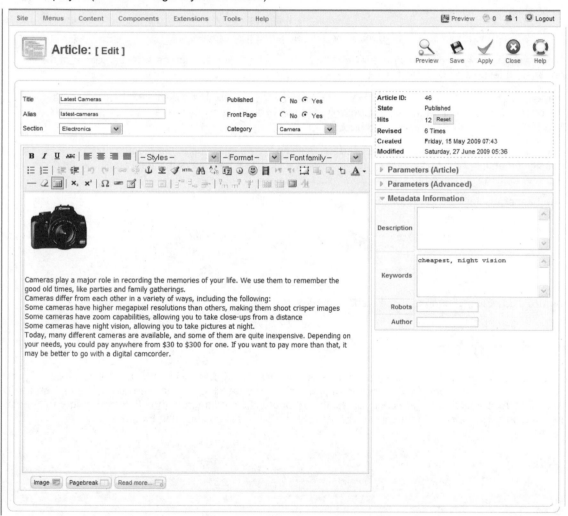

Figure 8-10. Specifying keywords for an article

Refer again to Figure 8-8 for the rest of the options. In the `Randomise` drop-down of the `Parameters` section for the Banners module, you select the order in which the banners will be displayed. There are two options:

- `Sticky, Ordering`, which means that the banners will be displayed in sequential order.

- `Sticky, Randomise`, which means the banners will be displayed in random order. This option has an impact only if more than one banner is being displayed.

Since we have only one banner on our website, we will not find any change on selecting either of the options. So let's keep its default value, `Sticky, Randomise`.

In the `Header Text` and `Footer Text` fields, you specify the text to be displayed before and after the banner (or group of banners), respectively. For this example, specify the text `Widest range` for the header text and `Lowest Price` for the footer text.

The `Module Class Suffix` field is used for applying individual styles to the module. In this field, you specify the suffix of the style class created in the template CSS file. Leave this field blank, as we don't want to apply any styles at this time.

The banner displayed on the website using this module will look as shown in Figure 8-11.

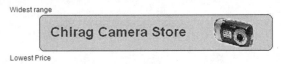

Figure 8-11. Client's banner on the website upon execution

Breadcrumbs

This module is helpful for quick navigation in a website. It not only displays your current location in the website, but also the parent web pages through which you've traveled to reach the current page. You can use the parent links to navigate back. Select the Breadcrumbs module from the Module Manager to open it in edit mode. The options in the `Parameters` section will appear as shown in Figure 8-12.

Figure 8-12. The parameters of the Breadcrumbs module

The `Show Home` option is used to decide whether to display the home page in the breadcrumbs path. For this example, let's set it to `Yes`.

The `Text for Home entry` field is for specifying the text to display for the home page in the breadcrumbs. Usually it is set to `Home`, but you can enter any text (e.g., Default or Index). Let's keep the default value `Home` in this field.

The `Show Last` option is for deciding whether to display the current location of the web page. If you set this field to `No`, it will display the links up to the parent web page, but not the current page. For example, suppose we select the Cell Phones category from the `News Feeds` menu. The breadcrumbs will display `Home >> News Feeds >> Cell Phones` if the `Show Last` field is set to `Yes`. If we set this field to `No`, the breadcrumb will display `Home >> News Feeds`, which excludes the location of the current web page. Let's set this field to `Yes`.

The `Text Separator` field specifies the text to be used to separate the navigation elements. Usually the default, `>>`, is used, but we can use any symbol. Keep this field blank to use the default.

The `Module Class Suffix` field is used for applying individual styles to the module. In this field, you can specify the suffix of the style class created in template CSS file. Let's keep this field blank.

After entering this information, the output on the website should look like Figure 8-13.

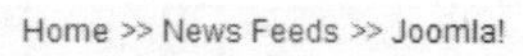

Home >> News Feeds >> Joomla!

Figure 8-13. The breadcrumb navigation upon execution

Feed Display

This module is for displaying news feeds from other websites. News feeds are usually used when you want to access certain information from other websites regularly. So, instead of visiting those websites continually for the updated information, news feeds allow you to merge the updated content from the specific websites into your pages. In other words, the Feed Display module is a facility that you can use to obtain new and updated content from the website(s) that the feed is linked with.

When you select the Feed Display module from the Module Manager, it opens in edit mode, and appears as shown in Figure 8-14.

Figure 8-14. The Feed Display module options

In the `Module Class Suffix` field, you specify the suffix of the style class created in the template CSS file. This option is used for applying individual styles to the module. In the `Feed URL` field, you specify the URL of the RSS feed. The `RTL Feed` option is used to specify whether the flow of information on your website should go from right to left (RTL). You'll usually set it to `Yes` for Arabic languages and the like, in which the flow of information is in the right-to-left direction. For this example, leave it at `No`. Set `Feed Title` to `Yes` to display the feed title, set `Feed Description` to `Yes` to display the feed description, and set `Feed Image` to `Yes` to display the feed image. The `Items` field is used to specify the number of news feed items to display. Set `Item Description` to `Yes` to display the description of individual items. The `Word Count` field is used to specify the maximum number of words to display in the item description (a value of `0` means that the entire item description will be displayed).

> Don't forget to set the value of the `Menus` option in the `Menu Assignment` section to
> `All` to keep the module visible on selection of any menu item of the website.

In the `Feed URL` field, let's specify the following URL, as shown in Figure 8-15:

http://rss.adobe.com/resources_flex.rss?locale=en_US

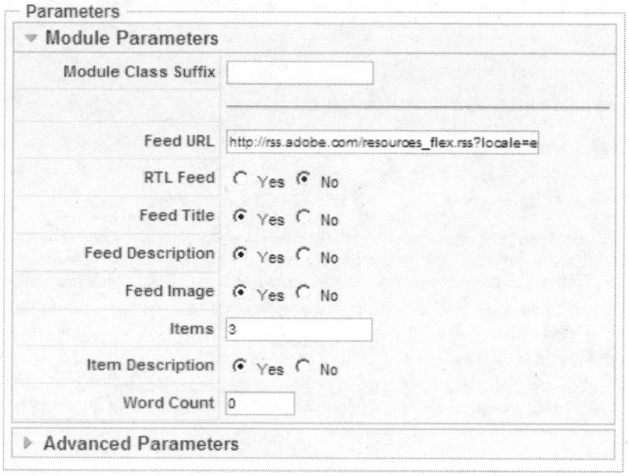

Figure 8-15. The module parameters of the Feed Display module

After entering the feed URL, click the `Save` icon from the toolbar to save the module. Since the module is disabled (by default) in the Module Manager, let's enable this module by clicking the red X in the `Enabled` column of this module. It will then be changed to a green check mark to signify that the module is now enabled and ready to use.

Open the Joomla website, and you'll see the news feed from the supplied website, as shown in Figure 8-16. Notice that the website displays links to certain articles. Any changes made by the source website in the feed contents will be reflected in your Feed Display module.

Feed Display

Flex News
Recent tutorials, updates, and
TechNotes for Adobe Flex

- Flex quick start guide
  for PHP developers
  Run these examples
  to get started using
  Flex with PHP.
- Flex 2.0.1 patch for
  Flash CS3
  Professional
  compatibility
  After adding a SWC
  compiled with Flash
  CS3 Professional to
  the Flex Builder
  library build path of
  the project, design
  view no longer
  works.The Flex
  debugger does not
  work with Flash
  Player 9 (9.0.45.0) in
  the Mozilla
  browser.This patch
  allows the Flex SDK
  and Flex Builder to...
- Designing Flex
  applications with
  Fireworks CS3
  Design the look of
  Flex applications

Latest News

- Content Layouts
- The Joomla! Community
- Welcome to Joomla!
- Newsflash 4
- Newsflash 5

Popular

- Welcome to Joomla!
- Content Layouts
- Joomla! Features
- The Joomla! Community
- Joomla! Facts

Welcome to the Frontpage

The Joomla! Community

Written by Administrator
Tuesday, 12 August 2008 16:50

Got a question? With more than 210,000 members, the Joomla! Discussion Forums at
forum.joomla.org are a great resource for both new and experienced users. Ask your
toughest questions the community is waiting to see what you'll do with your Joomla! site.

Do you want to show off your new Joomla! Web site? Visit the Site Showcase section of
our forum.

Do you want to contribute?

If you think working with Joomla is fun, wait until you start working on it. We're passionate
about helping Joomla users become contributors. There are many ways you can help
Joomla's development:

- Submit news about Joomla. We syndicate Joomla-related news on
  JoomlaConnect™. If you have Joomla news that you would like to share with the
  community, find out how to get connected here.
- Report bugs and request features in our trackers. Please read Reporting Bugs, for
  details on how we like our bug reports served up

Polls

Joomla! is used for?

- ○ Community Sites
- ○ Public Brand Sites
- ○ eCommerce
- ○ Blogs
- ○ Intranets
- ○ Photo and Media Sites
- ○ All of the Above!

[Vote] [Results]

Who's Online

We have 1 guest online

Advertisement

Figure 8-16. The feed display output upon execution

*Since the news feed is regularly updated by the source website, the list of items that you
see may be entirely different than that shown in Figure 8-16.*

Now let's supply the URL of another RSS feed location in the `Feed URL` field: http://feeds.joomla.org/
JoomlaMagazine. You'll see that in your Joomla website, the Feed Display module shows links to certain
articles supplied by the new RSS feed URL entered, as shown in Figure 8-17.

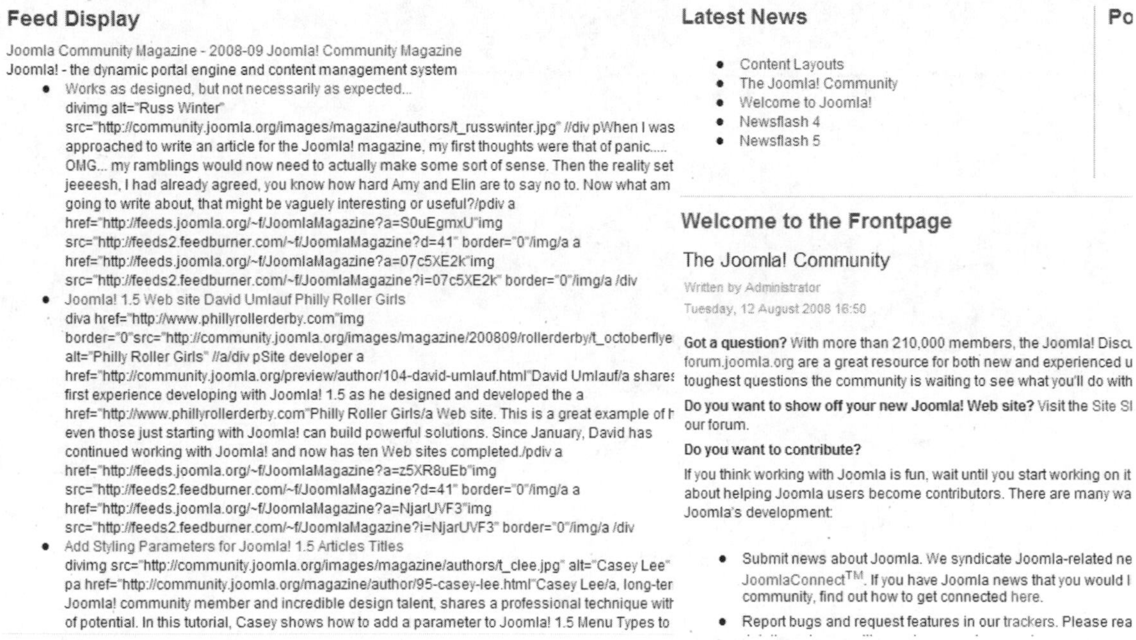

Feed Display

Joomla Community Magazine - 2008-09 Joomla! Community Magazine
Joomla! - the dynamic portal engine and content management system

- Works as designed, but not necessarily as expected...
  divimg alt="Russ Winter"
  src="http://community.joomla.org/images/magazine/authors/t_russwinter.jpg" //div pWhen I was
  approached to write an article for the Joomla! magazine, my first thoughts were that of panic.....
  OMG... my ramblings would now need to actually make some sort of sense. Then the reality set
  jeeeesh, I had already agreed, you know how hard Amy and Elin are to say no to. Now what am
  going to write about, that might be vaguely interesting or useful?/pdiv a
  href="http://feeds.joomla.org/~f/JoomlaMagazine?a=S0uEgmxU"img
  src="http://feeds2.feedburner.com/~f/JoomlaMagazine?d=41" border="0"/img/a a
  href="http://feeds.joomla.org/~f/JoomlaMagazine?a=07c5XE2k"img
  src="http://feeds2.feedburner.com/~f/JoomlaMagazine?i=07c5XE2k" border="0"/img/a /div
- Joomla! 1.5 Web site David Umlauf Philly Roller Girls
  diva href="http://www.phillyrollerderby.com"img
  border="0"src="http://community.joomla.org/images/magazine/200809/rollerderby/t_octoberflye
  alt="Philly Roller Girls" //a/div pSite developer a
  href="http://community.joomla.org/preview/author/104-david-umlauf.html"David Umlauf/a shares
  first experience developing with Joomla! 1.5 as he designed and developed the a
  href="http://www.phillyrollerderby.com"Philly Roller Girls/a Web site. This is a great example of h
  even those just starting with Joomla! can build powerful solutions. Since January, David has
  continued working with Joomla! and now has ten Web sites completed./div a
  href="http://feeds.joomla.org/~f/JoomlaMagazine?a=z5XR8uEb"img
  src="http://feeds2.feedburner.com/~f/JoomlaMagazine?d=41" border="0"/img/a a
  href="http://feeds.joomla.org/~f/JoomlaMagazine?a=NjarUVF3"img
  src="http://feeds2.feedburner.com/~f/JoomlaMagazine?i=NjarUVF3" border="0"/img/a /div
- Add Styling Parameters for Joomla! 1.5 Articles Titles
  divimg src="http://community.joomla.org/images/magazine/authors/t_clee.jpg" alt="Casey Lee"
  pa href="http://community.joomla.org/magazine/author/95-casey-lee.html"Casey Lee/a, long-ter
  Joomla! community member and incredible design talent, shares a professional technique with
  of potential. In this tutorial, Casey shows how to add a parameter to Joomla! 1.5 Menu Types to

Latest News

- Content Layouts
- The Joomla! Community
- Welcome to Joomla!
- Newsflash 4
- Newsflash 5

Welcome to the Frontpage

The Joomla! Community

Written by Administrator

Tuesday, 12 August 2008 16:50

Got a question? With more than 210,000 members, the Joomla! Discu
forum.joomla.org are a great resource for both new and experienced u
toughest questions the community is waiting to see what you'll do with

Do you want to show off your new Joomla! Web site? Visit the Site Sl
our forum.

Do you want to contribute?

If you think working with Joomla is fun, wait until you start working on it
about helping Joomla users become contributors. There are many wa
Joomla's development:

- Submit news about Joomla. We syndicate Joomla-related ne
  JoomlaConnect[TM]. If you have Joomla news that you would I
  community, find out how to get connected here.
- Report bugs and request features in our trackers. Please rea

Figure 8-17. The Feed Display output upon execution, for a different feed

You can select any link shown in the Feed Display module to see the corresponding information.

Footer

This module displays the website copyright and Joomla license information, as shown in Figure 8-18.

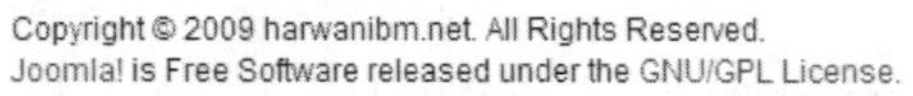

Copyright © 2009 harwanibm.net. All Rights Reserved.
Joomla! is Free Software released under the GNU/GPL License.

Figure 8-18. The footer, displaying copyright and license information

Latest News

This module shows a list of the most recently published articles. Select the Latest News module from the
Module Manager to open it in edit mode. The options will appear as shown in Figure 8-19.

313

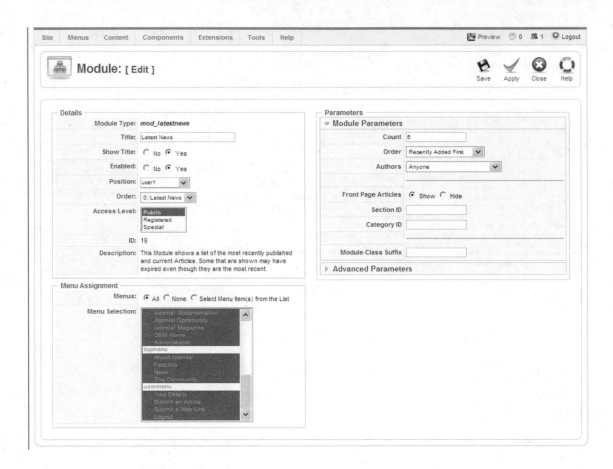

Figure 8-19. Latest News module options

The Count field is for specifying the number of articles to be displayed. Let's set it to 5.

The Order drop-down is used to specify the sequence in which the articles are to be displayed. The options are

- Recently Added First, which makes the articles that have recently been added appear first in sequence. Let's select this option.

- Recently Modified First, which makes the articles that have recently been modified appear first in sequence.

The `Authors` drop-down is used for watching the articles authored by a specific person. It has three options:

- `Anyone` will display all the articles, whoever the author may be.

- `Added or modified by me` will display only the articles written or modified by the current user.

- `Not added or modified by me` will display only the articles not written or modified by the current user.

The last two options are used only if the user is logged into the website. Since we want to see the articles written by anyone, set the `Authors` drop-down to `Anyone`.

Set the `Front Page Articles` option to `Show` if you want the titles of the articles displayed on the front page to appear in the Latest News module also.

The `Section ID` field is used to specify the section ID(s) for the articles you want to see. That is, this field is used to display articles only from the specific section(s). If you want to specify more than one section, you must separate them by commas—for example, 10,20. For this exercise, keep this field blank since we don't have any such requirement.

The `Category ID` field is for specifying the category ID(s) for the articles you want to see. Again, you can specify multiple category IDs separated by commas. As before, you can leave this field blank.

The `Module Class Suffix` field is used for individual module styling. Leave it blank, as we don't currently want to apply any style.

The output on the website should look something like Figure 8-20.

Latest News

- Content Layouts
- The Joomla! Community
- Welcome to Joomla!
- Newsflash 4
- Newsflash 5

Figure 8-20. The Latest News module upon execution

Login Form

This module displays a login form for entering a username and password. It also displays links for retrieving a forgotten password or username. A `Create an Account` link will also be displayed if user registration is enabled in the `User Settings` section of the Global Configuration file. This module functions in a similar way to the menu item of type Default Login Layout. When you select the Login Form module in the Module Manager, it will open in edit mode, and the options should appear as shown in Figure 8-21.

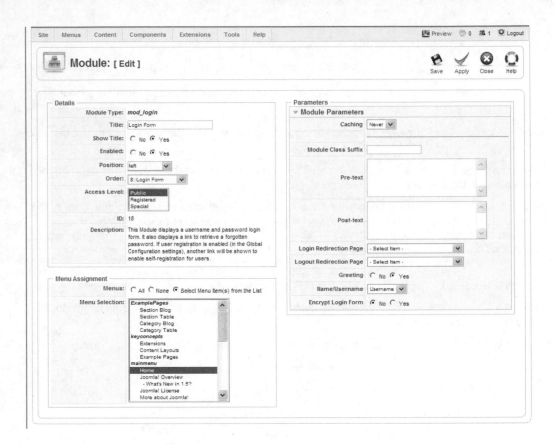

Figure 8-21. Options of the Login module

The `Caching` drop-down in the `Parameters` section allows you to control the speed of the loading process of a module by keeping the module in server memory. It takes less time to load the module from memory than it does to retrieve it from the disk drive. Caching is usually applied for modules that are frequently used but not frequently updated, such as the Footer module. In this case, set the `Caching` option to `Never` since we're not interested in caching.

The `Module Class Suffix` field is used to apply individual module styling.

The `Pre-text` box is for writing any text that you want to appear above the login form, and the `Post-text` box is for specifying any text that you want to appear below the login form. For this example, keep both of these fields blank since we don't want any text above or below the login form.

The `Login Redirection Page` drop-down is used to specify the page to be loaded after a successful login. It will display a list of pages like those shown in Figure 8-22, and you can select any web page. The item selected must be enabled or in published mode. If you don't make any selection here, the home page will be displayed.

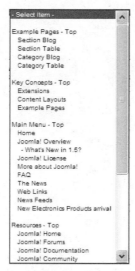

Figure 8-22. The list of login redirection pages

The `Logout Redirection Page` drop-down is used to specify the page to be loaded after a successful logout. You can select the desired page from the drop-down list. If you don't make any selection here, the home page will be displayed.

The `Greeting` option can be set to `Yes` to display a greeting message, such as "Hi *username*."

The `Name/Username` drop-down is used for deciding whether to display the name or username in the greeting message. The difference is that the username is a sort of user ID that is unique and used for login, and the name may be the complete name of the user. For this example, let's select `Username`.

The `Encrypt Login Form` option is set to `Yes` to encrypt the login form using SSL. It's used when Joomla is accessed using the https:// prefix. Let's set it to `No`.

Output on the website should appear as shown in Figure 8-23.

Figure 8-23. The Login Form module upon execution

Main Menu

The Main Menu module can be used to create your own menus and edit existing ones. You can also define the pages where you want the specific menus to appear and the location where you want the menus to appear on the desired web pages. When you select the Main Menu module from the Module Manager, it opens in edit mode. The options in the `Parameters` section are shown in Figure 8-24.

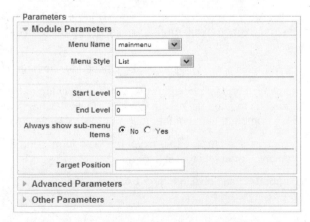

Figure 8-24. The parameters of the Main Menu module

From the `Menu Name` drop-down, you select the name of the menu. The default is `mainmenu`. More than one menu module can have the same menu name. Let's leave the menu name as `mainmenu`.

The `Menu Style` field is for selecting the style to be applied to the menu. The options are

- `List`: The default Joomla 1.5 style that's used by the menus on the sample website

- `Legacy Vertical`: A style that's compatible with Joomla 1.0 vertical style

- `Legacy Horizontal`: A style that's compatible with Joomla 1.0 horizontal style

- `Legacy Flat List`: A style that's compatible with Joomla 1.0 flat list style

The effects of these styles on a menu are depicted in Figures 8-25 through 8-28, respectively.

Figure 8-25. The Main Menu with the List style applied

Figure 8-26. The Main Menu with the Legacy Vertical style applied

Figure 8-27. The Main Menu with the Legacy Horizontal style applied

319

Figure 8-28. The Main Menu with the Legacy Flat List style applied

In the `Start Level` and `End Level` fields, you specify the level of depth of the menus. The top level is numbered 0. For example, if you set the start level to `0` and the end level to `1`, all the top-level menus will be displayed, along with all the menus at level 1. However, menus at level 2 or deeper will not be displayed. As you might expect, the **start level** is the highest level of menu to be displayed; the default is 0 (top level). For this example, keep the default value here. The **end level** is the lowest level in the menu hierarchy to be displayed; the default, 0, will display all menu levels. Again, for this example, keep the default value here.

The `Always show sub-menu Items` option is for deciding whether to display submenu items when the parent is not active. If `No`, a submenu item will be displayed only when the parent item is clicked. If `Yes`, submenu items will always be displayed in the menu.

The `Target Position` field is used to specify the location of the menu in pixels. If you don't specify any position here, it's supplied by the template being used. The position can be supplied in the following format: `top=20, left=20, width=200, height=200`.

Popular

This module displays a list of the articles with the highest hit counts—that is, the most popular articles among all visitors. Figure 8-29 shows the Popular module opened in edit mode.

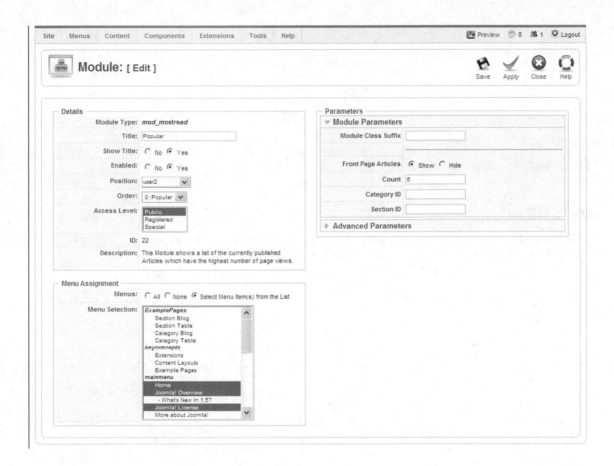

Figure 8-29. Options of the Popular module

I'll briefly go over the options in the `Parameters` section of this module. The `Module Class Suffix` field is used for individual module styling. The `Front Page Articles` option is used to decide whether to display the front page articles in the list. For this example, let's set this field to `Show`. The `Count` field is used to specify the number of articles to display in the list. The default value is `5`. Let's keep the default value.

The `Category ID` field is used for displaying articles only from specific categories. You specify the category ID(s) for the articles you want to see. To specify more than one category ID, separate them with a comma—for example, 10,20. In this case, keep this field blank since we don't want to see any particular articles. The `Section ID` field is used to specify the section ID(s) for the articles you want to display. Again, if you want to specify more than one section, they must be separated by a comma. Let's keep this field blank as well.

Output of the Popular module on the website should appear as shown in Figure 8-30.

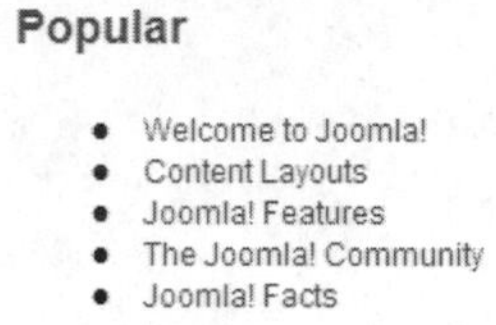

Popular

- Welcome to Joomla!
- Content Layouts
- Joomla! Features
- The Joomla! Community
- Joomla! Facts

Figure 8-30. The output of the Popular module upon execution

Newsflash

This module displays one or more articles from the selected category each time the page is refreshed. Figure 8-31 shows the Newsflash module opened in edit mode.

Figure 8-31. Options of the Newsflash module

In the `Category` drop-down list, you can select a category whose articles you want to display. Let's select `Electronics/Camera`, since we want to see the articles of the Electronics section and of the Camera category.

The `Layout` drop-down is used to decide the format in which to display the articles. There are three options:

- `Randomly choose one at a time` randomly displays an article from the selected category each time the page is refreshed. This is the default option.

- `Horizontal` displays horizontally the number of articles specified in the `# of Articles` field.

- `Vertical` displays vertically the number of articles specified in the `# of Articles` field.

For this example, let's select the `Vertical` option.

Set the `Show Images` option to `Yes` since we also want to display the images of the article.

The `Title Linkable` drop-down is for deciding whether you want the title of the article to act as a hyperlink to the article—that is, whether the contents of the article will be displayed upon clicking its title. Set this field to `Use Global` to get its value from the Global Configuration file.

Set the `Show last separator` option to `Yes` to display a separator after the last article.

The `Read more... Link` option is for deciding whether to show a `Read more` link (used in large articles to display the next portion of the article). In this case, set it to `Hide`.

The `Article Title` drop-down allows you to set whether the title of the article will be displayed. In this case, set it to `No`, since we don't want the title to be displayed.

As mentioned, the `# of Articles` field is used to specify the number of the articles to be displayed. The default is 5. You can leave this field blank to keep the default value.

Finally, the `Module Class Suffix` field is used for individual module styling. You can leave this field blank as well.

After choosing these settings, the `Parameters` section for your Newsflash module should appear as shown in Figure 8-32.

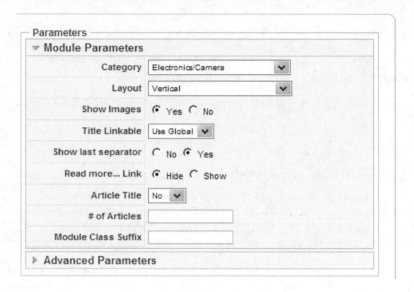

Figure 8-32. Parameters section of the Newsflash module

The output of this module should appear as shown in Figure 8-33.

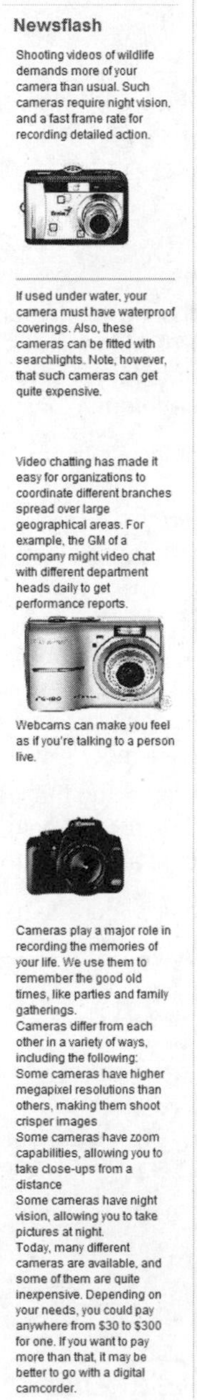

Newsflash

Shooting videos of wildlife demands more of your camera than usual. Such cameras require night vision, and a fast frame rate for recording detailed action.

If used under water, your camera must have waterproof coverings. Also, these cameras can be fitted with searchlights. Note, however, that such cameras can get quite expensive.

Video chatting has made it easy for organizations to coordinate different branches spread over large geographical areas. For example, the GM of a company might video chat with different department heads daily to get performance reports.

Webcams can make you feel as if you're talking to a person live.

Cameras play a major role in recording the memories of your life. We use them to remember the good old times, like parties and family gatherings.
Cameras differ from each other in a variety of ways, including the following:
Some cameras have higher megapixel resolutions than others, making them shoot crisper images
Some cameras have zoom capabilities, allowing you to take close-ups from a distance
Some cameras have night vision, allowing you to take pictures at night.
Today, many different cameras are available, and some of them are quite inexpensive. Depending on your needs, you could pay anywhere from $30 to $300 for one. If you want to pay more than that, it may be better to go with a digital camcorder.

Figure 8-33. Output of the Newsflash module upon execution

> *In case you find that too many modules are enabled and the screen appears cluttered, you can disable certain modules to make the front end appear neat and tidy.*

Polls

As you've seen, polls are the best way to get the views of your visitors on a particular subject. This section assumes that you've created a poll using the Poll Manager as instructed in Chapter 7. This module shows the selected poll, which the visitor can use to vote for an option or see the results of the poll. This module works in a similar fashion to the menu item type Internal Link: Poll Layout.

Figure 8-34 shows the `Parameters` section of the Polls module opened in edit mode.

Figure 8-34. Parameters section of the Polls module

In the `Poll` drop-down, you select the poll to display on the website. Select the "What you look for when purchasing a new cell phone" poll created in Chapter 7. Again, the `Module Class Suffix` field is used to apply individual module styles, and you can leave it blank for this exercise.

Output on the website should appear as shown in Figure 8-35.

Figure 8-35. Output of the Polls module upon execution

The user can select any of the available options and click the `Vote` button to enter his or her choice. The `Results` button can be clicked to see the current poll results.

Random Image

This module displays a random image from the selected directory. Figure 8-36 shows the Random Image module opened in edit mode.

Figure 8-36. Options of the Random Image module

The `Image Type` field is used to specify the type of image to be displayed (e.g., JPG, PNG, GIF, etc.). The default is JPG. In the `Image Folder` field, select the folder from which the images are to be displayed. The path specified is relative to the website URL. Let's enter the folder name `images/trialimg`, which is where we uploaded a few images during the discussion of the Media Manager. The `Link` field is used to specify the URL of the website to which you want the visitor to navigate if the image is clicked. You can enter http://www.bmharwani.com (though it can be any URL). In the `Width (px)` field, you specify the width of the image in pixels. The image will be resized to this width. In the `Height (px)` field, you specify the height of the image in pixels. The image will be scaled to the given height.

Output on the website should appear as shown in Figure 8-37. It displays a random image picked from the images/trialimg folder.

Random Image

Figure 8-37. Output of the Random Image module upon execution

If you click the `Refresh` button, the picture should change, as shown in Figure 8-38.

Random Image

Figure 8-38. The image changes upon clicking the Refresh button.

Related Items

This module displays a list of articles that are related to the current article being viewed. Related items are those articles that share at least one keyword in the article's metadata information.

When creating an article through the Article Manager, notice the `Keywords` field in the `Metadata Information` section. In this field, you specify certain words that best describe the characteristics of the article being created. To understand this better, let's edit the article we created earlier by the name of "Cameras for Safari," and enter the following in its `Keywords` field (as shown in Figure 8-39): `cheapest`, `night vision`, and `8 megapixel`. Click the `Save` icon to save the changes.

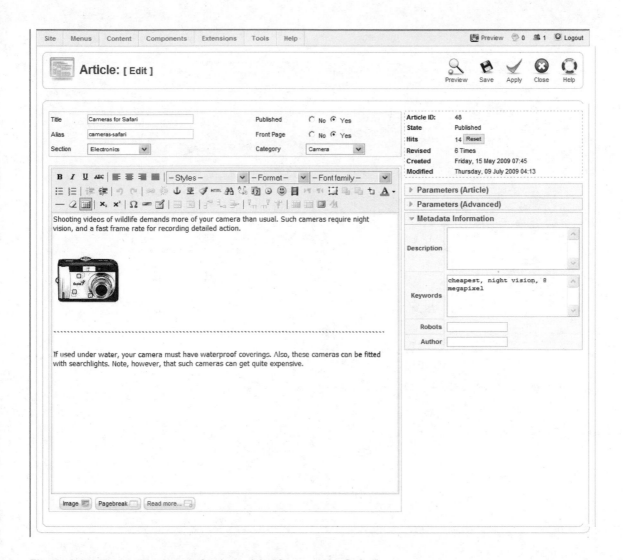

Figure 8-39. Entering keywords for the article "Cameras for Safari"

Similarly, edit the "Latest Cameras" article and enter `night vision`, `10 MB storage`, and `lightweight` in its `Keyword` field, as shown in Figure 8-40. Save the changes made to the article.

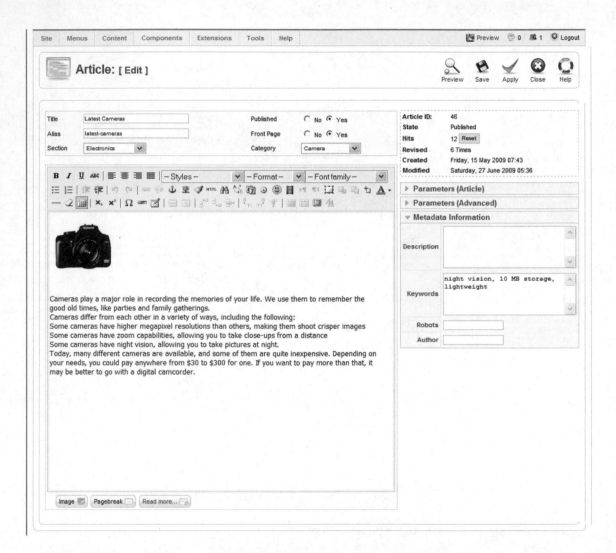

Figure 8-40. Entering keywords for the "Latest Cameras" article

Now, before we actually see the output of using this module, let's have a look at its parameters. Open the Related Items module in edit mode from the Module Manager, and you'll see the screen shown in Figure 8-41.

Figure 8-41. Related Items module in edit mode

The `Parameters` section prompts you to decide whether to display the date of creation of the related article(s). Let's set the `Show Date` option to `Hide` so that only the titles of the related articles will be displayed, not their date of creation. Also, leave the `Module Class Suffix` field blank, as we don't want to apply any styles.

Now take a look at the output of this module from the front end. If you open the "Cameras for Safari" article on the website, you'll find that a link to the "Latest Cameras" article appears under the title `Related Items`, as shown marked in Figure 8-42.

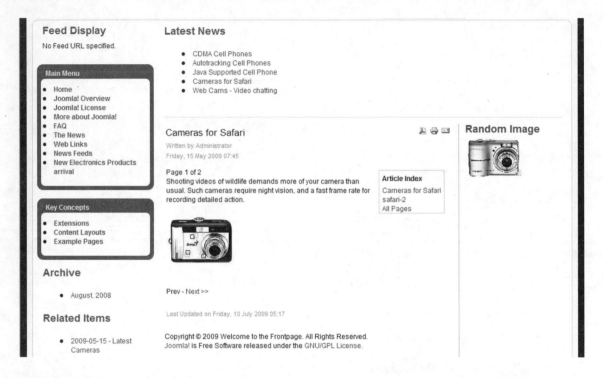

Figure 8-42. The article titles appear as related items when an article with common keywords is selected

The reverse will also happen. That is, if you open the "Latest Cameras" article, the "Cameras for Safari" article will appear under `Related Items`. In case we set the value of the `Show Date` field to `Show` (in the `Parameters` section), we will get the date of creation of the related articles along with their titles, as shown in Figure 8-43.

Related Items

- 2009-05-15 - Latest Cameras

Figure 8-43 The article titles along with their date of creation

If you don't see any module on the front end, confirm that it is enabled in the Module Manager, and also check that the `Menus` *option in the* `Menu Assignment` *section is not set to* `None`*. It is better to set the value of the* `Menus` *option to* `All` *to make the module appear on all menu items. In case the* `Menus` *options in* `Menu Assignment` *section is set to* `Select menu Item(s) from the List`*, then appropriate menu items must be selected to make the module appear on the front end.*

Search

This module displays a search box in which the user can enter a keyword for the information being sought on the website. This module works the same as the menu item type Internal Link: Search Layout. Figure 8-44 shows the Search module opened in edit mode.

Figure 8-44. Options of the Search module

The `Module Class Suffix` field is used for individual module styling. In the `Box Width` field, you specify the maximum number of characters for the search box. The default value is `20`. In the `Text` field, you specify the default text to appear in the search box. If it's left blank, the text `search...` will appear in the search box. If you set the `Search button` option to `Yes`, a search button will be displayed. The search button will be displayed beside the search box, as shown in Figure 8-45.

Figure 8-45. Search button displayed alongside the search box

If you set this option to `No`, the search button will not be displayed, and the search will begin when the user presses the Enter key. Let's set the value of this field to `No`.

The `Button Position` drop-down is used to select the position of the search button. The options are `Right`, `Left`, `Top`, and `Bottom`. This option is only useful when you want to display a search button; since we're not using a search button in this case, you can just leave the default value.

You can set the `Search button as image` option to `Yes` if you want the search button to appear as an image. In such a case, you need to specify the image that will appear as the search button. For that, you have to upload an image file with the name searchButton.gif in the images/M_images folder of the Media Manager. You set this option to `No` if you want the search button to appear as the default search button.

The `Button Text` field is used to specify the text to appear on the search button. If you leave it blank, the text `Search` will appear on the button, as in Figure 8-45. If you set the button text to, say, `Go` (provided the value of the `Search button` option is set to `Yes`), you get the output shown in Figure 8-46.

Figure 8-46. The button text set to Go

Since we have set the value of the `Search button` option to `No`, there is no point in assigning any button text, so let's leave the `Button Text` field blank. If you have kept the settings of the Search module as shown in Figure 8-44, the search box on the website will appear as shown in Figure 8-47. It displays a search box with the default text `search...` in it.

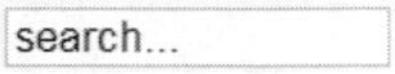

search...

Figure 8-47. The search box upon execution of the website

If you enter `Camera` in the search box and press Enter, you'll see all the articles that have the word *camera* in them, as shown in Figure 8-48.

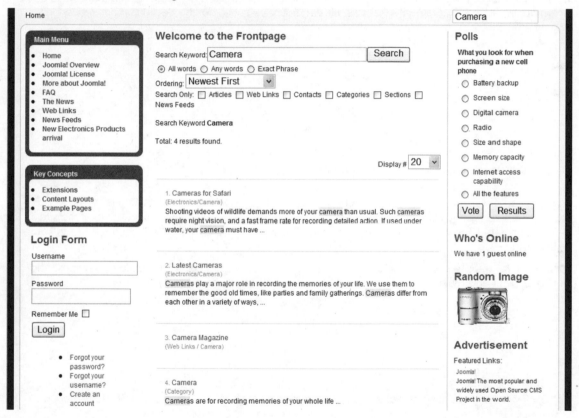

Figure 8-48. Display of all the articles that have *camera* in them

Sections

This module shows a list of all the sections in the website database. All the default sections provided by Joomla and the ones created by you using the Section Manager will be displayed (but only those that are in published mode). Figure 8-49 shows the `Parameters` section of the Sections module opened in edit mode.

Figure 8-49. Parameters section of the Sections module

In the `Count` field, you enter the number of sections to be displayed. The default value is `5`. The `Module Class Suffix` field is used to apply your own CSS class to certain modules, independent of the site's default template CSS classes. You can create a CSS class in the template CSS file and specify its name in this field.

Output on the website should appear as shown in Figure 8-50. It displays all the available sections, and you can select any to see the categories and finally the articles under them.

Sections

- Electronics
- News
- About Joomla!
- FAQs

Figure 8-50. All the existing sections of the website displayed upon execution of the Sections module

Statistics

This module shows a list of website statistics, including which operating system you're working on, which versions of PHP and MySQL you're using, your server time, and whether caching is enabled or disabled (see Figure 8-51).

Statistics

OS : Windows
PHP : 5.2.9
MySQL : 5.1.33-community
Time : 13:38
Caching : Disabled
GZIP : Disabled
Members : 2
Content : 43
Web Links : 7
Content View Hits : 662

Figure 8-51. Sample output of the Statistics module

Figure 8-52 shows the Statistics module opened in edit mode.

Figure 8-52. Options of the Statistics module

Set the value of the `Server Info` option to `Yes` to show server information. Also set `Site Info` to `Yes` to show site information. Set `Hit Counter` to `Yes` to show hit counter information. In the `Increase Counter` field, you enter a number to be added to the actual number of hits. The `Increase Counter` field is usually used when you want the hit counter to begin from a value other than the default 0. The `Module Class Suffix` field is used for individual module styling.

Syndication

This module creates an `RSS Feed` link for the page. This enables a user to create a news feed for the current page. Figure 8-53 shows the Syndication module opened in edit mode.

Before I describe the parameters, though, it's helpful to have a bit of background on RSS feeds. **RSS** stands for **Really Simple Syndication**. It's a technique by which visitors to your website can receive information about new and updated content on your website. It's the simplest way to have your information syndicated for others to read.

The procedure to syndicate your information is as follows:

1. First, you create an RSS feed for the information that you want to syndicate. Joomla has an integrated RSS feed; you just need to enable and configure it.
2. Then, visitors to your website add this feed to their RSS reader (known as an aggregator, which collects new content from your website and provides it to the visitor in a simple form). Joomla provides the Feed Display module for this purpose.
3. Whenever you add new content to your website, it's automatically sent directly to the readers—that is, it can be accessed via the Feed Display module.

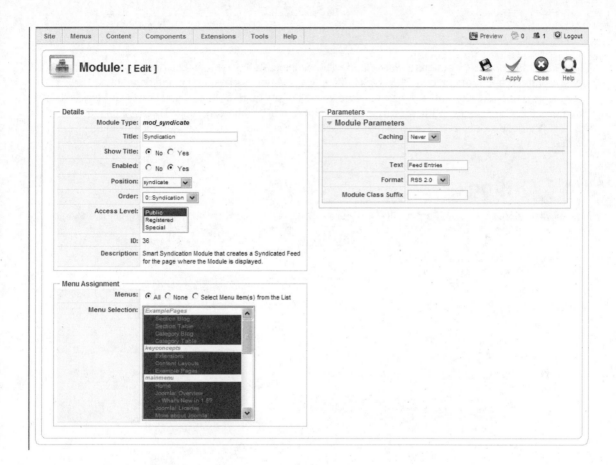

Figure 8-53. Options of the Syndication module

You can set the `Caching` option to `Never` to disable caching. In the `Text` field, you specify the text that you want to appear next to the `RSS` Link button. If you leave this field blank, the default text `Feed Entries` will appear. Alternatively, type a space inside double quotes (" ") if you don't want any text to appear. From the `Format` drop-down, you select the format of the news feed. The available options are `RSS 2.0` and `Atom 1.0`. As usual, the `Module Class Suffix` field is used for individual module styling.

Who's Online

This module displays information about users currently browsing the website. Figure 8-54 shows the Who's Online module opened in edit mode.

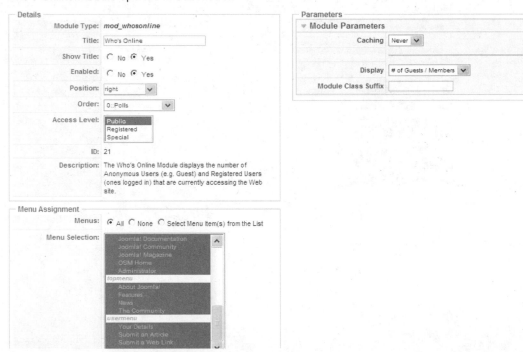

Figure 8-54. Options of the Who's Online module

The `Caching` field is set to `Never` by default as caching is usually disabled. The `Display` field is used to specify what is to be displayed. There are three options:

- `# of Guests / Members` displays the total number of guests (users who are not logged in) and members (users who are logged in), as shown in Figure 8-55.

- `Member Names` displays a list of the names of members logged in. No count of guests will be displayed, as shown in Figure 8-56.

- `Both` displays a count of users as well as a list of member names, as shown in Figure 8-57.

The `Module Class Suffix` field is used for individual module styling.

Who's Online

We have 1 member online

Figure 8-55. Count of members logged in

Who's Online

- roger

Figure 8-56. List of names of members logged in

Who's Online

We have 1 member online

- roger

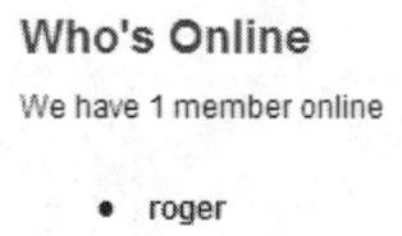

Figure 8-57. Count and names of online members displayed

Wrapper

This module is used to insert an external website into an iframe at the module position. An **iframe (inline frame)** is used for inserting frames (windows) into your web page, in which you can view another page inside your site. In other words, the Wrapper module enables you to visit an external website while remaining inside your website (both websites can be simultaneously accessed). If the external web page is bigger than the module, scrollbars will appear. This module provides functionality similar to the Internal Link: Wrapper Layout menu item type in the Menu Item Manager. Figure 8-58 shows the Wrapper module opened in edit mode.

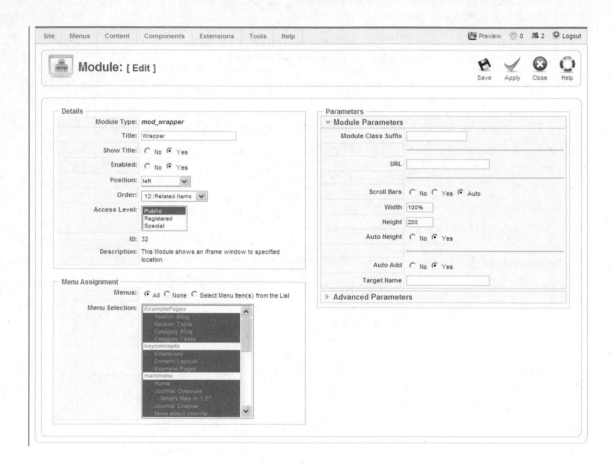

Figure 8-58. Options of the Wrapper module

The `Module Class Suffix` field is used for individual module styling. As usual, let's leave it blank.

In the `URL` field, you specify the URL of the website that you want to open in your web page. Let's specify the URL as http://bmharwani.com. The `Scroll Bars` option is used to decide whether to provide scrollbars for the iframe. If the setting is `Auto`, scrollbars will be provided automatically if required.

In the `Width` field, you enter the width of the iframe in pixels or as a percentage. Let's set it to `100%`. The `Height` field is used for specifying the height of the iframe in pixels. Let's set it to `400` pixels to have a better view of the external website. Set the `Auto Height` option to `Yes` since we want the height to automatically be set to the size of the external page.

The `Auto Add` option determines whether http: or https: is to be added to the beginning of the URL if it's missing. Set this field to `Yes`.

In the `Target Name` field, you specify the name of the iframe (it is optional). The name that you specify here can be used to display dynamic contents (contents of different websites) in the same iframe. In this case, let's leave it blank.

After setting the values as just discussed, the `Parameters` section of the module should appear as shown in Figure 8-59.

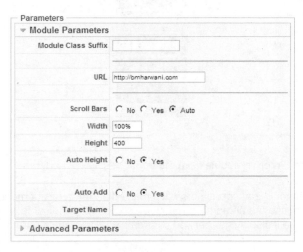

Figure 8-59. Parameters section of the Wrapper module

The output of the Wrapper module will appear as shown in Figure 8-60.

Figure 8-60. Output of the Wrapper module from the front end

The conclusion of this chapter is that Joomla provides many different types of modules, enabling you to create a fully functional website. As an administrator, you can enable or disable a module from the Module Manager, and you can make it display the desired information by setting its parameters.

Summary

In this chapter, you saw different built-in modules provided by Joomla and the roles they play in a website. You also saw how to set the parameters to get desired results.

In the next chapter, you will learn how to add more features to your website by installing different extensions. You will learn to download and install several extensions, including templates (to make your Joomla website appear more dynamic), e-commerce extensions (to create an online store and sell products via your website), an RSS feed reader (to get RSS feeds from the selected websites), and a chatting extension (to allow visitors of your website to communicate).

Chapter 9

Adding Extensions

In this chapter, you'll learn how to add more features to your Joomla website. To add a particular feature, you need to install the respective extension. Extensions are packages that can be downloaded from the Internet at no cost and easily installed on your Joomla website. Some examples of extensions are shopping carts, forums, social networking profiles, job boards, and estate listings. Basically, extensions are like add-ons to add features to your Joomla website that are not provided in the default Joomla package.

You'll learn how to download, install, and use the following extensions:

- Templates, to make your website appear more dynamic

- E-commerce extensions, to maintain an online store and sell products via your website

- RSS feed readers, to receive RSS feeds periodically from the selected websites

- Chatting, to allow visitors to your website to converse with one another

Extension Manager

Extensions, as the name suggests, are packages meant for extending features of a Joomla website. There are many extensions available on the Internet, ranging from large, complex components to small, lightweight modules and plug-ins. You can add features like chatting functionality, a discussion forum, or a shopping cart to your website by installing the respective extension. All types of extensions, as described in the following list, can be installed or uninstalled with the help of the Extension Manager.

- **Components**: A component is an independent application with its own functionality, database, and presentation. Installing a component in your website is just like adding an application to your website. For example, forums, shopping carts, newsletters, and guest books are all examples of components. A component may consist of one or more modules.

- **Modules**: Modules are meant for adding functions (features) to an existing component (application) of your website—for example, a login module, a sign-in module of a guest book component, a subscription module of a newsletter component, or a digital counter module of a guest book component. A module is one running unit of an application, and cannot be a stand-alone component.

- **Plug-ins**: Plug-ins were called mambots in Joomla 1.0.x, but since Joomla 1.5.x, they're called plug-ins. A plug-in is a function that can be applied to a particular component or an entire website—for example, a search plug-in that can be used by visitors to search our forum, or a bookmark plug-in to place bookmarks on desired contents of our website.

> *To understand the differences among components, modules, and plug-ins, consider this example: the shopping cart is a component that has several modules, including modules for maintaining inventory, storing payment information, and printing bills. Plug-ins can be added to the shopping cart component, including a plug-in to change the price of a particular product, or a search plug-in to enable searching for a desired product from the shopping cart.*

- **Languages**: This type of extension provides a facility for presenting the front end and back end of Joomla in any desired language. That is, you can present your Joomla website in different languages without much effort.

- **Templates**: The purpose of a template is to give a dynamic appearance to your website. A template contains the style sheets, locations, and layout of the web contents being displayed. It separates the appearance of the website from its content.

Let's open the Extension Manager by selecting `Extensions ➤ Install/Uninstall`. You'll see a screen like that shown in Figure 9-1.

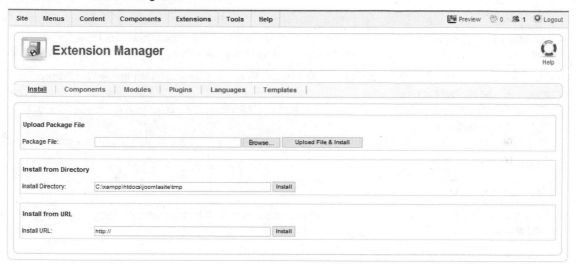

Figure 9-1. Extension Manager

The `Install` tab enables you to install all types of extensions. The remaining tabs—`Components`, `Modules`, `Plugins`, `Languages`, and `Templates`—are for uninstalling the respective extensions. That is, if you click the `Components` tab, you'll see a list of all the components installed on your Joomla website along with an `Uninstall` icon in the toolbar; you can then select any component from the list and click the `Uninstall` icon to remove it.

> *In Joomla 1.5, you can install an extension from any location on the Internet by providing the URL of the extension's installation package. That is, you can install an extension without downloading it to your local disk drive.*

Installing extensions

Joomla extensions can be installed using any of three methods:

- Package file

- Install directory

- Install URL

Let's take a quick look through the advantages and disadvantages of each method.

Package file

We use this method when we prefer installing the extension without unpacking the archive file. However, this method takes a long time to install the extension to a hosted website (on a remote server). The steps to follow are

1. Download one or more archive files (normally in .zip or tar.gz format) from the extension provider's website to your local disk drive.
2. Click the `Browse` button to specify the location to which the extension's archive file is to be downloaded.
3. Click the `Upload File & Install` button. Joomla will read the contents of the archive file and install the extension.

Install directory

Using this method, we unpack the archive file into a directory and upload that directory onto the server. The steps are

1. Download the extension's archive file to your local disk drive.
2. Create a temporary directory on the local disk drive and unpack the extension's archive file into this temporary directory.
3. Using FTP, upload the contents of this directory (including files and subdirectories) to a directory on the server.
4. In the `Install Directory` field, specify the directory to which you uploaded the files and subdirectories of the package.
5. Click the `Install` button. Joomla will install the contents of the given directory.

Install URL

Using this method, you don't download the archive file to your local computer, but instead just specify the URL of the target archive file. Then you click the `Install` button, and Joomla will automatically install the extension directly from this URL. This method is preferred when installing the extension on a hosted website (remote server). The archive file of the extension (to be installed on the website) is first uploaded to the remote domain, and then its URL is specified in the `Install URL` box.

When installation is done, the screen displays the message `Install Component Success`. If the installation is not successful, an error message is displayed.

By default, the newly installed extension is in unpublished mode, so we need to enable it from the respective manager, such as from the Module Manager or Plugin Manager.

Installing new templates

You can download any of hundreds of attractive templates that are available on the Internet. Let's download the CompuMan template, which is a free Joomla 1.5.x template. Its archive file is named

CompuMan.zip. Download it from www.joomportal.com to a folder on your local disk drive. Open the Extension Manager by selecting Extensions ➤ Install/Uninstall. Click the Install tab and, in the Package File area, click the Browse button to locate the archive file of the CompuMan template, as shown in Figure 9-2.

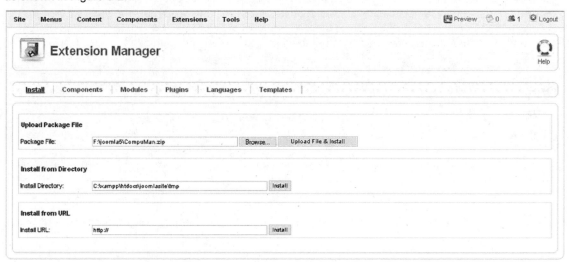

Figure 9-2. Locating the archive file of the CompuMan template

After specifying the template archive file, CompuMan.zip, click the Upload File & Install button to install the template. If the template is successfully installed, you'll see the message Install Template Success, as shown in Figure 9-3.

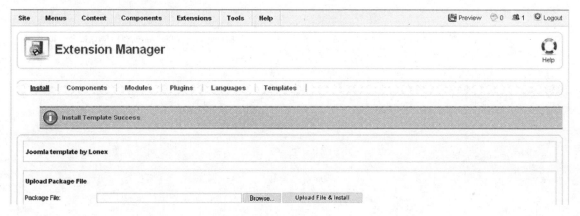

Figure 9-3. Message upon successful installation of the template

To apply the newly installed template to your website, you use the Template Manager, which you invoke by selecting `Extensions` ➤ `Template Manager`. The Template Manager opens, and you'll find that besides the three default templates provided by Joomla (beez, JA-Purity, and rhuk_milkyway), a new template named CompuMan also appears in the list, as shown in Figure 9-4. Let's select `CompuMan` from the list, and click the `Default` icon in the toolbar to make it the default template.

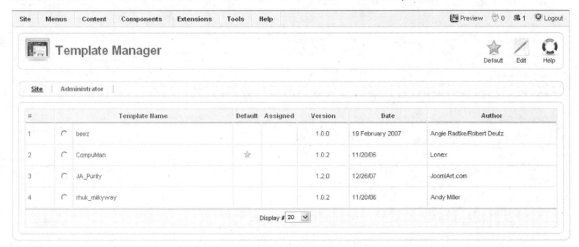

Figure 9-4. Newly installed template CompuMan listed in Template Manager

Now we're ready to see the impact of the newly applied template from the front end. Let's open the browser and point it to the address http://localhost/joomlasite to open our Joomla site's front end (alternatively, you can use the `Preview` button at the top right). Notice that our Joomla website's front end has changed, and the position of all the website contents—that is, menus and other components—are set according to the layout specified in the CompuMan template (as shown in Figure 9-5).

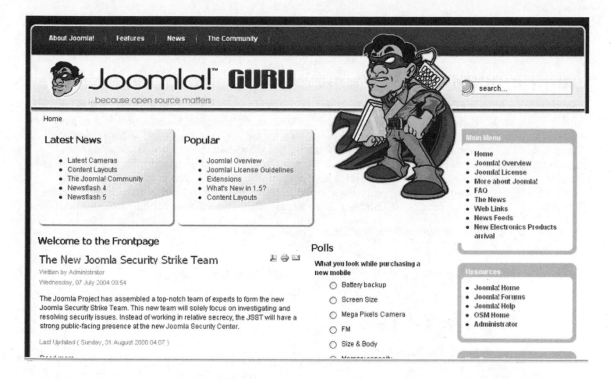

Figure 9-5. The impact of applying the CompuMan template on the front end of our Joomla website

So, you should see how easy it is to download and apply new templates to your website. Since we will be using the rhuk_milkyway template for the rest of the examples in this chapter, let's make it the default template again using the Template Manager.

Now let's make our website able to do some business selling certain products and services.

Adding e-commerce

Most of the websites that we see on the Internet do some type of e-commerce—that is, they publicize their products and services through the Internet and eventually do some business. E-commerce is a heavily desired feature in almost all websites. To add an e-commerce system to our website, we can download one of hundreds of components available on the Internet. I've downloaded one named VirtueMart. Its archive file is available on the Internet at http://virtuemart.net/, and the one I've used in this book is named VirtueMart_1[1].1.3-COMPLETE_PACKAGE.j15.zip. When you unzip this file, you will find two folders: modules and plugins, along with a file, com_virtuemart_1.1.3.j15.zip, which is the actual installation package. The VirtueMart component provides a complete store system. Its features include the following:

- You can have an unlimited hierarchy of products—that is, a category within a category, and so on.

- You can specify attributes of products, such as width, height, and color.

- You can use different currencies.

- You can specify different shipment methods.

- The component uses SSL encryption.

- You can do complete administration of inventory.

We'll see how the VirtueMart component can be installed on a hosted website rather than on a website located on a local server. You can use the package file method to specify the location of VirtueMart's archive file, but it may take a long time to install. A better option is to upload the archive file to your website. Assuming that the domain name of your website is bmharwani.net, you upload the archive file to this domain. Now, to install the component, you need to specify its location, http://www.bmharwani.net/com_virtuemart_1.1.3.j15.zip, in the `Install URL` field, and click the `Install` button, as shown in Figure 9-6.

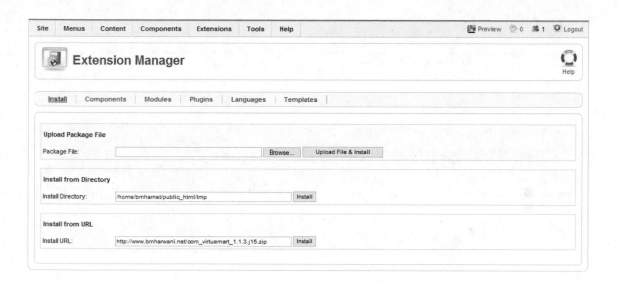

Figure 9-6. Specifying the location of the archive file for the VirtueMart component

The VirtueMart component is installed, and you'll see the message Install Component Success, as shown in Figure 9-7. Two buttons, Go directly to the Shop and Install SAMPLE DATA, enable you to decide whether you want to have an empty store or one with some dummy products. If you click the latter button, a wide range of products in different categories will be installed on your Joomla website, and the visitor will be able to view and purchase any of them. Instead, click Go directly to the Shop to have an empty store in which you can create your own product categories and add products of your own choosing to those categories.

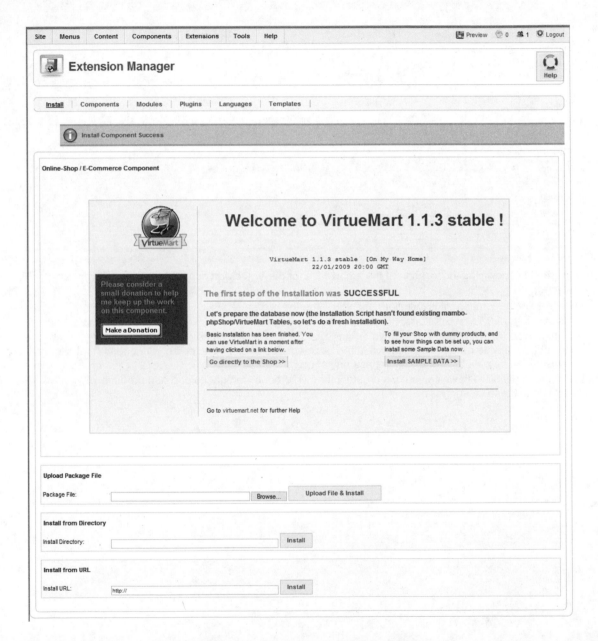

Figure 9-7. Welcome screen of VirtueMart displayed on successful installation

> *After successful installation of VirtueMart, it is accessible from the `Components` menu in the Administrator interface.*

The process of creating tables begins when you click the `Go directly to the Shop` button. These tables are required for keeping records of products, customers, and so on, so you'll see a message not to interrupt the next step (of table creation), as shown in Figure 9-8.

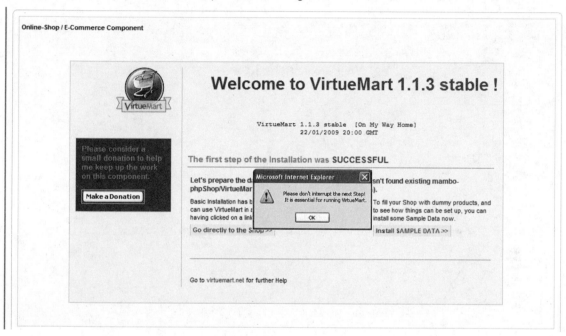

Figure 9-8. Dialog box asking you not to interrupt during the creation of tables

So click the `OK` button in the dialog box and wait until all the necessary tables are created. When all the tables and other configuration files required for e-commerce are created, you'll see the Control Panel for your store, as shown in Figure 9-9. The Control Panel contains icons for viewing and managing a product list, categories of products, orders placed, different payment methods, vendors, users, and so on. That is, all the maintenance tasks of e-commerce are performed here.

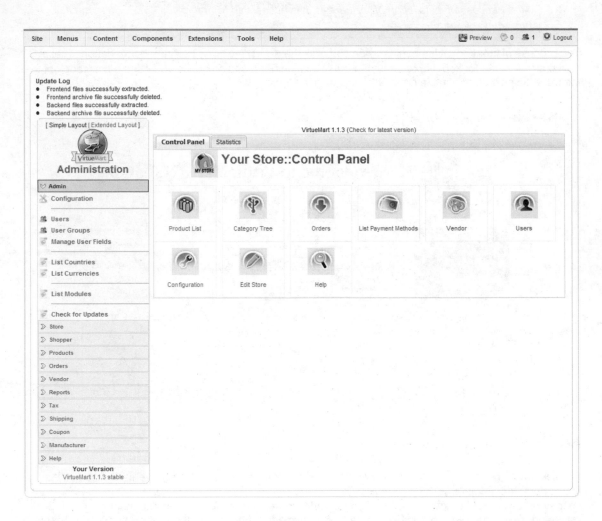

Figure 9-9. Control Panel of the store

Click the `Category Tree` icon to create different categories of products to be sold on your website. You should see a screen like the one shown in Figure 9-10. Notice that there are currently no categories in the category tree. You can create a new category by clicking the `New` icon in the toolbar. The remaining three icons in the toolbar, `Publish`, `Unpublish`, and `Remove`, are for publishing (displaying the products of the selected category), unpublishing (making the products of the selected category invisible), and removing the selected category, respectively.

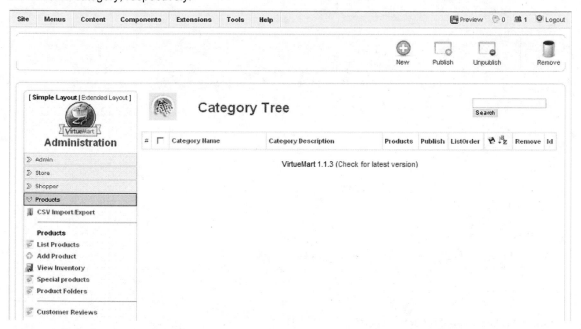

Figure 9-10. Category tree, currently blank

Upon clicking the `New` icon, you'll see a screen for creating a new category, as shown in Figure 9-11. The screen prompts for the category name and a description of it. You'll find that the `Publish` check box is already checked so as to display the category on the front end. Usually the newly added category appears last in the category tree, but you can easily change its order later if desired. We don't have any other categories, so we don't have to worry about ordering. Let's assume we want to sell products belonging to two categories: Tutorials CD and Computer Books. We create the first category by specifying the `Category Name` as `Tutorials CD`. In the `Category Description` column, enter a brief description of the category, as shown in Figure 9-11.

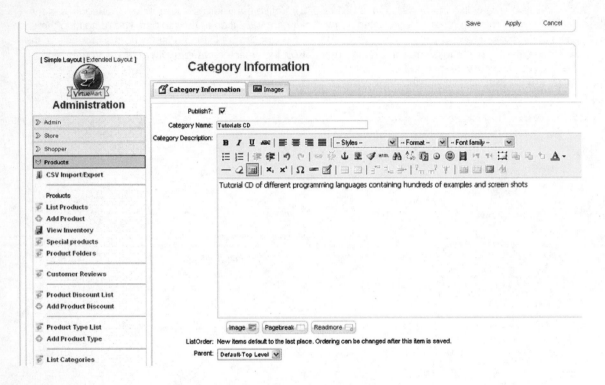

Figure 9-11. Creation of a new category, Tutorials CD

After entering the information for Tutorials CD, save it by clicking the `Save` icon in the toolbar. Using the same technique, create another category, named `Computer Books`. Our category tree now contains two categories, as shown in Figure 9-12.

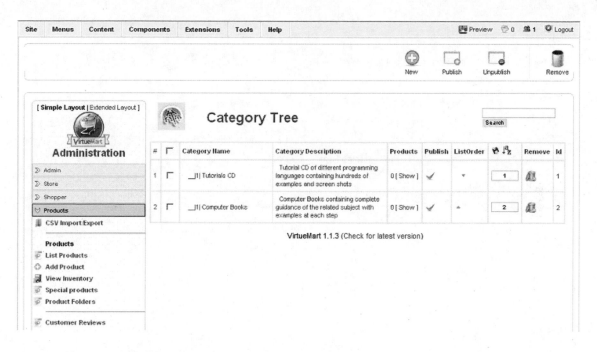

Figure 9-12. Two categories added to the category tree

To add products to these two newly created categories, click `Products` in the menu on the left. The `Products` menu will expand. From the expanded menu, select the menu item `List Products`. This will open the `Product List` screen. The product list is currently blank, since no product is present in the store. Notice in Figure 9-13 that this screen enables you to search for products with a particular keyword (if the volume of products is large). Also, you can look for products that have been added/modified before or after a particular date. These facilities are not applicable here, so click the `New` icon to add a new product. A new product can also be added by selecting the `Add Product` menu item from the menu on the left.

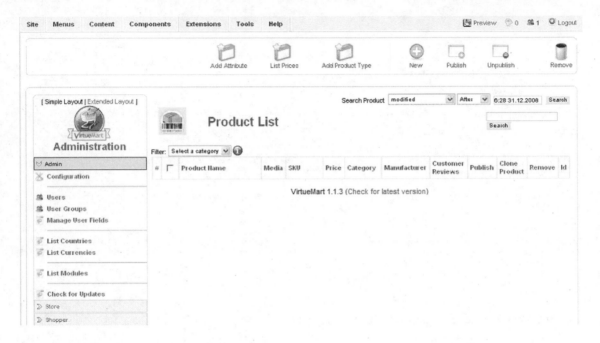

Figure 9-13. The product list, currently blank

You'll see a screen for specifying product information, which you can enter as follows:

- SKU: **SKU** is a common abbreviation used in catalog systems for **stock-keeping unit**. In the SKU field, enter a unique ID for the product—in this case, 101.

- Name: Name the product Unix Tutorial CD.

- URL: This field allows the visitor to navigate to a web page to see details of the products. In this case, you can leave it blank.

- Vendor: This is the name of the vendor supplying the product. It's not editable, so leave it as Washupito's Tiendita (the default).

- Manufacturer: This is the name of the manufacturer of the product. Let's keep it as Manufacturer (the default).

- Categories: In this box, you specify the category to which this product belongs. Let's select the category Tutorials CD.

- `Product Price (Net)`: Enter the price as `10`, and the currency for all of the prices for the product as `US Dollar`.

- `Product Price (Gross)`: Specify the gross product price as `10`.

- `VAT Id`: Since we don't have a VAT ID, leave it as `0 (none)`.

- `Discounted Price`: Set the discounted price to `9`.

- `Short Description`: In this box, you can include a short introduction of the product (that doesn't includes images).

- `Product Description`: Here, you enter a product description. This is a detailed description that can include images of the product, too.

After entering the information as shown in Figure 9-14, save it. Notice the other tabs at the top of the `New Product` window: `Display Options`, `Product Status`, `Product Dimensions and Weight`, `Product Images`, and so on. These tabs can be used to supply a lot more information about the product.

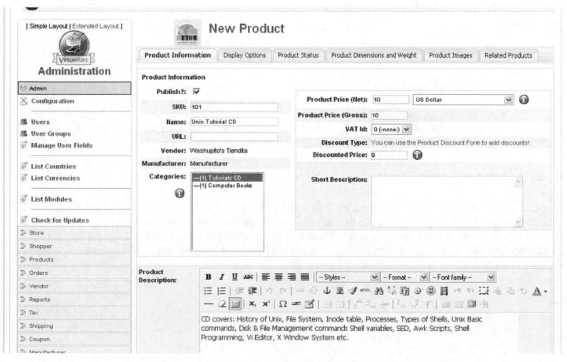

Figure 9-14. Adding a new product, Unix Tutorial CD, in the Tutorials CD category

On saving the product, you'll see a message confirming that the new product price along with the other product information has been added, as shown in Figure 9-15.

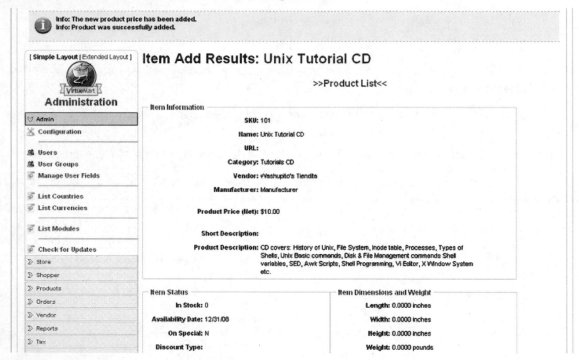

Figure 9-15. Message confirming the creation of product Unix Tutorial CD

To include an image for the next product we'll be adding, we need to load the image into the images/stories folder of the Media Manager. Assuming that we have an image in a file named datastucd.jpg, we open the Media Manager and select the stories folder. Click the Browse button (in the Upload File section) to locate the JPG file, and click the Start Upload button to upload that file into the images/stories folder, as shown in Figure 9-16.

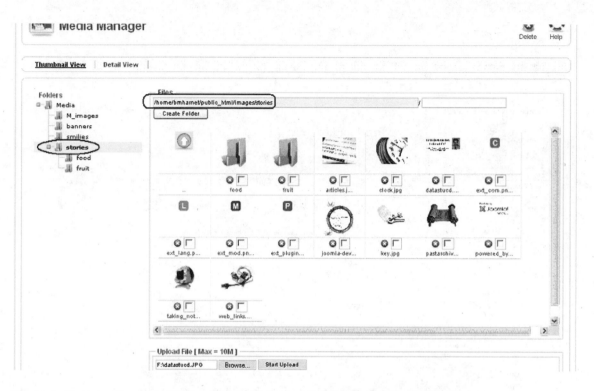

Figure 9-16. Uploading a product image into the images/stories folder of the Media Manager

Go back to the product list by selecting the `Products` tab in the menu on the left side and selecting the menu item `List Products` (refer to Figure 9-12). Here you'll find that our first new product, Unix Tutorial CD, in the Tutorials CD category, has been added, as shown in Figure 9-17.

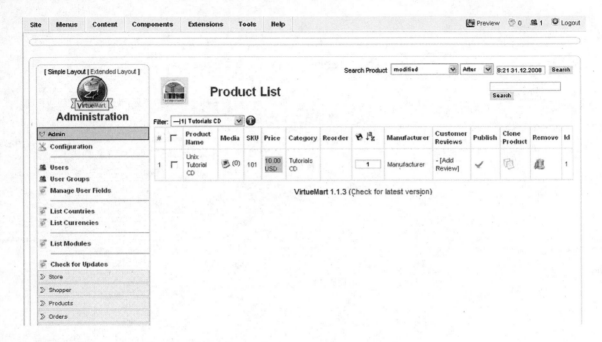

Figure 9-17. The product Unix Tutorial CD displayed in the product list

Let's enter information for another product, Data Structures Tutorial CD, by selecting the `Add Product` menu item from the menu on the left side. (If you don't find the `Add Product` menu item, select the `Products` tab in the menu to expand it, and you will see several menu items, along with `Add Product`). Let's enter the information about the new product as follows:

- `SKU`: As a unique ID for this product, enter `102`.

- `Name`: Enter `Data Structures Tutorial CD`.

- `URL`: Since we're not allowing the user to navigate to a web page to see details for this product, leave this field blank.

- `Vendor` **and** `Manufacturer`: Leave the vendor and manufacturer of the product at the defaults, `Washupito's Tiendita` and `Manufacturer`.

- `Categories`: Select `Tutorials CD` for the category for the product.

- `Product Price (Net)`: Enter `15`, and set the currency to `US Dollar`.

- `Product Price (Gross)`: Enter `15`.

- `Vat Id`: **Leave this at** `0` `(none)`.

- `Discounted Price`: **Leave this field blank (since we don't want to provide any discount for this product).**

- `Short Description`: **You can provide a very short introduction to the product (without an image). For this exercise, leave it blank.**

- `Product Description`: **Enter a detailed product description that may include the image(s) of the product, too.**

The information entered should look similar to Figure 9-18.

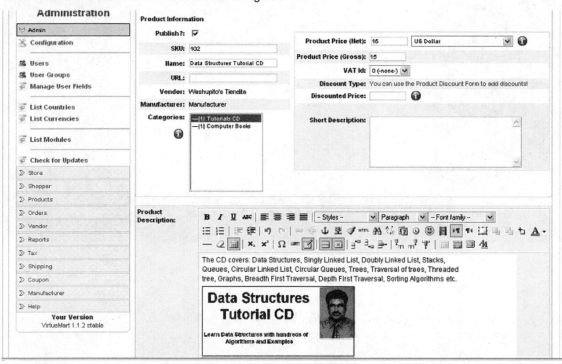

Figure 9-18. Creation of the Data Structures Tutorial CD product in the Tutorial CD category

To insert an image into the `Product Description` box, click the `Image` button below the rich text editor (similar to the one below the `Category Description` box in Figure 9-11).

The thumbnails of the images in the Media Manager will be displayed. In the `Image URL` field, select the image file you just loaded, datastucd.jpg, from the images/stories folder, to insert the picture into the product description (see Figure 9-19).

> *If you use the `Image` icon (which looks like a cactus tree) from among the tools in the editor box, then you'll get a different image load dialog box, which asks for the URL of the image (usually used to specify the images on the Internet).*

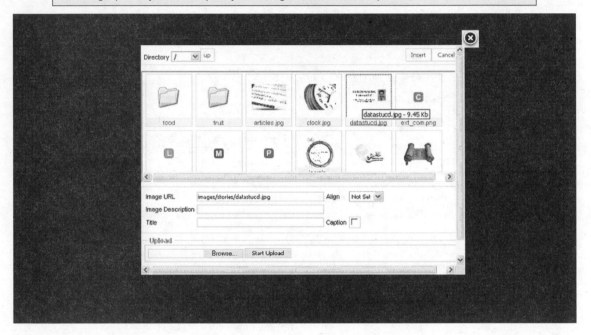

Figure 9-19. Screen for specifying the product image, opened upon clicking the Image icon in the Product Description area

After providing the information for the new product, as shown in Figure 9-18, save it. Again, you'll see a message confirming that the new product price along with the other product information has been added, as shown in Figure 9-20.

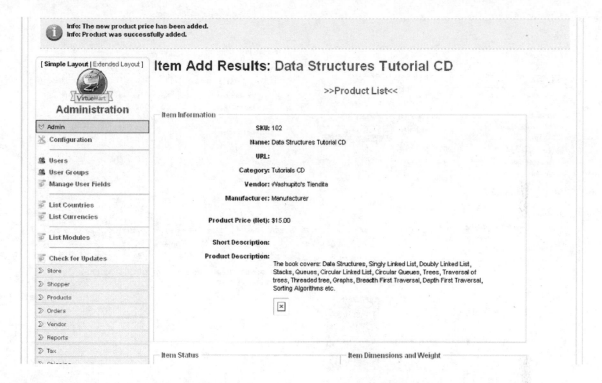

Figure 9-20. Message confirming the creation of the Data Structures Tutorial CD product

Up till now, we've been adding products of the category `Tutorials CD`. Now we'll add two products to the category `Computer Books`. Figure 9-21 shows the information entered to define a book product named 'C' Programming.

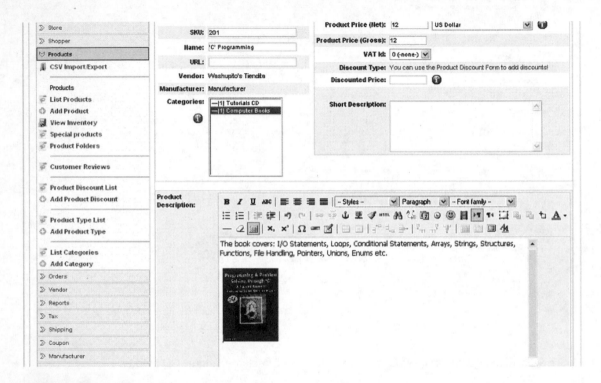

Figure 9-21. Adding the 'C' Programming product to the Computer Books category

Using the same technique, we'll define another product in the Computer Books category, named Business Systems, with a SKU of 202 and a price of $7. Now we have two categories defined in our online store, Tutorials CD and Computer Books, and each category has two products: Unix Tutorial CD and Data Structures Tutorial CD in the Tutorials CD category, and 'C' Programming and Business Systems in the Computer Books category.

Now it's time to access this VirtueMart component from the front end (our website). To do this, you need to install the component's module. The archive file for the VirtueMart module is named mod_virtuemart_1.1.2.j15.zip. Recall that on unzipping the VirtueMart archive file we downloaded (VirtueMart_1[1].1.3-COMPLETE_PACKAGE.j15.zip), we got two folders: modules and plugins, along with the file com_virtuemart_1.1.3.j15.zip. In the modules folder, along with several other files, is the module file mod_virtuemart_1.1.2.j15.zip . Let's upload it to the domain bmharwani.net. Open the Extension Manager by selecting Extensions ➤ Install/Uninstall. Specify the module file name along with the domain name in the Install URL field, and click the Install button to install the VirtueMart module, as shown in Figure 9-22.

Figure 9-22. Specifying the location of the VirtueMart module in the Extension Manager

You'll see the message `Install Module Success`, as shown in Figure 9-23, indicating that you'll find this module on the front end of your website.

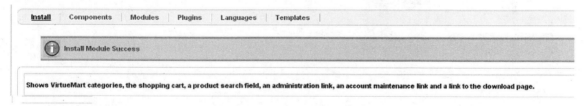

Figure 9-23. Message indicating successful installation of the VirtueMart module

But one step is still left. As shown in Figure 9-24, the newly added modules are in unpublished mode; that is, although they're installed on our website, they won't be displayed on the screen.

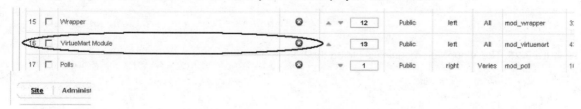

Figure 9-24. VirtueMart module listed in the Module Manager in unpublished mode by default

To set the VirtueMart module to published mode, open the Module Manager by selecting `Extensions` ➤ `Module Manager`. Select the check box of the VirtueMart module and click the `Enable` icon in the toolbar to make the module visible from the front end. Now if you open the front end by pointing the browser at the address http://localhost/joomlasite, or select the `Preview` button from the Administrator interface, you'll find that the VirtueMart module appears, along with the two categories of products, Tutorials CD and Computer Books, as shown in Figure 9-25.

Feed Display

No Feed URL specified.

Main Menu

- Home
- Joomla! Overview
- Joomla! License
- More about Joomla!
- FAQ
- The News
- Web Links
- News Feeds
- New Electronics Products arrival

Key Concepts

- Extensions
- Content Layouts
- Example Pages

VirtueMart Module

Tutorials CD
Computer Books

List All Products

Product Search

Search

Advanced Search

Show Cart
Your Cart is currently empty.

Latest News

- CDMA Cell Phones
- Autotracking Cell Phones
- Java Supported Cell Phone
- Cameras for Safari
- Web Cams - Video chatting

Cameras for Safari

Written by Administrator
Friday, 15 May 2009 07:45

Page 1 of 2
Shooting videos of wildlife demands more of your camera than usual. Such cameras require night vision, and a fast frame rate for recording detailed action.

Prev - Next >>

Last Updated on Saturday, 30 May 2009 13:09

Widest range

Article Index

Cameras for Safari
safari-2
All Pages

Random Image

Figure 9-25. The VirtueMart module visible on the front end

If you click the `Tutorials CD` link, it will display all the products in this category, as shown in Figure 9-26. Both products, Data Structures Tutorial CD and Unix Tutorial CD, will appear in the list. The products names are in the form of links that can be clicked to show detailed information for the product.

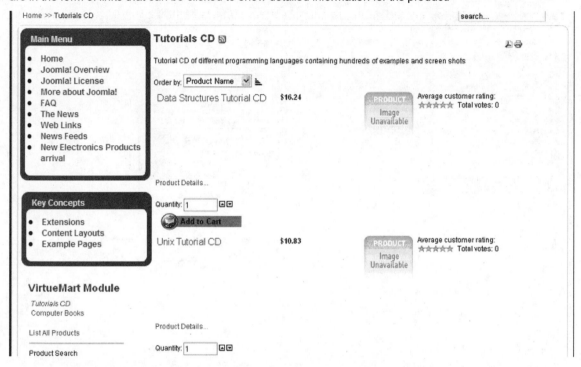

Figure 9-26. The products of the Tutorials CD category displayed

You can specify the desired quantity of a product in the `Quantity` field and click the `Add to Cart` button to add the product to the cart. You can also click the product name to see its details. Let's click `Data Structures Tutorial CD` to see the detailed information for it, along with the image and description, as shown in Figure 9-27.

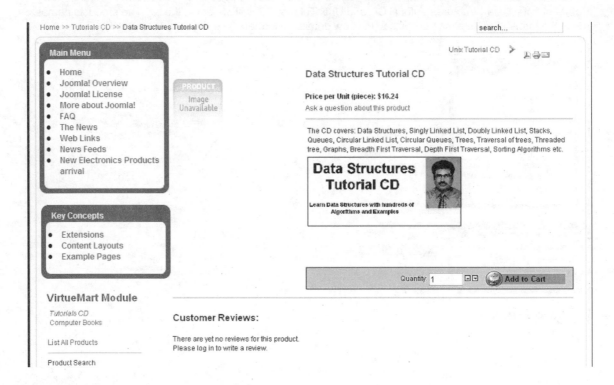

Figure 9-27. Detailed information for the Data Structures Tutorial CD product

You can select the product in the shopping cart at the time of product listing as well as when the details of an individual product are being displayed. You just need to specify the desired quantity of the selected product and click the Add to Cart button. Let's enter 1 in the Quantity field for this product and click the Add to Cart button. You'll see a screen showing that the product has been added to the cart, as shown in Figure 9-28.

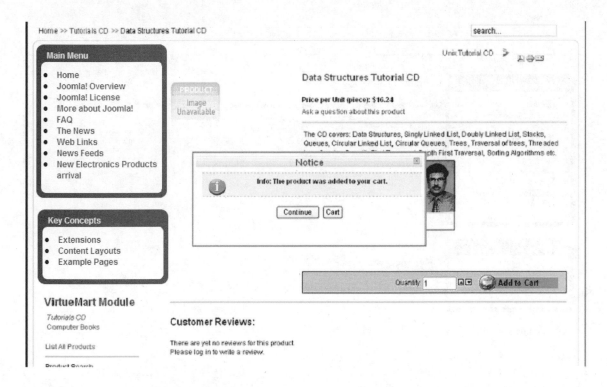

Figure 9-28. Message that the product has been added to the shopping cart

Two buttons are displayed in the dialog box: `Continue` and `Cart`. The `Continue` button is for viewing more products for shopping purposes, and the `Cart` button is for displaying the products in the shopping cart. Let's click the `Continue` button to see more products. This time, select `Computer Books` to see all the computer books that are available for sale on our website. The list of the books should look something like Figure 9-29.

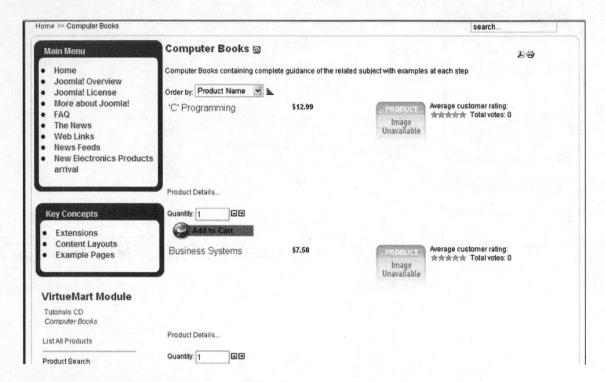

Figure 9-29. The products of the Computer Books category displayed

You can either select any book title to see its detailed information or directly select any book by specifying the quantity in the `Quantity` field for the product you want to purchase, and then click the `Add to Cart` button. Let's select `'C' Programming` to see the detailed information about the book, as shown in Figure 9-30.

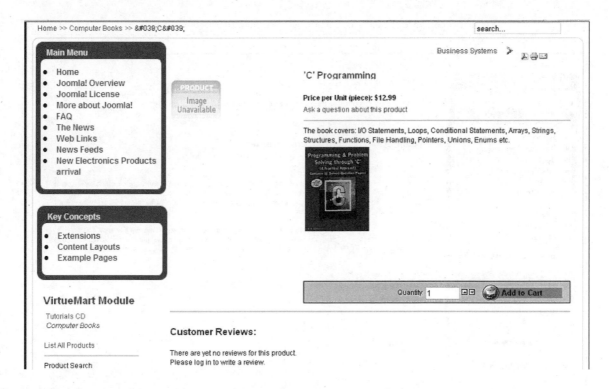

Figure 9-30. Detailed information of product 'C' Programming

Let's also add this book to our shopping cart, by specifying its quantity as 1 in the Quantity field and clicking the Add to Cart button. Again, you'll see the screen showing that the product has been added to the cart, along with the Continue and Cart buttons. Again, click Continue to see more products.

The VirtueMart module provides a link, Advanced Search (refer to the bottom left of Figure 9-25), that can be used for searching for products with the given keyword in the specific category. If you click the Advanced Search link, you'll see a screen like that shown in Figure 9-31.

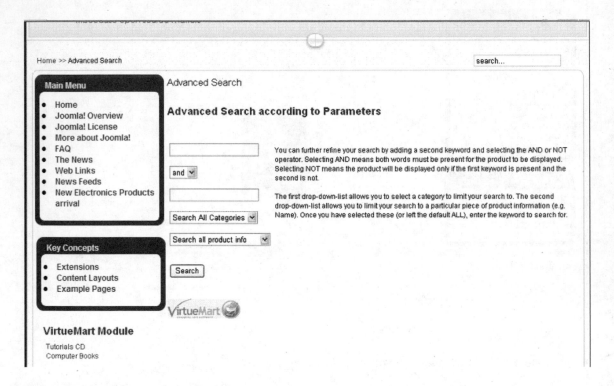

Figure 9-31. Advanced Search window

On this screen, you can enter a keyword for the product you're looking for. There are two text boxes so that you can perform a more advanced search by specifying an additional keyword. The two keywords can be connected with an "and" or "or" operator to search the desired product more accurately. You can also select a category to which to confine your search for the product.

Let's click the `Show Cart` link in the VirtueMart module (shown marked in Figure 9-32) to see the items that are in our shopping cart. Note that below this link is the count of the products in the cart along with their total price.

VirtueMart Module

Tutorials CD
Computer Books

List All Products

Product Search

[   ]

[Search]

Advanced Search

Show Cart
2 Products $29.23

Figure 9-32. The number of products in the cart along with their total price

Upon clicking the `Show Cart` link, you'll see a list of the products in your shopping cart. Before confirming the order, you can update the quantity of a selected product—that is, increase or decrease its quantity in the cart—or remove any product from the cart by clicking the `Remove` icon for that product. The tax is also automatically computed, according to the default tax rate. You can edit/enter the tax rates by clicking the `Tax` link in the menu on the left in the Administrator interface (refer back to Figure 9-21). In Figure 9-33, notice that below the list of products in your shopping cart is a `Checkout` link, which is used for confirming the order and leaving the module.

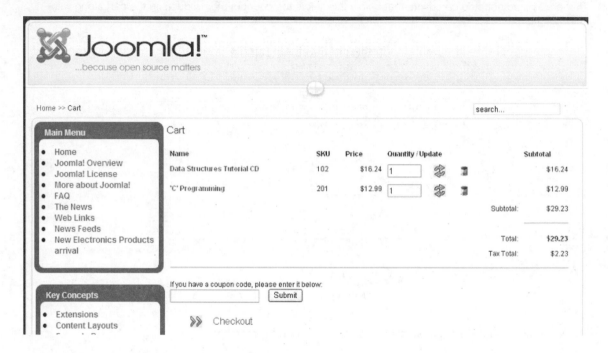

Figure 9-33. The list of products in the shopping cart

Before placing the order, the user has to be registered. On selecting the `Checkout` link, the user will be prompted to authenticate by entering a username and password on the screen that appears (see Figure 9-34). If the user has already created his or her account, there is no need to provide billing information, since this information is picked up from the account. Let's click the link `New? Please Provide Your Billing Information` to create a new account.

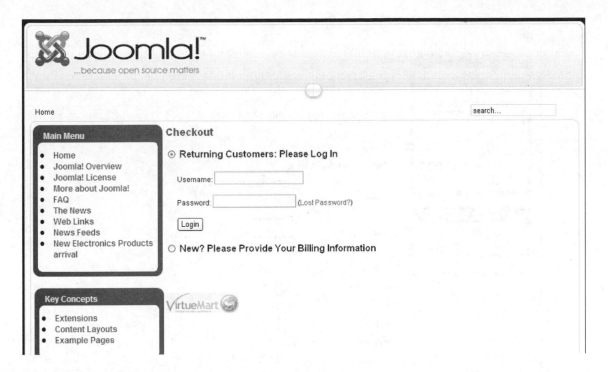

Figure 9-34. Screen for user authentication when checking out

Upon clicking the link New? Please Provide Your Billing Information, you'll see a screen for providing an e-mail address, username, and password, along with the address and other information for billing purposes, as shown in Figure 9-35. This information will be used when you make purchases in the future.

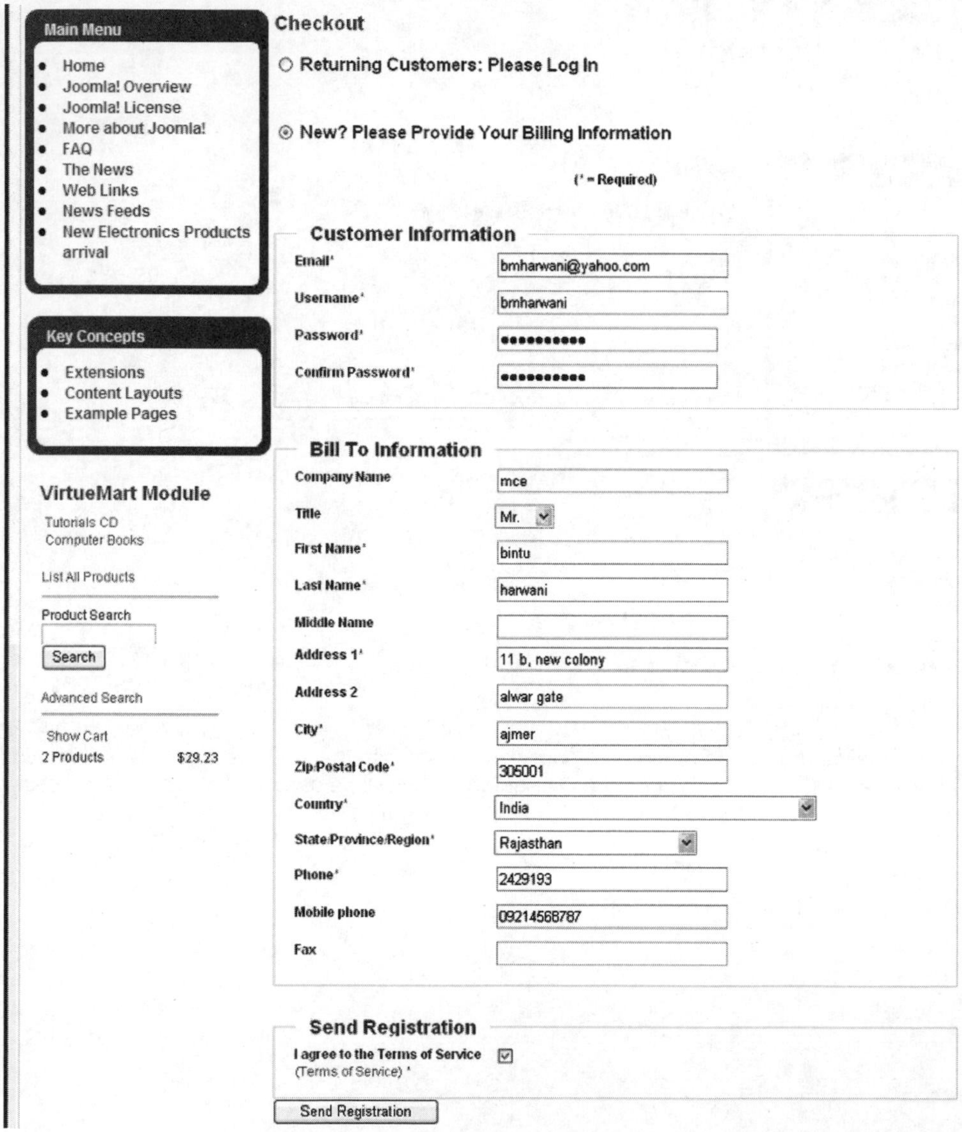

Main Menu

- Home
- Joomla! Overview
- Joomla! License
- More about Joomla!
- FAQ
- The News
- Web Links
- News Feeds
- New Electronics Products arrival

Key Concepts

- Extensions
- Content Layouts
- Example Pages

VirtueMart Module

Tutorials CD
Computer Books

List All Products

Product Search

[   ]
[Search]

Advanced Search

Show Cart
2 Products $29.23

Checkout

○ **Returning Customers: Please Log In**

◉ **New? Please Provide Your Billing Information**

(' = Required)

Customer Information

Email'	bmharwani@yahoo.com
Username'	bmharwani
Password'	••••••••••
Confirm Password'	••••••••••

Bill To Information

Company Name	mce
Title	Mr.
First Name'	bintu
Last Name'	harwani
Middle Name	
Address 1'	11 b, new colony
Address 2	alwar gate
City'	ajmer
Zip/Postal Code'	305001
Country'	India
State/Province/Region'	Rajasthan
Phone'	2429193
Mobile phone	09214568787
Fax	

Send Registration

I agree to the Terms of Service ☑
(Terms of Service) '

[Send Registration]

Figure 9-35. Customer and billing information entered on registration form, creating a new account

After entering the required information, click the `Send Registration` button. Don't forget to select the check box `I agree to the Terms of Service`, or else the account will not be created. An e-mail will be sent to you with a validation link, which needs to be clicked in order for the account to be activated. Again, you should see the list of products in the cart, with a `Checkout` link at the bottom. Upon clicking the `Checkout` link, you'll be prompted to authenticate by entering a username and password. Enter the username and password you specified when registering. Then you'll be prompted to specify the dispatch and payment terms, as well as the credit card details. Finally, click the `Confirm order` button to place the order. The VirtueMart module will display a `Thanks` message to ensure that the transaction was successful.

Installing an RSS feed reader

Joomla provides a feed reader for reading RSS feeds, but if you need more flexibility, you can install any of the RSS feed reader modules freely available on the Internet. In this section, you'll learn how to install an RSS feed reader module named Simple RSS Feed Reader, developed by JoomlaWorks (www.joomlaworks.gr) and released under the GNU General Public License. Simple RSS Feed Reader is based on the SimplePie PHP class. It supports both RSS and Atom formats. With an efficient caching system, it displays feeds quite fast. Upon selecting this module on the Internet, you'll see an introductory description, as shown in Figure 9-36.

Simple RSS Feed Reader - Easy and stylish content syndication!

★ ★ ★ ★ ☆ (189 votes)

Monday, 29 January 2007

If you came here via the menu link on the LEFT, then you should see the module in action, right BELOW this article. If you came here cause you clicked the "Read More" link, click again on the relevant menu item on the LEFT!

simple
rss feed
reader
by JoomlaWorks

Adding RSS syndicated content inside your Joomla! website is now super-easy and simple with the "Simple RSS Feed Reader" Module from JoomlaWorks. All you have to do is insert the Feed (RSS) URLs of the websites you want to syndicate in the module's settings, publish the module in some position and that's it!

No messing with the code and no worrying about feed encoding. You can publish right away english along with japanese feeds and have nothing to worry about!

The "**Simple RSS Feed Reader**" module is based on the very popular **SimplePie PHP Class**, which makes it easy to integrate syndicated content into your Joomla! website — and you don't even have to worry about what kind of feed it is! The "**Simple RSS Feed Reader**" module supports everything from the old-school RSS 0.91 and RSS 1.0 formats, to the ever-popular RSS 2.0 format, and also supports the emerging Atom format, in both 0.3 and 1.0 flavors. It has a very fast, very efficient caching system. By caching the processed data, rather than just the raw XML, the module is able to create a feed parser that's really, really quick.

The feeds are stored inside Joomla!'s **cache** folder and refreshed in a specific time interval, which you set in the module's parameters.

Figure 9-36. Introductory screen for the Simple RSS Feed Reader module

The module's archive file as I've downloaded it from the Internet is mod_jw_srfr-v1[1].4_j15.zip. You can download it from www.joomlaworks.gr to a folder on the local disk drive. To install the module, open the Extension Manager and select Extensions ➤ Install/Uninstall. The Extension Manager will open, and you can specify the location of Simple RSS Feed Reader's archive file by clicking the Browse button for the `Package File` option. After selecting the archive file on the local disk drive, click the `Upload File & Install` button to install the module, as shown in Figure 9-37.

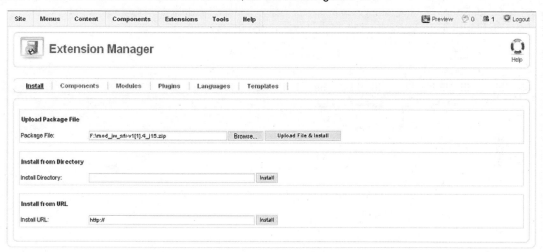

Figure 9-37. Specifying the location of the archive file for the Simple RSS Feed Reader module

The Simple RSS Feed Reader module is installed and can be seen listed in the Module Manager. To open the Module Manager, select `Extensions ➤ Module Manager`, and you'll find the newly installed module there, as shown marked in Figure 9-38. The module is in unpublished mode since that's the default for every newly installed module.

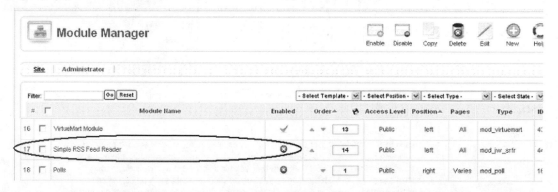

Figure 9-38. The Simple RSS Feed Reader module listed in the Module Manager upon successful installation

To convert Simple RSS Feed Reader to published mode, just select its check box in the Module Manager and click the `Enable` icon in the toolbar. The module will be changed to published mode and will be visible on the front end. Then click the `Edit` icon in the toolbar to edit the module. You'll see a screen like the one shown in Figure 9-39, displaying the module type and a description.

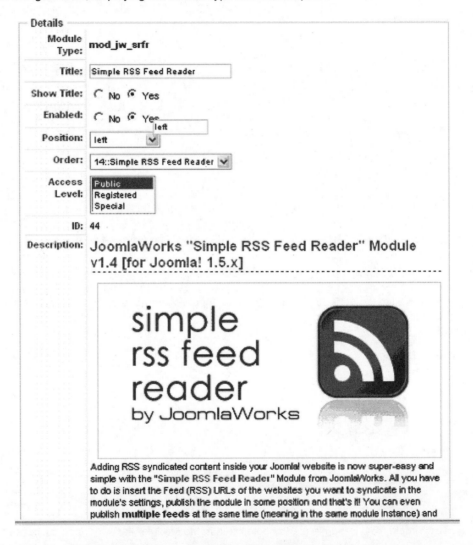

Figure 9-39. Module editing screen showing attributes of the RSS module

On this screen, you specify the position at which the module is to be displayed on the front end; let's select `Left`. You can also specify the access level—that is, whether the module can be used by any visitor of the website (`Public`), or is meant only for registered or special user groups. The `ID` is for internal use by Joomla (and is not editable).

The module also displays a screen for specifying `Parameters`, as shown in Figure 9-40. It's here that you specify the feed (RSS) URLs of the websites that you want to syndicate—that is, the URLs from which you want to receive RSS feeds. Let's specify the feed URL http://feeds.feedburner.com/joomlaworks, as shown in Figure 9-40.

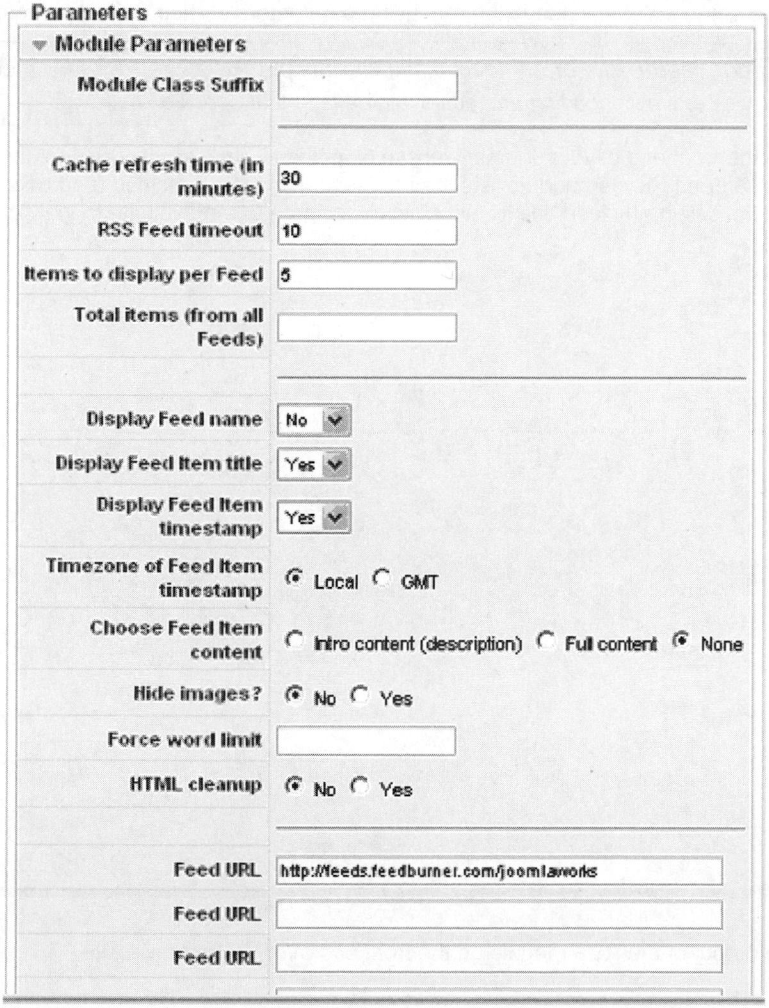

Figure 9-40. Parameters of the RSS module

Simple RSS Feed Reader performs caching for quicker feed display. You can specify certain parameters for caching. In this case, set `Cache refresh time (in minutes)` to `30` (so it will refresh the display every 30 minutes), `RSS Feed timeout` to `10` minutes, and `Items to display per Feed` to `5` (to show only five syndicated feed items at a time). Set the two fields `Display Feed Item title` and `Display Feed Item timestamp` to `Yes` to display the title of the feed item as well as the time it was last modified at the source. You can leave the remaining parameters at their default values.

> *You can add feed URLs of any encoding. The Simple RSS Feed Reader module will detect your website's encoding and adjust all feeds to that specific encoding.*

When you invoke the front end of your Joomla website by going to http://localhost/joomlasite, you'll see that the Simple RSS Feed Reader module lists the feed items from the specified feed URL, as shown in Figure 9-41. You can select any feed title from the list to navigate to that website to view details.

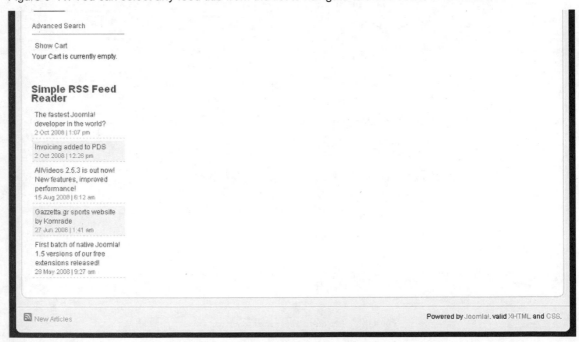

Figure 9-41. The output of the RSS module on the front end of the Joomla website

You can even publish multiple feeds at the same time (in the same module instance) by including more feed URLs. Let's include another feed URL, http://rss.news.yahoo.com/rss/sports, in the `Parameters` section of the module, as shown in Figure 9-42.

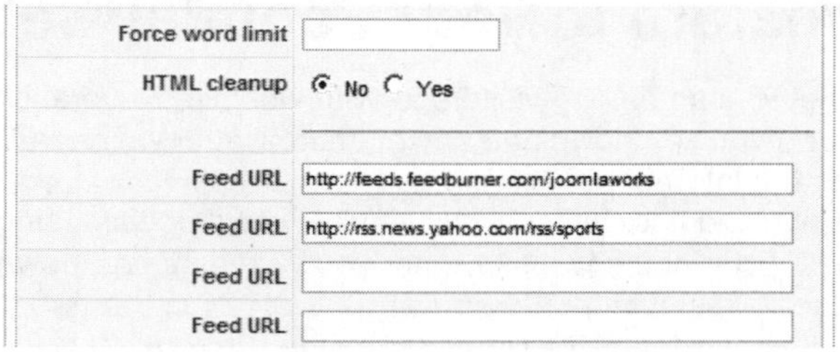

Figure 9-42. Adding another feed URL in the RSS module to receive feeds from both sites

Upon refresh, the front end will display the feed items from both the URLs, as shown in Figure 9-43.

Figure 9-43. RSS feeds from two sites combined and displayed in the Joomla website

Adding a chat feature to your Joomla! website

Chatting develops social networking among visitors to your website. Several chat components are available on the Internet, and you can download any of them. I've downloaded the jPFChat component, which is freely available on the Internet at www.jpfchat.com/index.php/downloads. Its archive file is com_jPFChat2d.zip. Let's download it to the local disk drive. Before downloading the archive file, however, you need to first register at the website. After you've registered, download the file, and then open the Extension Manager by selecting `Extensions` ➤ `Install/Uninstall`. In the `Package File` box, specify the location of the archive file and click the `Upload File & Install` button, as shown in Figure 9-44.

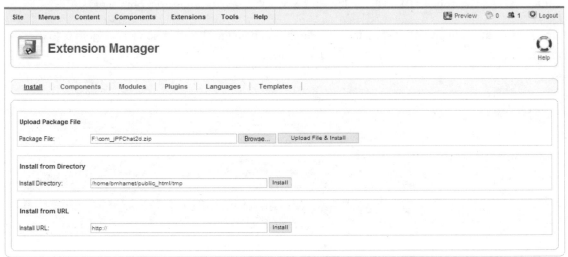

Figure 9-44. Specifying the location of the archive file for the jPFChat component

The jPFChat component will install, and you'll see the message `Install Component Success,` as shown in Figure 9-45.

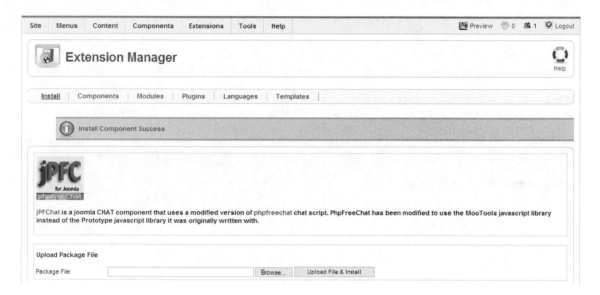

Figure 9-45. Message indicating successful installation of the jPFChat component

You'll also find the component included in the `Components` menu, as shown in Figure 9-46.

Figure 9-46. jPFChat component added to the Components menu

Upon selecting jPFChat from the Components menu, you'll see the jPFChat Administration dialog box, which allows you to specify certain settings, as shown in Figure 9-47. You can specify settings such as the type of user that can access the chat component (i.e., whether everyone or only users of a specific group can access it), the chat language, the size of the chat window, the maximum length of the nickname that a user can choose, the maximum number of chat rooms that can be opened for each user, and the number of private message rooms that can be opened for each user.

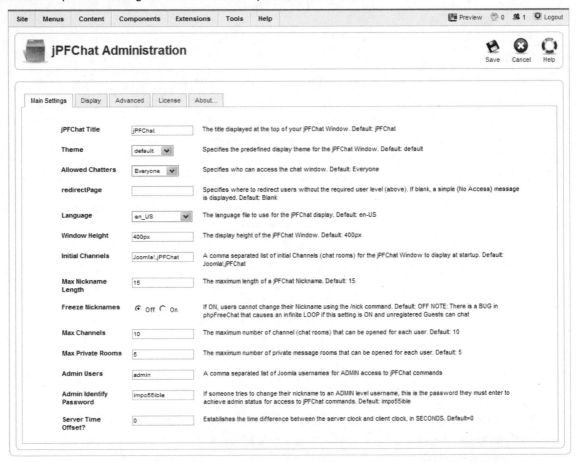

Figure 9-47. Default settings for the jPFChat component

To access this chat component from the front end, you need to assign it to a menu item in a menu on your Joomla website. Let's open the Menu Manager by selecting `Menus Menu Manager`. The Menu Manager will open, displaying all the menus that it contains, as shown in Figure 9-48.

Figure 9-48. List of menus in the Menu Manager

Select the icon in the `Menu Item(s)` column of the `Main Menu` row, since you want the chat component to be accessed via a menu item in the `Main Menu` (though you can choose any menu). The list of menu items present in the `Main Menu` is displayed on the `Menu Item Manager: [mainmenu]` screen, as shown in Figure 9-49.

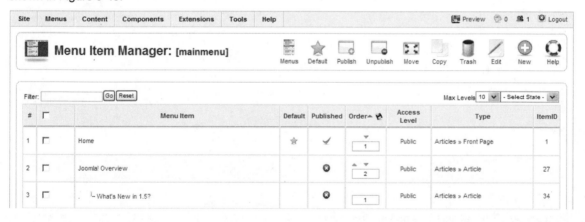

Figure 9-49. List of menu items in the Main Menu

Since we want to create a new menu item in the `Main Menu`, let's click the `New` icon in the toolbar. The list of all available menu item types will be displayed, as shown in Figure 9-50.

Figure 9-50. jPFChat listed as a menu item type

You'll find that a new menu item type, jPFChat, appears in the list of menu item types. Select it as your menu item type, and you'll see a screen to specify the menu item details, as shown in Figure 9-51.

Figure 9-51. Menu item attributes for the jPFChat menu item type

The Title field is used to specify the text of the menu item—that is, the title by which the menu item is to appear in the menu. You can enter any text here. Since we're making a menu item that will refer to a chat component, let's specify the title as Online Chat. Consequently, you'll see the menu item Online Chat in the menu, and when selected, it will invoke the chat component.

Alias, as you know, is a sort of secondary name meant for internal use. It must consist of lowercase letters without spaces (only hyphens are allowed). Let's enter the alias as online-chat.

The value of the Link field appears automatically and is not editable. It contains the address of the component to be invoked when the menu item is selected.

The Display in drop-down is used to specify the menu in which you want the menu item to appear. Set it to Main Menu.

Parent Item is used to specify whether you want the menu item to be a subitem of another menu item or to appear as the top item in the menu. Set the value of Parent Item to Top.

Set the Published option to Yes to make the menu item visible on the website.

Order specifies the location of the menu item. Usually it's at the last position, and it can also be set later from the Menu Item Manager.

Set the Access Level drop-down to Public to make the chat component publicly accessible.

In the On Click, Open in drop-down, select Parent Window with Browser Navigation so that the chat component will open in the same browser window instead of a new window.

Upon specifying the settings as shown in Figure 9-51, click the Save icon to save the menu item. You'll see the message Menu Item Saved, and the menu item will appear in the Menu Item Manager list, as shown in Figure 9-52.

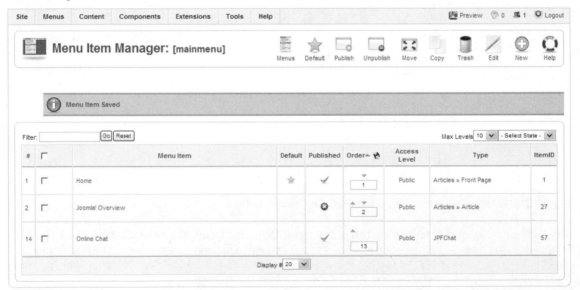

Figure 9-52. Menu item Online Chat added and listed in the Menu Item Manager

Now it's time to access the chat component from the front end. Let's access our Joomla website by pointing the browser to http://localhost/joomlasite. You'll find that a new menu item, `Online Chat`, appears in the `Main Menu`, as shown in Figure 9-53.

Figure 9-53. Menu item Online Chat appears on the front end of the Joomla website

When you select the `Online Chat` menu item, the chat component starts loading. You should see a message like that shown in Figure 9-54.

Figure 9-54. Online Chat component loading

When the chat component has finished loading, it will prompt the user to enter a nickname, as shown in Figure 9-55. You can enter any text up to 15 characters long (refer back to Figure 9-47, where we specified `Max Nickname Length` as `15`; you can increase this length if desired).

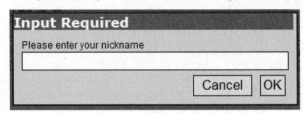

Figure 9-55. Dialog box asking for the nickname of the visitor wanting to chat

Let's enter the nickname as `bintu` (though it could be any name), and click the `OK` button. You'll find that a chat box appears and displays the message `bintu joins jPFChat`, as shown in Figure 9-56. Also, a user named `bintu` appears in the Users list on the right, and a text box is provided for the user to type the text for chatting. There are also some icons, formatting tools, and emoticons (smileys and other facial expressions) at the bottom of the chat box.

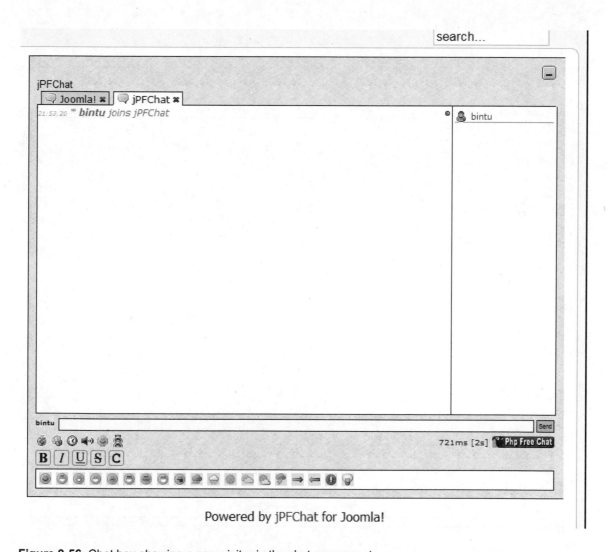

Figure 9-56. Chat box showing a new visitor in the chat component

Let's assume that the chat component is installed on a hosted website, and another user, with the nickname John, joins the chat by opening your website from some remote place. You'll see that the message John joins jPFChat appears in the chat box, and his name appears along with bintu in the Users list, as shown in Figure 9-57.

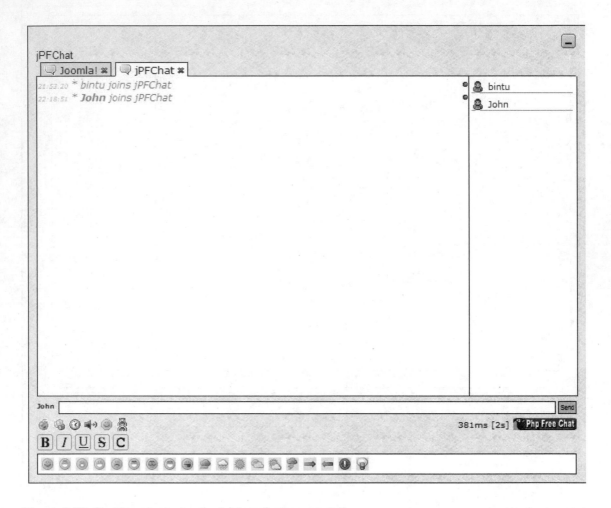

Figure 9-57. Chat box displaying the joining of one more visitor

If John writes a message—say, "Hello bintu"—you'll see the message in the chat box, as shown in Figure 9-58.

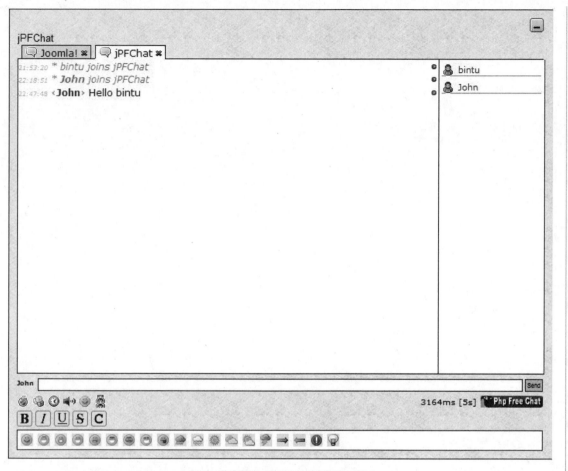

Powered by jPFChat for Joomla!

Figure 9-58. The message typed by John appears in the chat box

The user can also add an emoticon along with a text message by clicking the respective icon from the bottom of the chat box (see Figure 9-59).

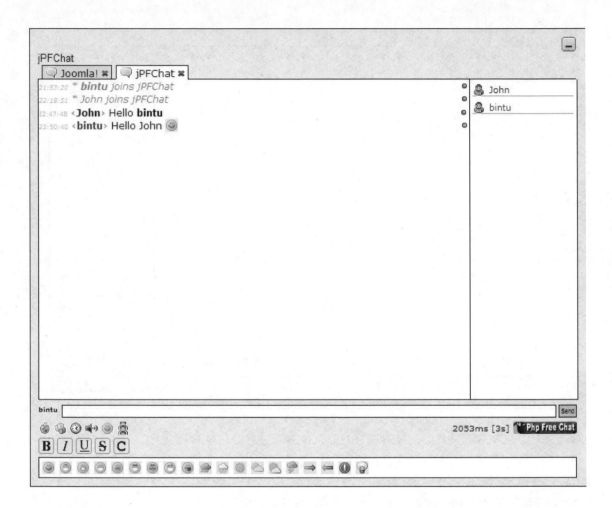

Figure 9-59. Emoticon included along with a message

You can perform a variety of formatting in your chats as well. For example, any text can be set to bold. One method for doing this is to type the text in the text field, select it, and then click the Bold formatting icon (the B near the bottom left of the window). (We'll look at another method shortly.) The message will be enclosed within the tags [b] and [/b], and when you press the Enter key to display it in the chat box, it will appear in bold, as shown in Figure 9-60.

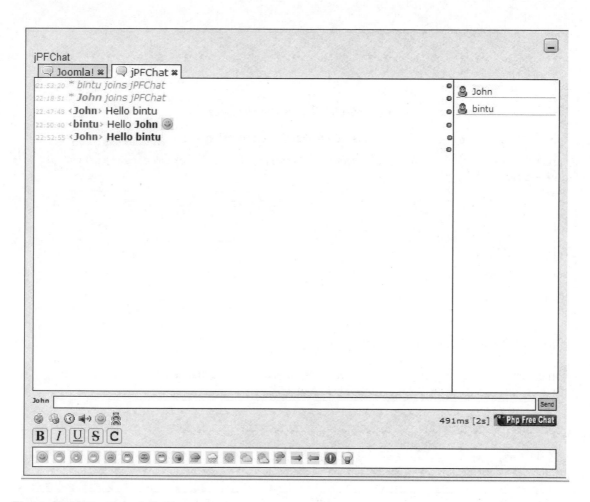

Figure 9-60. Messages in bold

There are also some icons above the formatting tools, which I'll describe in this list, from left to right:

- Connect/disconnect: If the user doesn't chat for some time, the time expires and the user is disconnected from the chat automatically. This icon can be used to reconnect, or to disconnect when the chatting is over.

- Hide nickname colors: The nicknames appear in red by default. This icon removes the color of the nicknames so that they appear in black.

- Hide dates and hours: The user messages in the chat box are normally preceded by the date and hour. This icon removes the date and hour.

- `Disable sound notifications`: This icon disables the sound that notifies the user of a chat message.

- `Hide smiley box`: This icon makes the smiley box invisible.

- `Hide online users box`: This icon makes the Users list invisible.

If you click the `Hide dates and hours` icon, the messages in the chat box will appear as shown in Figure 9-61.

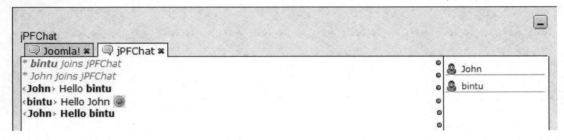

Figure 9-61. Messages after hiding dates and hours

Upon clicking the `Hide smiley box` icon, you'll see that the smileys that usually appear below the formatting icons become invisible, as shown in Figure 9-62.

Figure 9-62. Smiley box hidden

To make the smileys appear again, just click the `Hide smiley box` icon again.

If you click the `Hide online users box` icon, you'll find that the Users list that used to appear on the right will become invisible, as shown in Figure 9-63.

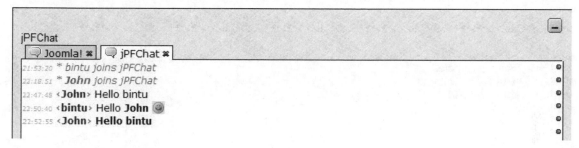

Figure 9-63. Users list hidden

The formatting icons are as follows:

- `Bold`: Makes the text bold

- `Italics`: Makes the text italic

- `Underline`: Underlines the text

- `Delete`: Draws a line through the text so that it appears struck out

- `Color`: Allows you to make the text appear in different colors

To make text appear struck out, type some text in the text field, select the text that you want to appear struck out, and then click the `Delete` formatting icon. The selected text will be enclosed in [s] and [/s] tags, and when you press the Enter key, the formatted text will appear struck out in the chat box, as shown in Figure 9-64.

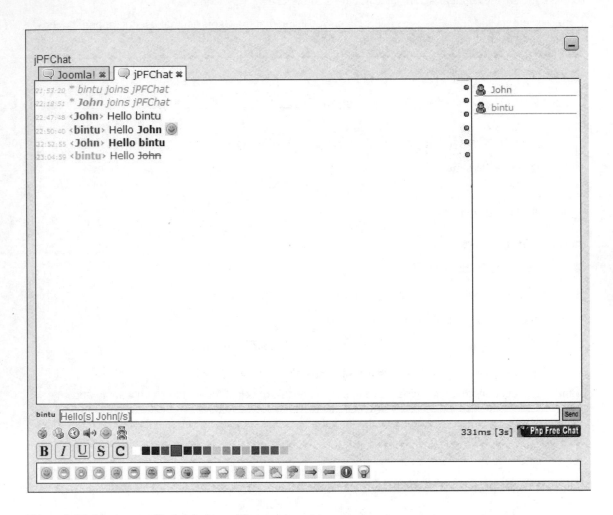

Figure 9-64. Message with delete formatting used

When you click the `Color` icon, you'll be presented a color palette with several colors in it, and you can simply select a color to make the text appear in that color. As shown in Figure 9-65, I've used the `Color` icon to open the color palette, and selected red to make the text appear in that color.

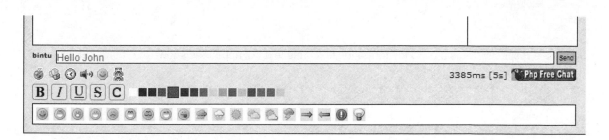

Figure 9-65. Entering messages in different colors

Another way to apply formatting to text, besides entering and selecting text in the text box and clicking the formatting icon of your choice, is to directly click a formatting icon without selecting any text in the text box. You'll then see a box like the one shown in Figure 9-66, asking you to enter the text that you want to appear in the chosen format.

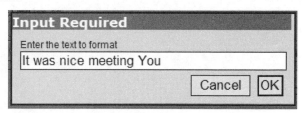

Figure 9-66. Applying formatting to the typed text

Type the text and click the OK button to make it appear in the chat box. The entered text will be enclosed in the respective tags to represent the formatting applied—that is, the tags [b] and [/b] for bold, [i] and [/i] for italic, and [u] and [/u] for underline. If you apply all three of these formats within a text message, it will appear as shown in Figure 9-67.

Figure 9-67. Message after applying bold, italic, and underline formatting

Notice the respective tags around the formatted text. This text will appear as shown in Figure 9-68 in the chat box.

‹bintu› **Hello** *John* It was nice meeting You

Figure 9-68. Output showing the three formats applied

The code that appears upon selecting the smileys in the smiley box is as follows:

- :)
- >(
- :-/
- :D
- :(
- :lol:
- :-}
- ;)
- :p
- :drizzle:
- :***:
- >O<
- :clouds:
- :cloudly:
- :$:
- >>>
- <<<
- :!:

For example, let's enter a text message with smileys, as shown in Figure 9-69.

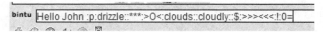

Figure 9-69. Code that appears after using different smileys

The output will appear as shown in Figure 9-70.

Figure 9-70. Output upon applying different smileys

Users can also send private messages to each other that will not be visible to the rest of the users. Suppose user John wants to send a private message to user bintu. John clicks `bintu` in the Users list, and a box will pop up displaying a `Private message` option in it, as shown in Figure 9-71.

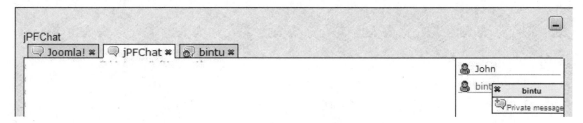

Figure 9-71. Private message box appearing upon selection of a user in the Users list

John can now enter the private message in the text box that appears and press the Enter key. The message, which only user bintu can see, appears as shown in Figure 9-72.

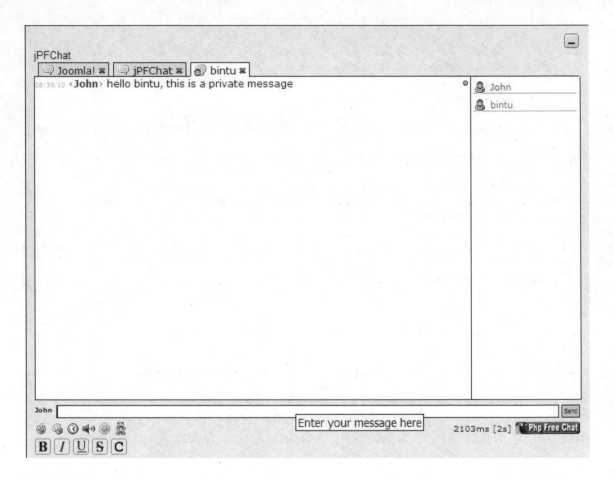

Figure 9-72. Private message for user bintu

Now, if John wants to send a private message to bintu, he can click the `bintu` tag (at the top of the chat box) and enter the text. To send a public message (visible to everyone), he can select the `jPFChat` tag and enter the message.

So, you should see that the jPFChat component provides an easy way to support a chatting facility in your Joomla website.

Summary

In this chapter, you learned how to add extra facilities to your Joomla website by installing a wide variety of extensions available on the Internet. You saw how commonly used extensions such as templates, e-commerce extensions, RSS feed readers, and chatting extensions can be downloaded, installed, and used in a Joomla website. In the next chapter, you will learn the techniques for configuring global settings of Joomla. Also, you will see the steps of installing an editor. You will also learn how to make search engine–friendly (SEF) URLs. Additionally, you will see how activation links can be sent to visitors registering to your website (in order to activate their account). You'll also see how to change the language of the front end of your website and provide a multilingual facility to your visitors—that is, the ability to translate the contents of your website into different languages. Finally, you will learn to make your own local help server.

Chapter 10

Making It Global

In the previous chapter, you learned how to add extra features to a Joomla website by installing various extensions. You saw how the most commonly required extensions, such as templates, e-commerce extensions, RSS feed readers, and chatting extensions, can be downloaded, installed, and used in a Joomla website. In this chapter, you'll learn how to

- Configure global settings for Joomla
- Install an editor
- Make search engine–friendly (SEF) URLs
- Allow visitors to register at your website and send them an activation link to activate their account
- Change the language of the front end of the website
- Provide a multilingual facility to your visitors—that is, the ability to translate the contents of your website into different languages

Global Configuration settings

Global settings, made using the Global Configuration menu, enable us to apply global features to your website. These settings play a major role in

- Enabling visitors to create an account by registering on your website
- Making SEF URLs
- Highlighting the description of your website in the form of metadata to be caught by search engines
- Getting help screens from a local or remote help server
- Setting the upper limit of the size of MIME files and verifying whether they are valid

> *MIME stands for Multipurpose Internet Mail Extensions, and is a specification for formatting non-ASCII messages, including graphics, audio, and video files to be sent over the Internet. Verification of MIME files means assuring that the MIME file uploaded to your website is a valid MIME file.*

- Setting the session lifetime and caching time
- Configuring mail settings and database settings
- Selecting the local time zone
- Applying compression techniques to increase site performance

Global Configuration can be invoked by either selecting its icon from the control panel or selecting Site ➤ Global Configuration. It contains three tabs: Site, System, and Server.

Site tab (Global Configuration)

Using the Site tab (Figure 10-1), you can set a message that your website is offline, select an editor for managing site contents, set the size of the lists and feeds, specify metadata information for search engines, make SEF URLs, and so on.

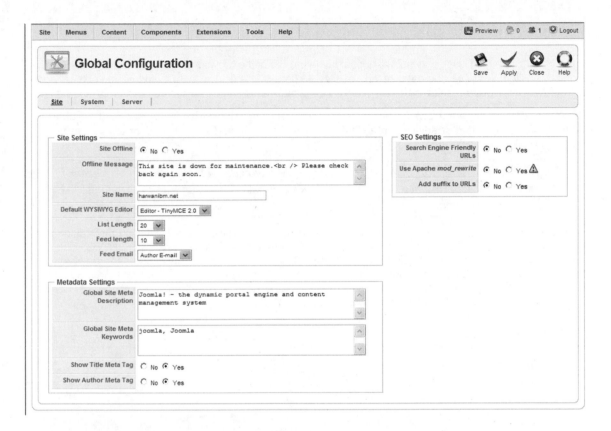

Figure 10-1. Site tab of Global Configuration

As you can see in the figure, there are three sections within the Global Configuration `Site` tab, and I'll explain them each in detail in the following sections.

Site Settings (Site tab)

The `Site Offline` field is used to inform visitors whether your Joomla website is temporarily shut off for a maintenance task. When you're performing a maintenance task on your website (this might include installing new extensions, adding or editing content, etc.), you can set the value of this option to `Yes` to inform visitors that the website is currently offline. They will receive a message (which you enter in the next field) telling them about the unavailability of the site and when it will be available again. If users visit your website while you're making changes and you haven't set this option, your visitors will get a `Page not found` error message, and won't understand why they're unable to view the site.

The text in the `Offline Message` field will be displayed to the visitor if the `Site Offline` option is set to `Yes`. You can use standard HTML code in the message entered in this field (e.g., `<br />`, to break the message into multiple lines).

In the `Site Name` field is the text that will appear in the title bar of the browser when a user is visiting your Joomla website (usually it is the name of the website). By default, this field is set to the name you originally gave for your website. However, this field allows you to change the website name anytime after Joomla installation.

The editor you select from the `Default WYSIWYG Editor` drop-down list will be used as the global default editor for creating or editing content items (articles) on your website. This editor will be used for front-end as well as back-end purposes.

> **WYSIWYG** is an acronym for "What you see is what you get," used to describe a system in which content displayed during editing appears exactly the same in the final output (such as in printing).

By default, the editor is TinyMCE 2.0, which provides a standard toolbar that's helpful in most editing and formatting tasks. TinyMCE is a platform-independent, web-based JavaScript HTML WYSIWYG editor control that can very easily be integrated into a CMS. It's an open source, lightweight editor that's Ajax compatible. It loads quickly and supports multiple languages through the use of different language packs. To see the toolbar that TinyMCE provides, select the title of an article from the Article Manager to open it in the TinyMCE editor; the result is as shown in Figure 10-2.

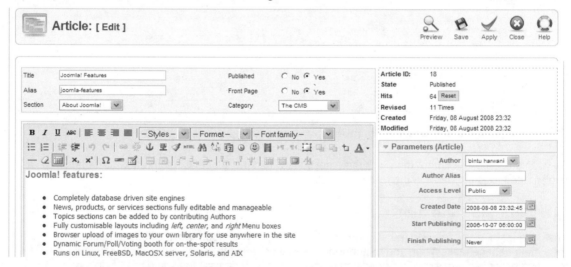

Figure 10-2. Article opened in the TinyMCE editor

Keep in mind that you can always install more editors as well; so let's do that now. From among the many editors that are freely available on the Internet, I've downloaded JoomlaFCK, a lightweight, fast, advanced, feature-rich editor built on the FCK code. This editor has the same sophisticated interface as Microsoft Word 2007, making our content management task much easier. The editor has image and document management capabilities that assist in uploading and administering files within the editor's GUI. Its archive file name is bot_JoomlaFCKeditor2[1].6.3.9b.zip. You can download it from the following address to your local disk drive: http://webscripts.softpedia.com/scriptDownload/JoomlaFCK-Download-2711.html. Note that you need to register at the website before downloading the archive file. To install the editor, invoke the Extension Manager by selecting Extensions ➤ Install/Uninstall. You'll see a dialog box like the one shown in Figure 10-3. In the Upload Package File section, click the Browse button to locate the archive file, and then click the Upload File & Install button.

Figure 10-3. Using the Extension Manager to install the JoomlaFCK editor

Once the editor is installed, you'll see the message Install Plugin Success, as shown in Figure 10-4.

Figure 10-4. Success message upon installation of the JoomlaFCK editor

Now, in the Site Settings section of the Site tab of Global Configuration, you'll see an extra option in the Default WYSIWYG Editor list: Editor - JoomlaFCK, as shown in Figure 10-5. Let's select it to see what facility it provides.

Figure 10-5. The Default WYSIWYG Editor drop-down list showing the JoomlaFCK editor

If you now edit an article by selecting its title in the Article Manager, the article will open in the JoomlaFCK editor and you'll see its toolbar, as shown in Figure 10-6. This toolbar looks quite a bit more advanced than that of the TinyMCE editor.

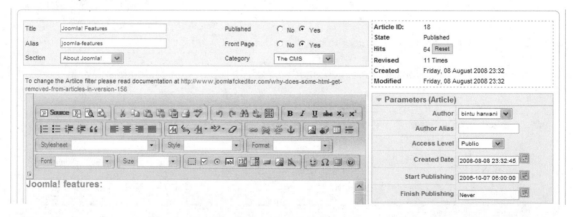

Figure 10-6. Tools of the JoomlaFCK editor

Now, let's go back to see the rest of the settings in the `Site` tab of Global Configuration (by selecting its icon from the control panel or selecting `Site` ➤ `Global Configuration`).

The `List Length` drop-down determines how many items can appear in a list. By default, its value is `20`, which means that if you're looking at the articles list on your website (from the front end), you'll see the articles in a group of 20. If you have more than 20 articles, they'll appear on the next page (or pages). You can change the value of this option to any value from 5 to 100, in increments of 5.

For example, suppose there's a menu item named `Books Published` that displays a list of all books published by our organization. If we've published eight books to date and the length of the list is the default, 20, all the titles of the books appear on the first page, as shown in Figure 10-7. The list length is also displayed in the `Display #` drop-down list. You can even change it from the front end to set the desired number of articles to be displayed at one time, but this setting is temporary and vanishes when you select another menu item.

Figure 10-7. The list of eight books when the list length is 20

If you set the list length to 5 in the Global Configuration settings, you'll see that only five book names appear in a list at one time, and again, pagination occurs if there are more books. The links are displayed as `Start Prev 1 2 Next End` to navigate you to any page, as shown in Figure 10-8.

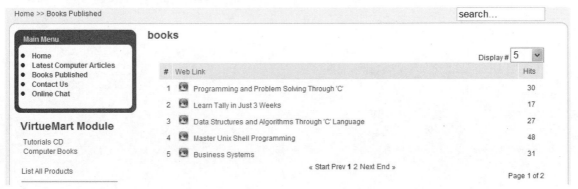

Figure 10-8. The list of books is paginated when the list length is 5.

Upon clicking the 2 link to see the second page, you'll see the titles of the rest of the books, as shown in Figure 10-9.

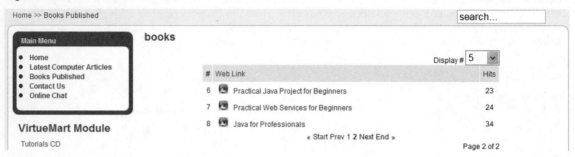

Figure 10-9. Second page of list of books

The Feed length drop-down determines the number of content items to be shown in the specific feed. By default, its value is 10. We'll use the Feed Display module for checking this setting. First, open the Module Manager by selecting Extensions ➤ Module Manager. Then, from the list of modules, select the Feed Display module to open it in edit mode, as shown in Figure 10-10. Specify the URL of the RSS feed as http://rss.news.yahoo.com/rss/sports in the Feed URL field. Note that the Items field must be blank—that is, it must not have any value in it, or else the value will override the Global Configuration settings. For example, if the value in this field is 3, the number of items displayed by the RSS feed will always be three, no matter what value we specify in the Feed length drop-down of the Global Configuration settings.

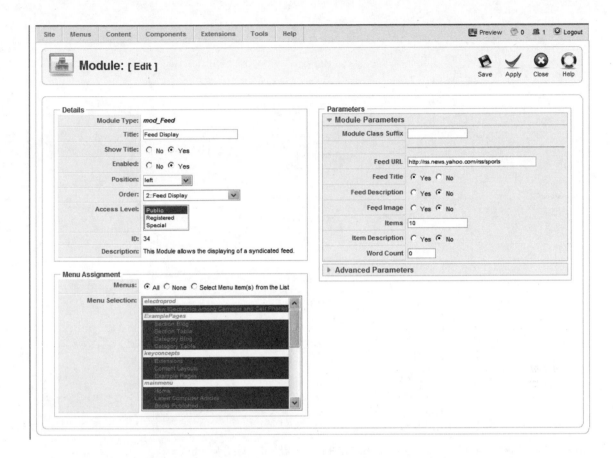

Figure 10-10. Feed Display module in edit mode

Since the default value of the `Feed length` field is `10`, a total of ten Items are displayed in the RSS feed, as shown in Figure 10-11.

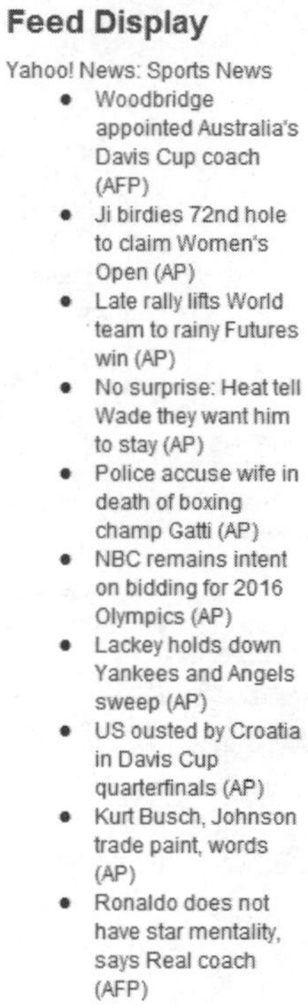

Feed Display

Yahoo! News: Sports News

- Woodbridge appointed Australia's Davis Cup coach (AFP)
- Ji birdies 72nd hole to claim Women's Open (AP)
- Late rally lifts World team to rainy Futures win (AP)
- No surprise: Heat tell Wade they want him to stay (AP)
- Police accuse wife in death of boxing champ Gatti (AP)
- NBC remains intent on bidding for 2016 Olympics (AP)
- Lackey holds down Yankees and Angels sweep (AP)
- US ousted by Croatia in Davis Cup quarterfinals (AP)
- Kurt Busch, Johnson trade paint, words (AP)
- Ronaldo does not have star mentality, says Real coach (AFP)

Figure 10-11. Ten items are displayed in the RSS feed when the feed length is 10.

If we set `Feed length` to `5`, the front end of our Joomla website will show five items of the RSS feed, as shown in Figure 10-12.

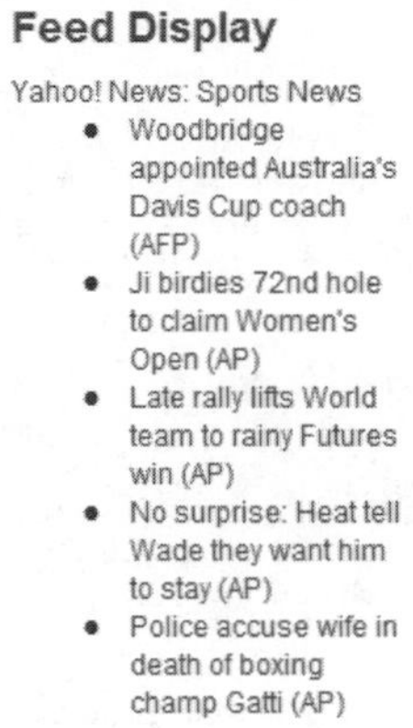

Feed Display

Yahoo! News: Sports News
- Woodbridge appointed Australia's Davis Cup coach (AFP)
- Ji birdies 72nd hole to claim Women's Open (AP)
- Late rally lifts World team to rainy Futures win (AP)
- No surprise: Heat tell Wade they want him to stay (AP)
- Police accuse wife in death of boxing champ Gatti (AP)

Figure 10-12. Five items are displayed in the RSS feed when the feed length is 5.

Again, let's go back to see the rest of the settings in the Site tab of Global Configuration (by selecting its icon from the control panel or selecting Site ➤ Global Configuration).

The Feed Email drop-down determines whether to display the e-mail addresses along with the RSS/news feeds. It has two options: Author Email and Site Email. If Author Email is selected, the e-mail addresses of the feed authors will be displayed. Similarly, if Site Email is selected, then along with the feed contents, the front end will display the website e-mail address (if any) of the site from which the feeds are accessed.

Metadata Settings (Site tab)

These settings are used by search engines searching your website.

In the Global Site Meta Description, you can enter a brief description of your website that will be used by search engines for searching your website—that is, the description will be indexed by search engine spiders. This information will be displayed along with your website name when users perform a search via any search engine, as shown in Figure 10-13. The description should be to the point and explanatory, since the user will decide whether to visit the site or not depending on the description given. It's best to limit the description to 20 words, as any extra words will be ignored by the search engines.

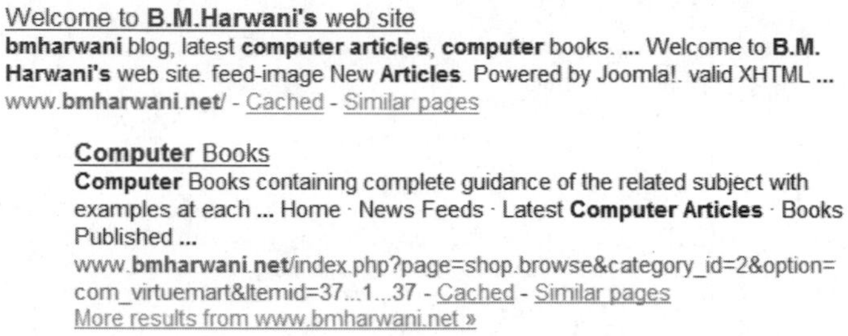

Welcome to **B.M.Harwani's** web site
bmharwani blog, latest **computer articles**, **computer** books. ... Welcome to **B.M. Harwani's** web site. feed-image New **Articles**. Powered by Joomla!. valid XHTML ...
www.**bmharwani**.net/ - Cached - Similar pages

Computer Books
Computer Books containing complete guidance of the related subject with examples at each ... Home · News Feeds · Latest **Computer Articles** · Books Published ...
www.**bmharwani**.net/index.php?page=shop.browse&category_id=2&option= com_virtuemart&Itemid=37...1...37 - Cached - Similar pages
More results from www.bmharwani.net »

Figure 10-13. Brief description of website along with website link

In the `Global Site Meta Keywords` field, you can enter the keywords that best describe your website, to be used for improving the ability of search engine spiders to index the site. Usually, you should enter keywords that briefly and precisely explain the products, services, facilities, and so on provided by your organization. The keywords should be limited to a total of 1,000 characters, since the search engines will not read more than that. Separate the keywords with a comma. Think about the keywords that are likely to be searched from the visitor's point of view, and include them in the keywords list.

> Nowadays, search engines like Google do not use any content in the meta keywords section when indexing.

Let's specify a meta description and keywords for our website. Assuming our site sells computer books and tutorial CDs, publishes computer-related articles, and offers virtual classes, let's set the `Global Site Meta Description` and `Global Site Meta Keywords` as shown in Figure 10-14.

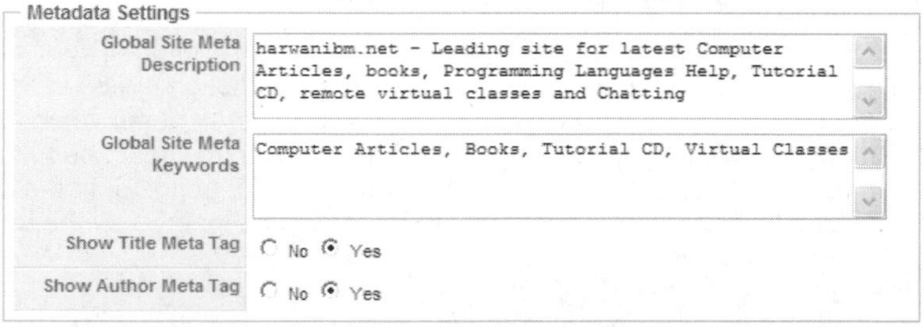

Metadata Settings

Global Site Meta Description	`harwanibm.net - Leading site for latest Computer Articles, books, Programming Languages Help, Tutorial CD, remote virtual classes and Chatting`
Global Site Meta Keywords	`Computer Articles, Books, Tutorial CD, Virtual Classes`
Show Title Meta Tag	○ No ● Yes
Show Author Meta Tag	○ No ● Yes

Figure 10-14. Metadata settings

You can see the meta description and keywords from the front end of your Joomla website. Just right-click the website and select `View Source` from the shortcut menu that appears. You might see something like the following:

```
<!DOCTYPE html PUBLIC "-//W3C//DTD XHTML 1.0 Transitional//EN"
```

```
http://www.w3.org/TR/xhtml1/DTD/xhtml1-transitional.dtd">
<html xmlns="http://www.w3.org/1999/xhtml" xml:lang="en-gb" lang=
"en-gb" >
<head>
  <meta http-equiv="content-type" content="text/html; charset=utf-8" />
  <meta name="robots" content="index, follow" />
  <meta name="keywords" content="Computer Articles, Books,
Tutorial CD, Virtual Classes" />
  <meta name="description" content="harwanibm.net - Leading site for
latest Computer Articles, books, Programming Languages Help,
Tutorial CD, remote virtual classes and Chatting" />
  <meta name="generator" content="Joomla! 1.5 - Open Source Content
Management" />
  <title>Welcome to the Frontpage</title>
```

Notice that the `<meta name="keywords">` and `<meta name="description">` tags display what we specified in these fields in the Global Configuration settings.

The `Show Title Meta Tag` options allows you to choose whether to show the title meta information for each article, which is used by search engine spiders when indexing the site. Each article on your website can have its own meta information. Let's open the "Latest Cameras" article that we created in Chapter 3 by selecting the `New Electronics Products arrival` menu item from the main menu. When the article is displayed, view the source code, which should look something like the following. The main thing to observe here is that the `<meta name="title">` tag shows the title of the article as `Latest Cameras`, which may be used by search engines.

```
<!DOCTYPE html PUBLIC "-//W3C//DTD XHTML 1.0 Transitional//EN"
"http://www.w3.org/TR/xhtml1/DTD/xhtml1-transitional.dtd">
<html xmlns="http://www.w3.org/1999/xhtml" xml:lang="en-gb"
lang="en-gb" >
<head>
  <meta http-equiv="content-type" content="text/html; charset=utf-8" />
  <meta name="robots" content="index, follow" />
  <meta name="keywords" content="Night vision, 10 MB storage,
Light weight, advt_shooting" />
  <meta name="title" content="Latest Cameras" />
  <meta name="author" content="Administrator" />
  <meta name="description" content="harwanibm.net - Leading site for
latest Computer Articles, books, Programming Languages Help,
Tutorial CD, remote virtual classes and Chatting" />
  <meta name="generator" content="Joomla! 1.5 - Open Source Content
Management" />
  <title>Latest Cameras</title>
```

If you set the value of the `Show Title Meta Tag` option to `No`, you'll find that the `<meta name="title">` tag disappears, as shown in following source code:

```
<!DOCTYPE html PUBLIC "-//W3C//DTD XHTML 1.0 Transitional//EN"
"http://www.w3.org/TR/xhtml1/DTD/xhtml1-transitional.dtd">
```

```
<html xmlns="http://www.w3.org/1999/xhtml" xml:lang="en-gb"
lang="en-gb" >
<head>
  <meta http-equiv="content-type" content="text/html; charset=utf-8" />
  <meta name="robots" content="index, follow" />
  <meta name="keywords" content="Night vision, 10 MB storage,
Light weight, advt_shooting" />
  <meta name="author" content="Administrator" />
  <meta name="description" content="harwanibm.net - Leading site for
latest Computer Articles, books, Programming Languages Help,
Tutorial CD, remote virtual classes and Chatting" />
  <meta name="generator" content="Joomla! 1.5 - Open Source Content
Management" />
  <title>Latest Cameras</title>
```

The `Show Author Meta Tag` option allows you to show the author meta information for each article—that is, information about the creator of the article. This information is used by search engine spiders when indexing the site. Note the `<meta name="author">` tag in the preceding source code. If you set the value of the `Show Author Meta Tag` option to `No`, this tag will disappear, as you can see in the following code:

```
<!DOCTYPE html PUBLIC "-//W3C//DTD XHTML 1.0 Transitional//EN"
"http://www.w3.org/TR/xhtml1/DTD/xhtml1-transitional.dtd">
<html xmlns="http://www.w3.org/1999/xhtml" xml:lang="en-gb"
lang="en-gb" >
<head>
  <meta http-equiv="content-type" content="text/html; charset=utf-8" />
  <meta name="robots" content="index, follow" />
  <meta name="keywords" content="Night vision, 10 MB storage,
Light weight, advt_shooting" />
  <meta name="description" content="harwanibm.net - Leading site for
latest Computer Articles, books, Programming Languages Help,
Tutorial CD, remote virtual classes and Chatting" />
  <meta name="generator" content="Joomla! 1.5 - Open Source Content
Management" />
  <title>Latest Cameras</title>
```

The conclusion is that by using `Show Title Meta Tag` and `Show Author Meta Tag`, you can control the display of all of these header elements.

SEO Settings (Site tab)

Joomla has built-in SEO (search engine optimization) functionality. The `SEO Settings` section of the `Site` tab handles global SEO settings for your Joomla site.

SEF URLs change the way site links are presented and optimize them so that search engines can access more of your website. The `Search Engine Friendly URLs` option is available only to sites hosted on

Apache servers. Select Yes, as shown in Figure 10-15, to enable Joomla to create SEF URLs rather than normal, database-generated URLs.

Figure 10-15. SEO settings

Usually, when the Search Engine Friendly URLs option is set to No, the URL of an item selected on your website is difficult to remember. For example, if you click the Online Chat link on your website, the URL will appear as shown in Figure 10-16.

Figure 10-16. URL when Search Engine Friendly URLs is set to No

You can see that the URL contain symbols and numbers. After you enable SEF URLs, the symbols and numbers will disappear, and the URL will appear as shown in Figure 10-17.

Figure 10-17. Friendly URL that appears when Search Engine Friendly URLs is set to Yes

> *The alias text autogenerated by Joomla (or specified by you) is set as the SEF URL.*

When the Search Engine Friendly URLs option is set to Yes, the URL that appears in your browser is friendly—that is, easy to remember (by our search engines); however, the SEF URLs feature works only when the Use Apache mod_rewrite option is enabled, as shown in Figure 10-18. That is, you need a running Apache web server, the mod_rewrite module on Apache must be active (most hosting companies have this module installed), and you need the Apache configuration to allow .htaccess files.

Figure 10-18. Apache mod_rewrite in enabled mode

Joomla uses the mod_rewrite setting of Apache when creating SEF URLs. In order to use this setting, you need to use the `.htaccess` file provided with Joomla, which means you need to rename the `htaccess.txt` file (found in the root directory where Joomla is installed) to `.htaccess`.

> *Don't forget to remove the .txt and add the . (dot) before htaccess.*

If you enable SEF URLs and Apache mod_rewrite, your URLs will be simplified further in the browser's address bar; for example, `http://www.bmharwani.net/index.php/online-chat` will become `http://www.bmharwani.net//online-chat`.

When the `Add suffix to URLs` option is set to `Yes`, Joomla will add `.html` to the end of the URLs. The default setting is `No`. For example, after this option is enabled, the URL for `Online Chat` will appear as shown in Figure 10-19.

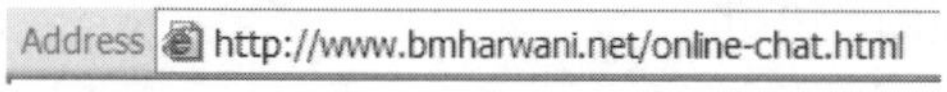

Address   http://www.bmharwani.net/online-chat.html

Figure 10-19. Suffix .html added to URL

System tab (Global Configuration)

The `System` tab (Figure 10-20) is used for various configurations, including setting the path of the log folder; specifying the location of the help server; enabling or disabling visitor registration at your website; setting the default user group for new accounts; setting the maximum size of MIME files; and enabling, disabling, or setting the time for caching and sessions.

Figure 10-20. System tab of Global Configuration

System Settings (System tab)

The `Secret Word` setting is an encrypted word generated automatically when Joomla is first installed, and is not changeable. It is used internally by Joomla for security purposes.

In the `Path to Log folder` field, you specify the location where the logs will be stored. This path is automatically filled in by the Joomla installer. You can use the log files to see information about the latest visitors to your website, the bandwidth used by the site, errors, and so on. You don't need to open the logs with a text editor; the control panels of most hosting companies provide a GUI (something like Figure 10-21) that reads the information from the log files and presents it in an easily understandable format.

Figure 10-21. Sample control panel provided by a web hosting company

Some web hosting companies provide icons, as shown in Figure 10-22, to extract information from the log files and present a report in the desired format.

Figure 10-22. Tools of analysis and log files

You set the value of the `Enable Web Services` option to `Yes` so that Joomla can make RPCs (remote procedure calls) using HTTP as the transport medium and XML as the encoding language. Several extensions related to e-commerce, mobile iPhone plug-ins, and so on, need this option to be enabled for proper functioning. The default value is `No`.

The help server is used to display help screens when the user clicks the `Help` icon. By default, the server that's specified in the `Help Server` drop-down is a remote server, `help.joomla.org`, but you can also set up your own local help sever (see this book's page on `www.apress.com` for a bonus section on how to do this).

User Settings (System tab)

These settings determine whether visitors to your website will be able to register themselves, whether an activation link will be sent for e-mail verification, what the default user group for a new user should be, and so on.

Set the `Allow User Registration` option to `Yes` if you want to enable a visitor to your website to create an account. If this option is enabled, you'll see a `Create an account` link in the Login module, as shown in Figure 10-23. If you set this field to `No`, the `Create an account` link disappears; no visitor can create an account from the front end, and only existing users can log in and access the member areas of the website. The administrator can still create new users from the back end.

Figure 10-23. Login module on the front end

When the `Create an account` link is clicked, a sign-up form appears (Figure 10-24) on which visitors can enter their information. All the fields marked with an asterisk (*) must be filled in; otherwise, an error will occur and the visitor will be asked to provide the missing information.

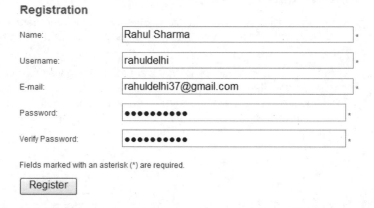

Figure 10-24. Sign-up form to create an account

Via the `New User Registration Type` drop-down, you can select any of the predefined user groups shown in Figure 10-25 to define the default group for newly created accounts. (The rights and limitations of each user group are covered in Chapter 5.)

Figure 10-25. Types of user groups for new users

To validate the e-mail address provided by a visitor when creating an account, an activation link is sent to the e-mail address specified, and the account will not be created until the visitor accesses the account and clicks the activation link. The activation link is sent to the e-mail address of a newly created account only if the `New User Account Activation` option is set to `Yes`. For example, suppose that this option is enabled and the user Rahul Sharma creates an account, as shown earlier in Figure 10-24. After filling in the desired information and clicking the `Register` button, the user will see a message (Figure 10-26) saying that the account has been created, and an activation link has been sent to the specified e-mail address, asking the visitor to click the activation link to activate the account.

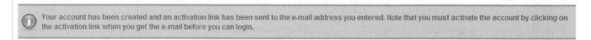

Figure 10-26. Message upon submitting the sign-up form

Upon accessing this e-mail, the visitor will find a message sent by the owner of the website. In the example shown in Figure 10-27, we assume that the name of the owner of the Joomla website (where the account was created) is bintu and the Joomla website name is `bmharwani.net`. Assuming that the user has a Gmail account, on opening Gmail, we find the user receives an e-mail with the subject "Account Details for Rahul Sharma at bmharwani.net," as shown in Figure 10-27.

Archive	Report spam	Delete	Move to▼	Labels▼	More actions▼	Refresh		1 - 1 of 1

Select: All, None, Read, Unread, Starred, Unstarred

☐ ☆	bintu	**Account Details for Rahul Sharma at bmharwani.net** - Hello Rahul S	11:23 pm

Figure 10-27. E-mail sent to the user upon creating an account

Upon opening the e-mail message, Rahul will see a message like the one as shown in Figure 10-28. It consists of a "Thank you" message for creating an account and an activation link to be clicked by the user to activate the account. In addition, it displays the username and password to be used for logging into the website in the future.

433

Figure 10-28. Information sent in an e-mail to the new user

When the activation link is clicked, the user's account is activated and an `Activation Complete!` message appears, as shown in Figure 10-29. The message also says that the user can now log in using the username and password supplied at the time of registration.

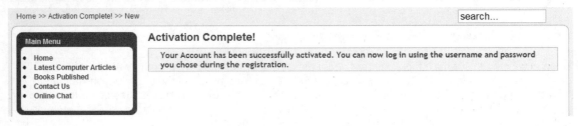

Figure 10-29. Message after clicking the activation link

If the value of `New User Account Activation` is set to `No`, no activation link will be sent to the visitor's e-mail address; instead, the account will be directly activated. To understand this better, let's set this field to `No` and click the `Create an account` link from the Login module to create a new account. Assuming that the name of the user is `Peter David`, fill in the registration information as shown in Figure 10-30.

Figure 10-30. Sign-up form for the user without the activation facility

After we fill in the registration information and click the `Register` button, the message `You may now log in` immediately appears, as shown in Figure 10-31.

Figure 10-31. Message to directly log in without the activation link formality

The message sent by our Joomla website to the user Peter David will be similar to the one shown in Figure 10-32. It includes a "Thank you" message and asks the user to log in with the username and password supplied at the time of registration.

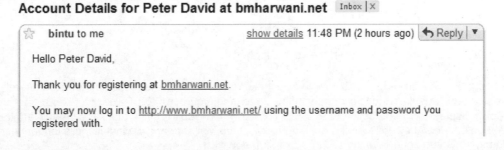

Figure 10-32. Information in e-mail message sent to the user without an activation requirement

435

The `Front-end User Parameters` option provides the user with the flexibility to edit the information specified during account creation from the front end. A user who successfully logs into the system sees a `Your Details` link, which when clicked enables the user to see and edit the user information. Only if the value of this field is `Yes` will the user be able to edit the information. In addition to being able to edit personal information, the user can choose the type of editor (if the user is a member of the Author group or higher), the local time zone, the front-end language, and so on. Let's see what happens when the user peter logs onto our website, as shown in Figure 10-33.

Login Form

Username

peter

Password

●●●●●●●●●

Remember Me ☐

Login

Figure 10-33. User peter logging in

You should see two links appear, `Your Details` and `Logout`, as shown in Figure 10-34.

Login Form

Hi peter,

Log out

Figure 10-34. Links that appear when the user is logged in

The `Your Details` link allows this user to select the front-end language (if that language is already installed on your website) and to change the time zone (see Figure 10-35). The `Front-end Language` drop-down displays only one option, `English (United Kingdom)`, since that's the default language installed on our Joomla website, but more language options will appear if we install more languages. You can change the time zone from the `Time Zone` drop-down list.

Edit Your Details

Username: peter

Your Name: Peter David

E-mail: harwanibm@gmail.com

Password:

Verify Password:

Front-end Language: English (United Kingdom)

Time Zone   (UTC 00:00) Western Europe Time, London, Lisbon, Casablanca

Save

Figure 10-35. Front-end parameters for changing front-end language and time zone

If the value of the `Front-end User Parameters` field is `No`, clicking the `Your Details` link that appears after a successful login will not enable the user to change the front-end language or time zone. The screen will instead look like the one shown in Figure 10-36, in which the options of selecting the front-end language and time zone are missing.

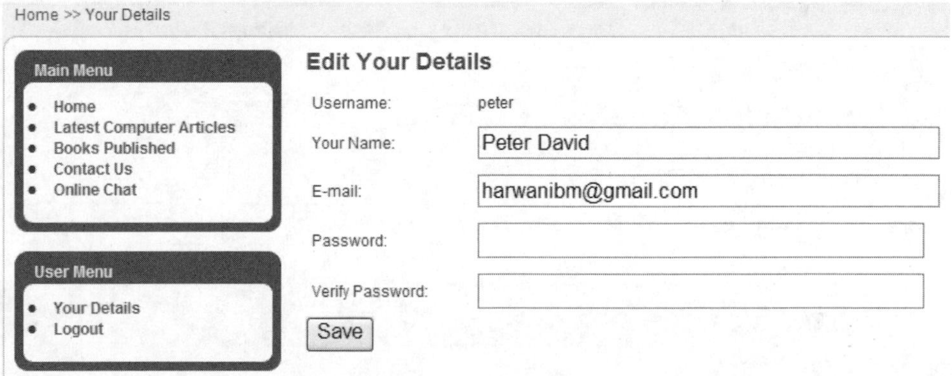

Home >> Your Details

Main Menu
- Home
- Latest Computer Articles
- Books Published
- Contact Us
- Online Chat

User Menu
- Your Details
- Logout

Edit Your Details

Username: peter

Your Name: Peter David

E-mail: harwanibm@gmail.com

Password:

Verify Password:

Save

Figure 10-36. Front-end parameters not displayed

Changing the language of the front end of the website

Let's install a language to see how the front end of our website can appear in a language other than English. The extensions for almost all languages are freely available on the Internet. For this example, let's download the extension for French. The archive file for the French language is `fr-FR_joomla_lang_full.1.5.10.v1.zip`, which you can find at `http://joomlacode.org/gf/project/french/frs/`. Download it to a local disk drive. To install this language, open the Extension Manager by selecting `Extensions` ➤ `Install/Uninstall`. In the

Upload Package File section, click the Browse button to locate the French language archive file, and click the Upload File & Install button to install this language in your website, as shown in Figure 10-37.

Figure 10-37. Installing the French language pack

You'll see the message Install Language Success, confirming that the French language pack has been installed (Figure 10-38).

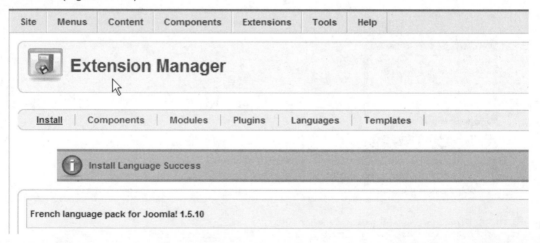

Figure 10-38. Installation success message

Now let's click the Your Details link in the Login module to edit the user information. You'll see a screen like that shown in Figure 10-39, where the Front-end Language list now offers two language options: English and French. Let's select the French language.

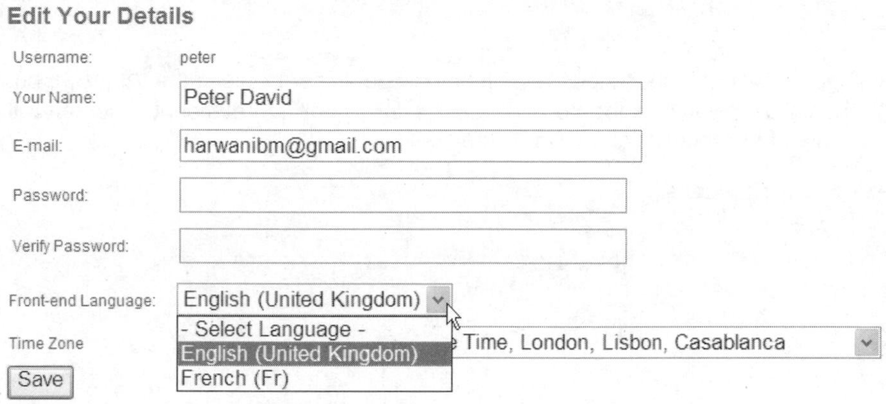

Edit Your Details
Username:
peter
Your Name:
Peter David
E-mail:
harwanibm@gmail.com
Password:
Verify Password:
Front-end Language:
English (United Kingdom)
- Select Language -
English (United Kingdom)
French (Fr)
Time Zone
Time, London, Lisbon, Casablanca
Save

Figure 10-39. French now appears as an option in the Front-end Language list.

Now click the `Save` button to save the information and apply the chosen front-end language. You'll see the message `Your settings have been Saved`, as shown in Figure 10-40.

Home
recherche...
Your settings have been Saved.
Main Menu
Home
Latest Computer Articles
Books Published
Contact Us
Online Chat
Welcome to B.M.Harwani's web site
User Menu
Your Details
Logout
Login Form
Bonjour peter,
Déconnexion

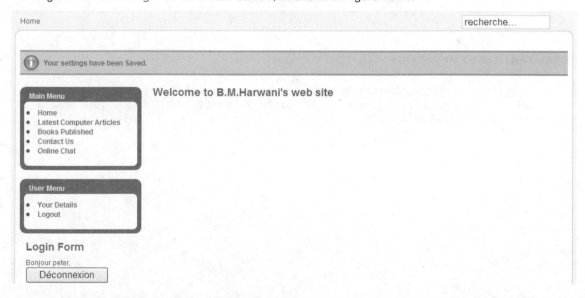

Figure 10-40. Front end of website changed to French

Also notice in Figure 10-40 that the language of the message `Hi peter` and the `Log out` button have changed to French. Now if you click the `Your Details` link to edit information, the screen will be completely translated to French, as shown in Figure 10-41.

Figure 10-41. Labels on the front end changed to French

Likewise, the results that appear upon performing any search on your website are translated. For example, assuming the current default language is English, if you search for the keyword `Java` on your website, you'll see the output shown in Figure 10-42.

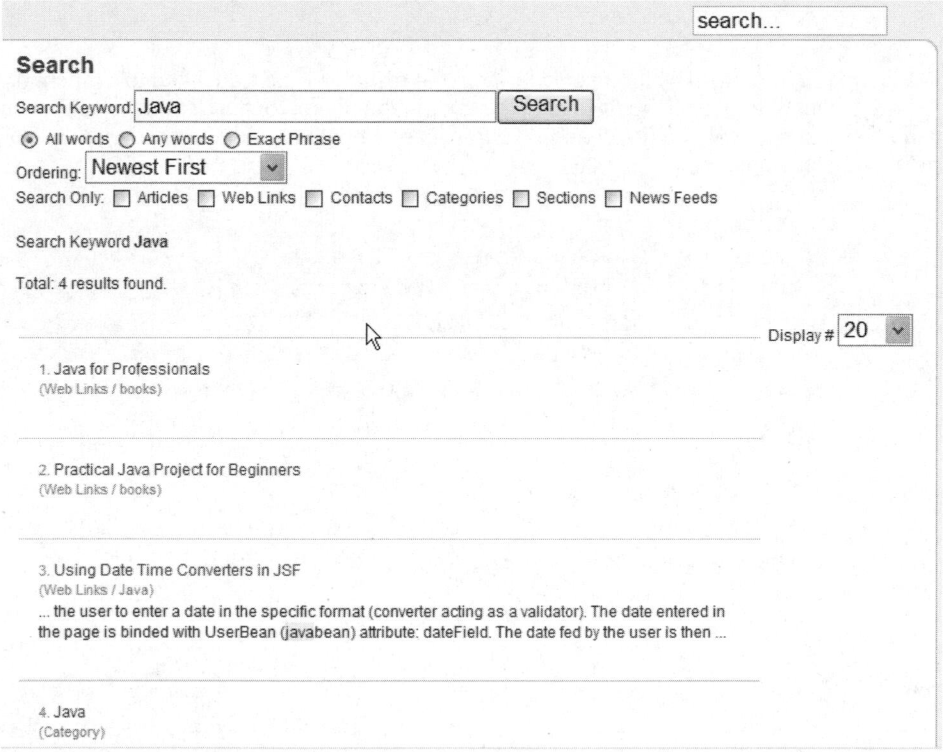

Figure 10-42. Search results in English

If the front-end language chosen by the user is French, the results will be translated to French, as shown in Figure 10-43. Notice that everything, including the text on the search button, changes to French. The content of the articles, however, do not change. To translate the language of the articles, we would need to install translation extensions.

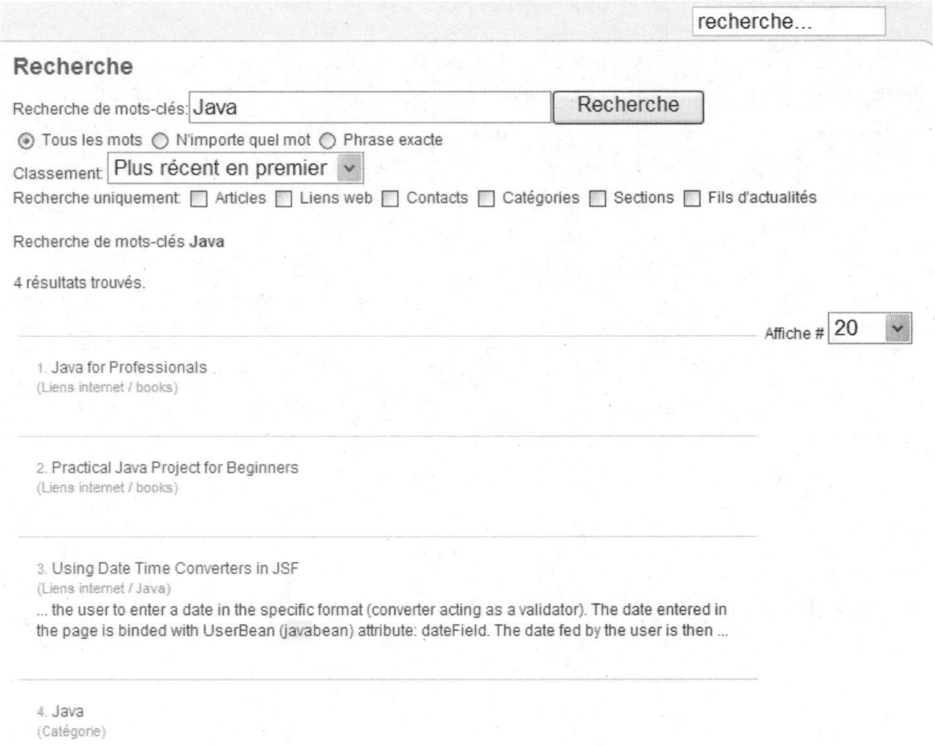

Figure 10-43. Search results in French

Similarly, if you click the `Logout` link (below the `Your Details` link) in the Login module (see Figure 10-40, earlier), you'll see the message shown in Figure 10-44 if English is the front-end language.

Figure 10-44. Logout message in English

This message will change to French if the front-end language chosen is French, as shown in Figure 10-45.

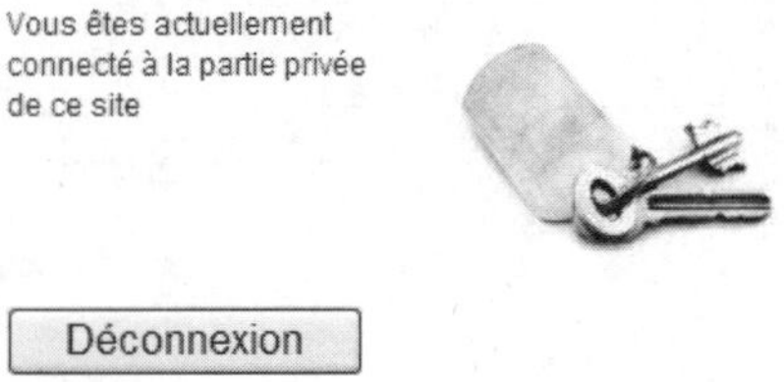

Figure 10-45. Logout message in French

Media settings (System tab)

The Media settings are for setting certain checks on the files being uploaded to your website. The idea is to upload only legal and verified files. The options in this section are shown in Figure 10-46, and explained following.

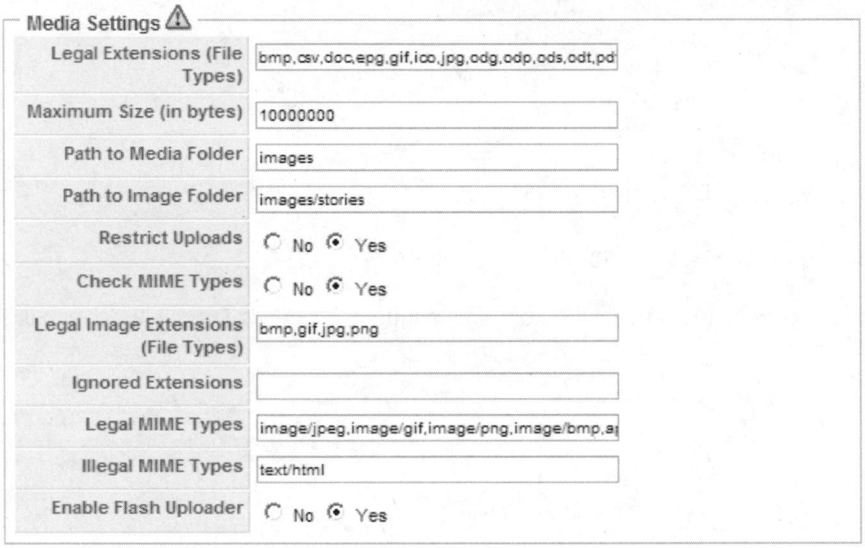

Figure 10-46. Media settings

The `Legal Extensions (File Types)` field contains the list of file types that users are allowed to upload. By default, Joomla allows the basic image and document files: BMP, CSV, DOC, EPG, GIF, ICO, JPG, ODG, ODP, ODS, ODT, PDF, PNG, PPT, SWF, TXT, XCF, and XLS. You can edit this list to suit your needs.

The `Maximum Size (in bytes)` field contains the maximum file size that users are allowed to upload. The default setting is 10000000 (10MB). You can edit it according to your requirements.

You can specify the path of non-image media files in the `Path to Media Folder` field. These files include videos and document files. The default path is `<Joomla! home>/images`, but you can create a new folder and specify its path in this field to use it with the Media Manager.

> *Don't delete or rename the existing `<Joomla! home>/images` folder, because this folder and its subfolders—images/banners, images/M_images, images/smiles, and images/stories—are used by Joomla.*

In the `Path to Image Folder` field, you specify the path to the directory where images are to be stored. The default is `<Joomla! home>/images/stories`, but you can create a new folder to store your images and specify its path in this field to use it with the Media Manager. The `images/stories` folder is used by Joomla, so you should not delete or rename this folder.

The `Restrict Uploads` option is for restricting uploads to the server. If you set this to `Yes`, only authorized users will be able to upload documents or images to the website. The default value of this option is `Yes`.

The `Check MIME Types` option is for assuring that the MIME files uploaded to your website are valid. Valid MIME types include GIF, JPEG, PNG (and most other file types that support audio, video, and graphics). Recall that MIME files make it possible to include graphics, audio, and video to be sent over the Internet. To verify files, MIME Magic or Fileinfo are used. If the value of this field is set to `Yes` (the default), users will be restricted from uploading malicious files onto the website. MIME Magic and Fileinfo contain vast databases of file extensions with detailed information about the associated file types. The file extensions of all three platforms are included in the database: Macintosh, Windows, and Linux. Each entry in the database contains information about the file format, a description of the file, and the program that opens the file. If the user tries to upload a file with an unknown file extension (i.e., one that doesn't exist in the MIME Magic or Fileinfo databases), an error will occur and the file will not be uploaded.

The `Legal Image Extensions (File Types)` field allows you to specify the types of images that can be uploaded to your Joomla website. It operates by checking the file image headers. By default, Joomla allows only images of type BMP, GIF, JPG, and PNG. For example, if you want to upload an image file with the extension `.tiff`, it will not be uploaded unless `tiff` is entered in this field.

The `Ignored Extensions` field is used for specifying the extensions that are to be ignored for MIME type checking. By default, this field is blank to indicate that no extensions are ignored, but you can always add an extension that you want to be uploaded without any checking.

The Legal MIME Types field contains the list of legal MIME types, making them valid for uploading. By default, Joomla automatically includes certain standard file types, including image/jpeg, image/gif, image/png, image/bmp, application/x-shockwave-flash, application/msword, application/excel, application/pdf, application/
powerpoint, text/plain, and application/x-zip. You can edit this list to suit your requirements.

In the Illegal MIME Types field, you specify the list of illegal MIME types so that these types won't be uploaded. By default, Joomla automatically blocks text/HTML types.

You set the Enable Flash Uploader option to Yes to enable the integrated Flash Uploader, which makes the task of uploading files to the web server much easier. Flash Uploader is based on Adobe Flash technology; it not only allows you to upload several files simultaneously (to the Media Manager), but also displays a progress bar indicating what percentage of the file has been uploaded. You can preview images and also resize images after the upload. To use this component, you need Flash 8 installed on your server. The default value of this option is No.

Debug Settings (System tab)

The Debug, Cache, and Session Settings sections are shown in Figure 10-47.

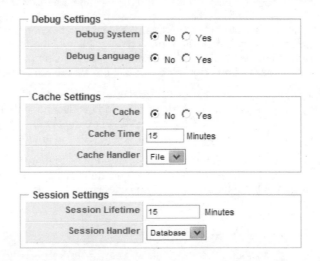

Figure 10-47. Debug, cache, and session settings

With the debug settings, you can decide whether to apply the debug system on your Joomla website and whether to display debug indicators in case of bugs.

The `Debug System` option is used to detect any bugs that may occur during an operation performed on the front end or back end of your Joomla website. If you set this option to `Yes`, it will activate Joomla's debug system, and you will start getting diagnostic information, language translations, and SQL errors. That is, you will start getting debugging information at the end of each page of your website that includes the following:

- Profile information (the amount of time it takes to execute code up to various points in the code)
- Memory usage (the amount of RAM used)
- SQL queries executed for building the page
- Language files loaded (all the language files loaded for building the page along with their full path and the number of times the file was referenced)
- Untranslated string diagnostics (list of all the untranslated strings found)
- Untranslated string designer (list of all the untranslated strings found in a key = value format).

On setting the `Debug System` option to Yes, the debug information may be something like that shown in Figure 10-48.

Profile Information

Application afterLoad: 0.005 seconds, 0.27 MB
Application afterInitialise: 0.115 seconds, 2.59 MB
Application afterRoute: 0.142 seconds, 3.17 MB
Application afterDispatch: 0.426 seconds, 5.99 MB
Application afterRender: 0.748 seconds, 6.98 MB

Memory Usage

7364672

27 queries logged

```
1.  SELECT *
      FROM jos_session
      WHERE session_id = 'ef183eea16c0477d65b462d6a39c4f22'
2.  DELETE
      FROM jos_session
      WHERE ( time < '1244736232' )
3.  SELECT *
      FROM jos_session
      WHERE session_id = 'ef183eea16c0477d65b462d6a39c4f22'
4.  UPDATE `jos_session`
      SET `time`='1244737132',`userid`='0',`usertype`='',`username`='',`gid`='0',`guest`='1',`client_id`='0',`data`='__default|a:8:
      {s:15:\"session.counter\";i:2;s:19:\"session.timer.start\";i:1244736994;s:18:\"session.timer.last\";i:1244736994;s:17:\"session.timer
      (compatible; MSIE 6.0; Windows NT 5.1; SV1)\";s:8:\"registry\";O:9:\"JRegistry\":3:
      {s:17:\"_defaultNameSpace\";s:7:\"session\";s:9:\"_registry\";a:1:{s:7:\"session\";a:1:{s:4:\"data\";O:8:\"stdClass\":0:{}}}
      s:7:\"_errors\";a:0:{}}s:4:\"user\";O:6:\"JUser\":19:
      {s:2:\"id\";i:0;s:4:\"name\";N;s:8:\"username\";N;s:5:\"email\";N;s:8:\"password\";N;s:14:\"password_clear\";s:0:\"\";s:8:\"usertype\
      {s:4:\"_raw\";s:0:\"\";s:4:\"_xml\";N;s:9:\"_elements\";a:0:{}s:12:\"_elementPath\";a:1:
      {i:0;s:66:\"C:\\xampp\htdocs\\joomlasite\\libraries\\joomla\\html\\parameter\\element\";}
      s:17:\"_defaultNameSpace\";s:8:\"_default\";s:9:\"_registry\";a:1:{s:8:\"_default\";a:1:{s:4:\"data\";O:8:\"stdClass\":0:{}}}
      s:7:\"_errors\";a:0:{}}s:9:\"_errorMsg\";N;s:7:\"_errors\";a:0:{}}
      s:13:\"session.token\";s:32:\"153580bdefe3a3fbf696271904c9855d\";}'
      WHERE session_id='ef183eea16c0477d65b462d6a39c4f22'
```

Figure 10-48. Debug information displayed at the end of each web page

The Debug Language option is used for switching on the debugging indicators for the Joomla language files. That is, all translatable text is enclosed in special characters that reflect their status. Any text enclosed in bullets indicates that a match has been found in the language definition file and the text has been translated. Any text enclosed in pairs of question marks (??) indicates that the string is translatable but no match was found in the language definition file. Text with no surrounding characters indicates that the string is not translatable. You can use language debugging without enabling the Debug System option, but if you do, you won't get additional detailed information about the bugs to help you correct them. An example of the use of the Debug Language option on the front end of a Joomla website (displaying text enclosed in bullets) is shown in Figure 10-49.

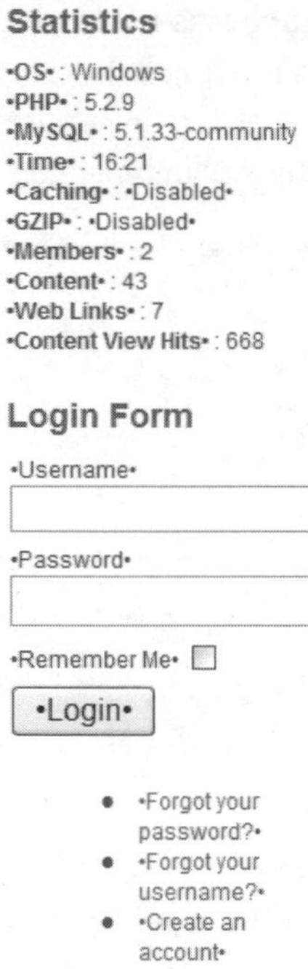

Statistics

•OS• : Windows
•PHP• : 5.2.9
•MySQL• : 5.1.33-community
•Time• : 16:21
•Caching• : •Disabled•
•GZIP• : •Disabled•
•Members• : 2
•Content• : 43
•Web Links• : 7
•Content View Hits• : 668

Login Form

•Username•

•Password•

•Remember Me• ☐

•Login•

• •Forgot your password?•
• •Forgot your username?•
• •Create an account•

Figure 10-49. Text enclosed in bullets when the Debug Language option is set to Yes

Cache Settings (System tab)

The cache is a small, temporary storage area on the hard drive where browsers keep website contents that have been repeatedly viewed by visitors. In this way, caching is a technique to improve the speed of displaying contents of a website. Recall that since our website is a CMS, whatever contents we see on it are accessed from the MySQL database. Using caching, Joomla creates a local copy of the contents being viewed (a cache) on the server's hard disk, so that the next time the contents are requested by the visitor, Joomla can access them from there. The options in the `Cache Settings` section of Global Configuration are as follows:

- `Cache`: You can set the value of this option to `Yes` to allow caching of your Joomla website and hence improve its performance.
- `Cache Time`: This is the amount of time to keep the local copy of the contents before refreshing it. Upon expiration of the time specified in this field, Joomla updates the local copy maintained in the cache with that of the MySQL database contents (to display the latest updated information). The default value is 15 minutes—that is, after every 15 minutes, the contents of the cache will be refreshed automatically
- `Cache Handler`: This field displays how the caching is performed. There's only one caching mechanism: file-based. **File-based caching** means reading and writing operations are performed using the **file cache**. That is, the read operations read from an area in system memory known as the system file cache, rather than from the physical disk. Similarly, for write operations, the data is written to the system file cache rather than to the disk.

Session Settings (System tab)

Sessions allow your system to recognize that requests are being generated by the same client (visitor). This not only helps in remembering the options selected by a particular visitor on your website (such as products selected in a shopping cart), but also prevents visitors from having to perform repetitive tasks (e.g., a visitor who has logged in once should not be asked to log in again when accessing another page of your website). The options in the `Session Settings` section of Global Configuration are as follows:

- `Session Lifetime`: This field determines how long a session should last and how long a user can remain signed in after being inactive. The default value is 15 minutes, which means that a visitor who logs into your website and doesn't perform any action for more than 15 minutes will be prompted to log in again.
- `Session Handler`: This drop-down determines how the session should be handled once a user connects and logs into the site. The default setting is `Database`, which means that all the actions taken by the visitor on the webpage are temporarily stored in a database until the visitor either logs out or closes the browser window. If you set the value of this option to `None`, your Joomla website won't be able to maintain the session (i.e., it won't be able to recognize whether the requests are being made by the same user).

Server tab (Global Configuration)

The `Server` tab of Global Configuration (Figure 10-50) is used for configuring several servers, including FTP, database, and mail. You can use this tab to apply a compression technique to enhance your website performance; set the local time zone to display the time to your visitors; specify the FTP host, username, and password; specify the type and name of the database where your Joomla website is stored; specify the mailer to be used for sending e-mail; and so on.

Figure 10-50. Server tab of Global Configuration

Server Settings (Server tab)

In the `Path to Temp-folder` field, the location of the folder where files are temporarily stored is specified. It is filled in by default when Joomla is installed, but you can edit it later.

If you set the `GZIP Page Compression` option to `Yes`, the web pages will be stored in compressed form when in an inactive state and will be uncompressed when invoked by the visitor. This increases your website's speed. The only drawback of GZIP compression is that it consumes valuable CPU bandwidth on the web servers. Hence, the default value of this option is No.

> *GZIP is a software application used for file compression. Compression is a simple and effective way to save bandwidth and speed up a site. The reason is quite simple. HTML files are very bulky, since every <html>, <table>, and <div> tag has a corresponding closing tag—that is, words are repeated throughout the document. Compression, however, reduces the file size by removing the repetitions without loss of information. The browser can easily download the zipped file, extract it, and then show it to the user. This compression results in quick page loading.*

The Error Reporting drop-down allows you to set the appropriate level of reporting. The error reporting options are as shown in Figure 10-51, and described following.

Figure 10-51. Error reporting options

- System Default: This value (the default) allows the level of error reporting to be determined by the php.ini file on the web server.
- None: This turns error reporting off.
- Simple: This turns error reporting to E_ERROR | E_WARNING | E_PARSE. These are the standard error types in PHP, as explained here:
  - **E_ERROR**: It is the most serious error type; it represents errors that PHP is unable to recover from. The error handler in this case stops execution of the script and displays the error number and message to the user.
  - **E_WARNING**: This is the intermediate error type, and doesn't lead to stopping script execution. The error handler displays a warning message with the error number to the user.
  - **E-PARSE**: This is the lowest error type, and is generated by the PHP parser to denote that some syntax error has occurred in the script. The error handler in this case also stops execution of the script and displays the error number and message to the user.
- Maximum: This turns error reporting to the maximum level (E_ALL).

> *The output from the error reports is displayed at the bottom of every page of the website.*

The Force SSL setting makes the website more secure. **SSL (Secure Sockets Layer)** is a protocol developed by Netscape and a security technology used for establishing an encrypted link between a web server and a browser. The encryption in the link ensures that all data passed between the web server and browser remains private and is not visible to unauthorized persons. To encrypt data, two cryptographic keys—a **private key** and a **public key**—are used. The public key is known to everyone and the private key is known only to the recipient of the message.

To establish an SSL connection, a web server requires an **SSL certificate**. To get an SSL certificate, the steps are as follows:

1. You choose to activate SSL on your web server.
2. You are asked to provide information about your website and your company.
3. On the basis of the information provided, the web server creates two cryptographic keys: a private key and a public key. The public key is placed in a certificate signing request (CSR)—a data file containing information about you and your website. Then the CSR is submitted to the web server.
4. Upon submission of the CSR, the certification authority (CA) validates your details and issues an SSL certificate, which allows you to use SSL.
5. The web server matches the issued SSL certificate with your private key and then establishes an encrypted link.

> *URLs that require an SSL connection start with* https: *instead of* http:.

The options in the `Force SSL` drop-down are as follows:

- `None`: SSL is not activated.
- `Administrator Only`: SSL is valid only for the back end.
- `Entire Site`: SSL is valid for the whole site (front and back end).

Locale Settings (Server tab)

The only option in the `Locale Settings` section is `Time Zone`, which identifies the time zone in which the website is to operate. You can set the time zone so that your website displays local times to your visitors. The time should reflect where the site's server is located. The default setting is `(UTC 00:00) Western Europe Time, London, Lisbon, Casablanca`.

FTP Settings (Server tab)

The FTP settings made in this section play an important role in the way files are uploaded to the web server. The options in this section are as follows:

- `Enable FTP`: You can set the value of this field to `Yes` to enable Joomla to use its built-in FTP function instead of the normal upload process used by PHP.
- `FTP Host`: In this field, you specify the URL of the host server with which you will be performing FTP.
- `FTP Port`: In this field, you specify the port that is used by FTP. The default setting is `21`.

- `FTP Username`: In this field, you specify the name of the user who is allowed to access the FTP server.
- `FTP Password`: The password that Joomla will use when accessing the FTP server is specified in this field.
- `FTP Root`: In this field, you specify the root directory where you want the uploaded files to be kept initially.

Database Settings (Server tab)

The database settings include information about the database used for your Joomla website, including the type of database, the location of the database server, the name of the database, and the users who have permission to access the database. The options in the `Database Settings` section are as follows:

- `Database Type`: This is the type of database to be used. The default setting is `mysql`, but this can be changed during Joomla installation.
- `Hostname`: This is the server where the database exists. The server IP address is entered here. It is typically set to `localhost` by default.
- `Username`: The username with which you access the database is entered in this field.
- `Database`: The name of the database where the Joomla website is stored is specified here.
- `Database Prefix`: In this field, you specify the term to be used before every table in the selected database. This enables you to have multiple Joomla installations in the same database. The default setting is `jos_`, but it can be changed. There is a warning attached to this setting, which reads, `Do not change unless you have a database built using tables with the prefix you are setting`. So, you should only change the database prefix if you have already created a database with tables having the prefix that you are going to specify here.

Mail Settings (Server tab)

The mail settings are set during the initial setup of Joomla, but they can be changed whenever needed. The following are the options in the `Mail Settings` section of Global Configuration:

- `Mailer`: This setting determines which mailer to use to deliver e-mail from the site. The default setting is `PHP Mail Function`. This can also be changed during the initial setup of Joomla. Figure 10-52 shows the different mailer options, and they're described following.

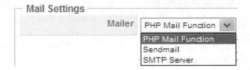

Figure 10-52. Mailer options

- `PHP Mail Function`: This uses the mail function that is built into PHP.
- `Sendmail`: This uses the Sendmail program, which is typically used when creating HTML e-mail forms. Sendmail is a widely used **mail transport agent (MTA)**. MTAs are meant for sending mail from one machine to another—that is, they work internally to move e-mail over networks or the Internet to their destinations. Sendmail supports a variety of mail transfer protocols, including SMTP, ESMTP, HylaFAX, QuickPage, and UUCP. Most of the mail servers on the Internet today run Sendmail.
- `SMTP Server`: This uses the site's SMTP (Simple Mail Transfer Protocol) server. SMTP is a network protocol used to send messages from the mail client to the mail server. Messages can only be pushed with this protocol, meaning that they can only be sent to the server, not retrieved from it. The protocols POP and IMAP are used to retrieve the message from the server.

An SMTP server, after verifying the configuration, gives permission to the sending machine to send an e-mail message. The message is sent to the specified destination and a validation that it has been delivered successfully is performed. If the message has not been delivered successfully, an error message is sent to the sending machine. There are two limitations of SMTP: it cannot authenticate the senders and hence cannot stop e-mail spamming, and it's a text-based protocol in which message text is specified along with the recipients of the message.

- `Mail From`: The e-mail address used by Joomla to send site e-mail is specified in this field.
- `From Name`: This is the name that Joomla will use when sending site e-mail messages. By default, Joomla uses the site name specified during the initial setup.
- `Sendmail Path`: This is the path where the Sendmail program is located. This field is typically filled in by Joomla during the initial setup. This path is used only if `Mailer` is set to `Sendmail`.
- `SMTP Authentication`: If the SMTP server requires authentication to send mail, set this to `Yes`. Otherwise, leave it at `No`. This is used only if `Mailer` is set to `SMTP`.
- `SMTP Username`: This is the username to use for access to the SMTP host. This is used only if `Mailer` is set to `SMTP`.
- `SMTP Password`: This is the password to use for access to the SMTP host. This is used only if `Mailer` is set to `SMTP`.
- `SMTP Host`: This is the SMTP address to use when sending mail. This is used only if `Mailer` is set to `SMTP`.

Providing a multilingual facility to visitors

You can translate the contents of your website to different languages to make it readable by people all around the globe. There are a number of freely available modules on the Internet that can be downloaded and installed on your Joomla website to translate web contents to different languages. This section will discuss two modules for language translations for your website: Google Dictionary and Browse Your Website in 35 Languages.

Google Dictionary

Google Dictionary allows visitors to your website to type sentences and then translate them into several languages, including Chinese (simplified and traditional), Italian, French, Dutch, German, Spanish, Russian, Portuguese, Japanese, Korean, Arabic, and English. In order to use Google Dictionary, you need to download the `unzip_first_mod_googleDictionary.zip` file from `http://vivociti.com/component/option,com_remository/` (before you can download the file, you will first need to register on the website). On unzipping the `unzip_first_mod_googleDictionary.zip` file, you'll find two files in it: `mod_googleDictionary.zip` and `mod_googleDictionary15.zip`, along with a `readme` file. The two files are for Joomla versions 1.0 and 1.5, respectively. The archive file that we will be using is `mod_googleDictionary15.zip`. Open the Extension Manager by selecting `Extensions ➤ Install/Uninstall`. In the `Upload Package File` section (see Figure 10-53), click the `Browse` button to search for and select the archive file, and then click the `Upload File & Install` button.

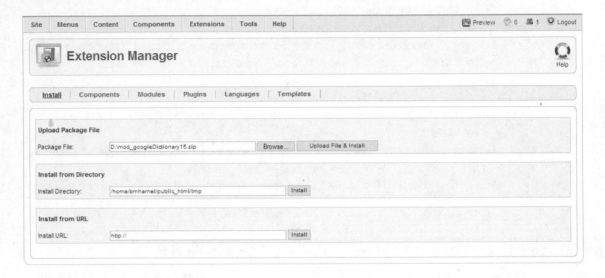

Figure 10-53. Installing Google Dictionary

The Google Dictionary module will be installed on your website, and you'll see the message `Install Module Success`, as shown in Figure 10-54. You'll also see the developer's name and a brief introduction to what this module can do.

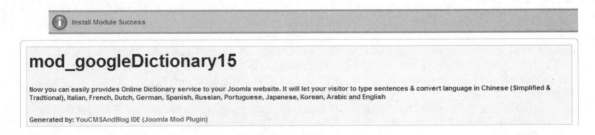

Figure 10-54. Installation success message of Google Dictionary

By default, all newly installed modules are set to disabled mode, so they will not appear on the front end of your website until you enable them. So, to use the Google Dictionary module on your Joomla website, you need to enable it from the Module Manager. Open the Module Manager by selecting `Extensions ➤ Module Manager`. In the Module Manger, you'll find your Google Dictionary module, `mod_googleDictionary15`, in disabled mode, as shown in Figure 10-55. (A red *X* in the `Enabled` column indicates that the module is currently disabled, and a check mark indicates that the module is enabled). To enable this module, either click the red *X* (which toggles the mode), or select the check box of the module and then click the `Enable` icon in the toolbar.

Figure 10-55. Google Dictionary module in disabled mode in the Module Manager

The module `mod_googleDictionary` will now be visible on the front end of your Joomla website, as shown in Figure 10-56.

Figure 10-56. Google Dictionary module from the front end

Notice that the module displays two text boxes: one for typing the sentences to be translated and the other for displaying the translated text. The drop-down list is for selecting the language to which you want to translate the sentence. Let's see how the sentence "Hello how are you?" appears in French. Type the sentence in the first text box, select `French` from the drop-down list, and click the `Translate To` button. You should see the French version of your sentence in the second text box, as shown in Figure 10-57.

Figure 10-57. Converting an English sentence to French

Similarly, follow the same process to see the Russian version of your sentence (the results are shown in Figure 10-58).

Figure 10-58. Converting an English sentence to Russian

The drop-down list offers the languages that the text can be translated to, as shown in Figure 10-59.

| Select language... |
| English |
| Arabic |
| Chinese(Simplified) |
| Chinese(Traditional) |
| Dutch |
| French |
| German |
| Italian |
| Japanese |
| Korean |
| Portuguese |
| Russian |
| Spanish |

Figure 10-59. Language options of Google Dictionary

The Google Dictionary module works perfectly well for translation of sentences. Next, we'll look at a technique for automatically translating contents of our website.

Browse Your Website in 35 Languages

There are many modules on the Internet that may be used to translate the contents of your website to any desired language. The one that we're going to use in this example is Browse Your Website in 35 Languages. This module enables a visitor to your website to browse its contents in 35 supported languages, including English, Chinese (simplified and traditional), Italian, French, Dutch, German, Spanish, Russian, Portuguese, Japanese, Korean, Arabic, Catalan, Filipino, Hebrew, Indonesian, Latvian, Lithuanian, Serbian, Slovak, Slovenian, Ukrainian, and Vietnamese. The module uses the Google Translate translation machine.

To use this module, you need to download the `mod_browsein35lang_unzip_me_1st.zip` file from `http://vivociti.com/component/option,com_remository/` (before you are able to download the file, you will first need to register on the website). On unzipping the `mod_browsein35lang_unzip_me_1st.zip` file, you'll find two files in it: `mod_browsein35lang.zip` and `mod_browsein35lang-15.zip`, along with a `readme` file. The two files are for Joomla version 1.0 and 1.5, respectively.

The archive file that we will be using is `mod_browsein35lang-15.zip`. To install the module, open the Extension Manager by selecting `Extensions` ➤ `Install/Uninstall`. In the Extension Manager, specify the archive file of the module in the `Package File` field and click the `Upload File & Install` button, as shown in Figure 10-60.

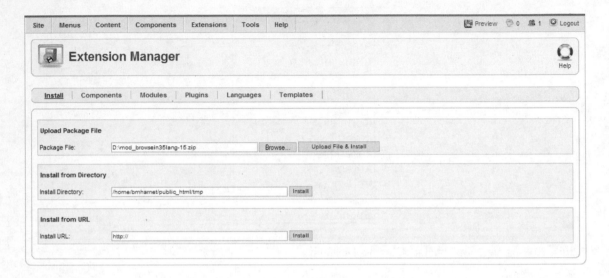

Figure 10-60. Installing the Browse Your Website in 35 Languages module

Once the module is installed, you'll see the message `Install Module Success`. A brief introduction to the capabilities of the module will appear, along with an identification of the module's developers, as shown in Figure 10-61.

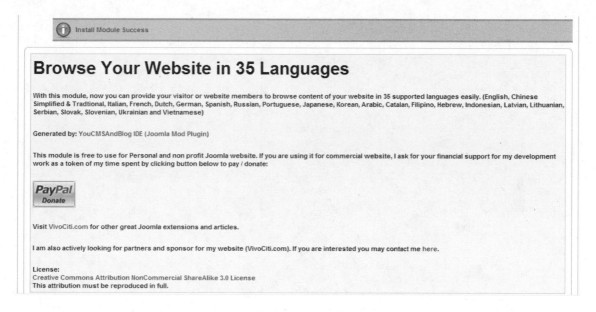

Figure 10-61. Installation success message

The module is in disabled mode initially, so you need to enable it from the Module Manager. Just select the red *X* in the `Enabled` column (Figure 10-62) to toggle it to enabled mode.

Figure 10-62. The Browse Your Website in 35 Languages module in disabled mode in the Module Manager

The module will become visible on the front end of your website, as shown in Figure 10-63.

BrowseIn35Languages

Browse this website in:

Spanish ▾ Go

Figure 10-63. The module from the front end

The drop-down list (Figure 10-64) provides a listing of all 35 languages to which the contents of your website can automatically be translated.

Figure 10-64. Language translation options

To compare the original contents to that of the translated version, we will first see how the original contents appear in English when we select certain menu items on our website. Let's assume that the initial screen displaying the Main Menu and the Login module of our website appears as shown in Figure 10-65.

Figure 10-65. Main Menu and Login module in English

Again, let's assume that when we select the menu item Latest Computer Articles from the Main Menu, it displays the categories of articles shown in Figure 10-66.

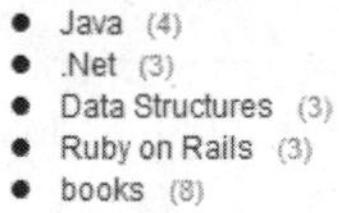

- Java (4)
- .Net (3)
- Data Structures (3)
- Ruby on Rails (3)
- books (8)

Figure 10-66. List of Latest Computer Articles categories in English

The article category Java contains four articles that will be displayed, as shown in Figure 10-67.

	Display #	20 ⌄
#	Web Link	Hits
1	Accessing data from a database using JSP All the steps involved in Accessing data from a database using JSP are explained with diagrams	60
2	Creating Custom Component in JSF The idea behind developing Custom UI components is to hide the complexity of UI functionality. A JSF component is typically combination of three classes working closely together : renderer, subclass of IOComponent (the component class) and the tag handler.	46
3	Using Date Time Converters in JSF This application asks a user to enter a date which is then displayed in different styles and formats. For this application, we are going to develop two pages index.jsp and response.jsp. The index.jsp prompts the user to enter a date in the specific format (converter acting as a validator). The date entered in the page is binded with UserBean (javabean) attribute: dateField. The date fed by the user is then displayed after converting in different formats through response.jsp page.	28
4	Demonstration of selectOneMenu tag in JSF selectOneMenu tag displays its child items in a listbox and the number of items displayed is always one. It displays a element with the size attribute set to 1. All of its items configured by child UISelectItem or UISelectItems components are rendered as elements.	47

Figure 10-67. List of articles about Java in English

To translate the website contents to French, select the option French and click the Go button. The initial welcome screen containing the Main Menu and Login module will appear as shown in Figure 10-68.

Figure 10-68. Main Menu and Login module in French

If you move the mouse pointer over any menu item, a pop-up will appear that displays the original English text of the menu item, as shown in Figure 10-69.

Figure 10-69. Pop-up in original language

Upon selecting the menu item `Derniers articles Computer`, you'll see the list of categories of articles in French, as shown in Figure 10-70.

- Java (4)
- . Net (3)
- Structures de données (3)
- Ruby on Rails (3)
- livres (8)

Figure 10-70. List of latest computer articles in French

Finally, upon selecting the `Java` category, you'll see the list of articles in that category. Notice in Figure 10-71 that the titles and introductory descriptions of the articles also appear in French. You can select the title of any article to see it in full.

Affiche # 20

#	Web Link	Hits
1	Accès aux données d'une base de données utilisant des JSP Toutes les étapes nécessaires à l'accès aux données à partir d'une base de données en utilisant JSP sont expliqués avec des schémas	60
2	Création personnalisée de composants JSF dans L'idée de développement de composants de l'interface utilisateur personnalisée permet de masquer la complexité de l'interface utilisateur de fonctionnalités. Un composant JSF est généralement la combinaison de trois classes, travaillent en étroite collaboration: moteur de rendu, de la sous-classe IOComponent (la classe de composant) et le gestionnaire de balise.	46
3	Date Heure en utilisant des convertisseurs de JSF Cette application demande à un utilisateur d'entrer une date qui est ensuite affichée dans différents styles et de formats. Pour cette application, nous allons développer deux pages et response.jsp index.jsp. Le index.jsp invites à l'utilisateur d'entrer une date dans le format spécifique (agissant comme un convertisseur de validation). La date est entré dans la page est lié avec UserBean (JavaBean) attribut: dateField. La date alimenté par l'utilisateur est affichée après la conversion en différents formats à travers response.jsp page.	28
4	Démonstration de selectOneMenu balise JSF selectOneMenu tag affiche son enfant des objets d'une listbox et le nombre d'éléments affichés est toujours un. Il affiche un élément avec l'attribut de taille 1. Tous ses articles configurés par enfant UISelectItem ou UISelectItems sont rendus comme des éléments.	47

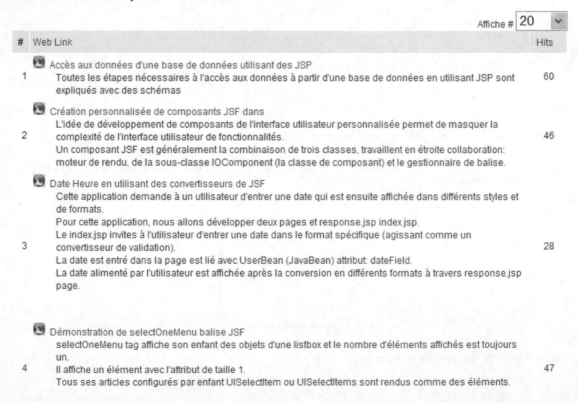

Figure 10-71. List of articles about Java in French

The list of language options also changes to French, as shown in Figure 10-72.

Figure 10-72. Language options changed to French

Summary

In this chapter, we dealt with Joomla's Global Configuration settings. You saw how to install an editor and how to make SEF URLs. You learned how to enable visitors to register on your website, as well as how an activation link is sent, and its role in activating a new account. You saw how the language of the front end of your website can be changed. To make your website readable by everyone, you learned how to translate your website contents into different languages

Index

You Need the Companion eBook

Your purchase of this book entitles you to buy the companion PDF-version eBook for only $10. Take the weightless companion with you anywhere.

We believe this Apress title will prove so indispensable that you'll want to carry it with you everywhere, which is why we are offering the companion eBook (in PDF format) for $10 to customers who purchase this book now. Convenient and fully searchable, the PDF version of any content-rich, page-heavy Apress book makes a valuable addition to your programming library. You can easily find and copy code—or perform examples by quickly toggling between instructions and the application. Even simultaneously tackling a donut, diet soda, and complex code becomes simplified with hands-free eBooks!

Once you purchase your book, getting the $10 companion eBook is simple:

❶ Visit **www.apress.com/promo/tendollars/**.

❷ Complete a basic registration form to receive a randomly generated question about this title.

❸ Answer the question correctly in 60 seconds, and you will receive a promotional code to redeem for the $10.00 eBook.

THE EXPERT'S VOICE™

233 Spring Street, New York, NY 10013

All Apress eBooks subject to copyright protection. No part may be reproduced or transmitted in any form or by any means, electronic or mechanical, including photocopying, recording, or by any information storage or retrieval system, without the prior written permission of the copyright owner and the publisher. The purchaser may print the work in full or in part for their own noncommercial use. The purchaser may place the eBook title on any of their personal computers for their own personal reading and reference.

Offer valid through 4/10.